THE VALUE MANDATE

Other Books by Peter J. Clark and Stephen Neill

netValue

Other books by Peter J. Clark

Beyond the Deal

THE VALUE MANDATE

MANDATE

MAXIMIZING SHAREHOLDER VALUE ACROSS THE CORPORATION

Peter J. Clark and Stephen Neill

www.vbm-consulting.com

AMACOM

American Management Association

New York • Atlanta • Boston • Chicago • Kansas City • San Francisco • Washington, D.C.
Brussels • Mexico City • Tokyo • Toronto

Library of Congress Cataloging-in-Publication Data

Clark, Peter J.
    The value mandate: maximizing shareholder value across the
corporation / Peter J. Clark and Stephen Neill.
        p. cm.
    Includes bibliographical references and index.
    ISBN 0-8144-0605-X
    1. Corporate profits. 2. Investments—Valuation.
3. Corporations—Finance. I. Neill, Stephen II. Title.

HG4028.P7 C58 2000
658.15'5—dc21

                                                    00–060585

Printing number

10 9 8 7 6 5 4 3 2 1

For
Lillian, Jane, Bob, Dot, COL

Contents

List of Exhibits

Abbreviations Used in This Book

Following are explanations of some abbreviations that are used in this book, including their location in the book where applicable:

APV   Adjusted Present Value. A cash flow–based valuation methodology developed by Professor Timothy A. Luehrman, as introduced in the May–June 1997 issue of *Harvard Business Review*. (Appendix A)

CAPEX   Company's CAPital EXpenditure evaluation methodology and decision systems.

CF   Cash flow. Usually defined as net income plus depreciation plus or minus changes in deferred taxes.

CFE   Cash flow per employee. An emerging broad measure of staffing efficiency and overall organizational effectiveness. At this writing, not as extensively used as Revenue/Employee, but should gradually displace the latter measure.

CKC   Corporate Key Contributors. Refers to a very small number of nearly irreplaceable employees who can be directly linked to the generation of significant amounts of corporate cash flow, net of investment. (Chapter 3)

DFT™   Demand Flow Technology™. Proprietary "flow" production/assembly approach of John Costanza, Jc-I-T Technology, Denver. (Chapter 5)

EPS   Earnings per share.

FTE   Full-time equivalent. Typically refers to combinations of activities or time by several employees which, when combined, represent the equivalent work of a single, full-time employee. Issue arises in some instances of staff reductions when fractions of activities of numerous employees occur because of consolidation and/or elimination.

G&A   General and administrative expenses. Administrative overhead and other expenses, including indirect employees. SG&A has typically been used as a primary indicator of corporate expense and efficiency performance, but with sales ("S") now highly volatile with introduction of new channels such as the Net, G&A grows with importance as a measure. (Chapter 8)

G&A/R   General and Administrative Expenses, combined, as a percentage of revenues. A useful overall indicator of company progress in extracting value from the administration. (Chapter 8)

IRR   Internal rate of return. Project/asset/investment return on investment on a discounted cash flow basis, over the economic life or period of utilization.

JIT   Just-in-Time. Inventory delivery approach calling for supplier to deliver precise quantities of raw materials, parts, components, or other supplies to a particular cell on the production or assembly floor, at the point of need. Replaces advance excess ordering and storage known as "stack and wait." (Chapter 5)

LERC   Lean Enterprise Research Centre, Cardiff Business School, University of Wales, Professor Daniel T. Jones, Director, lerc@cardiff.ac.uk. LERC is an academic research center helping manufacturers improve performance, in part through implementation of lean management principles.

MSV   Maximum shareholder value.
MV   Market value, or share price.

PCF   Share price to cash flow multiple.
PE   Multiple of share price to reported net income per share.

TSR   Total shareholders return. Refers to appreciation in stock price plus dividends received, over analysis period. Often compared to investment alternatives, e.g., near risk-free debt, overall indices, industry competitors.

Vn   Value now. Current value: analyzed current value of company based on valuation method used, e.g., APV.

Vp   Value potential. The corporation's potential based on the sum or current value (Vn) plus additional value from timely and complete execution of a full agenda of maximum value actions in all sectors of the business: financial, operational, administrative.

VOG   Value Opportunity Gap. Difference between current value (Vn) and potential value (Vp), expressed either in terms of an amount or a percentage. (Throughout book, all of Chapter 2)

VCF   Value to cash flow multiple. An approximate factor for quick estimation of the minimal value effect from changes in continuing cash flows.

WACC   Weighted average cost of capital. Sum of weighted average cost of debt (WACD) plus weighted average cost of equity (WACE), in proportion to each element's percentage of company's total capital.

WACD   Weighted average cost of debt. After-tax cost of all forms of debt, based on rate, in proportion to each element's percentage of total debt.

WACE   Weighted average cost of equity.

WIP   Work in process of being manufactured or assembled.

Preface

Finally, Value Gets Down to Business

We wrote *The Value Mandate* to help corporate leaders achieve their mandate to reach *full* shareholder value, through a comprehensive, systematic approach, directed at the major new value creation opportunities across the corporation.

This book starts where theoretical "value" overviews leave off: with pursuit of the lion's share of the corporation's untapped, unrealized wealth. We focus on the operations and administration of the corporation, where most of the missing value resides.

Value emerges from under theory. Value gets down to business.

The pragmatic chief executive already suspects the truth shown in Figure P-1. Less than one-fifth of the corporation's missing value comes from financial restructuring tactics, such as increasing the debt-to-capital ratio somewhat or altering cash dividend policy.

Such tactics are well known and extensively adopted in the new millennium. The corporation just now getting around to developing its optimal value capital approach is merely catching up, rather than pulling ahead.[1]

Your corporation is underperforming by 50 percent, in value terms. "Pulling ahead" means meeting this challenge as posed in the first line of the first chapter of this book: implementing a consistent, rigorous value strategy, better, faster, and more completely than the competition.

Without specific value initiatives in each of the four key areas shown in Figure P-1 (and Chapters 5–8 in this book), your value program will be a shadow of what it could be.

Figure P-1. Finding the missing value: operations-driven approaches come of age.

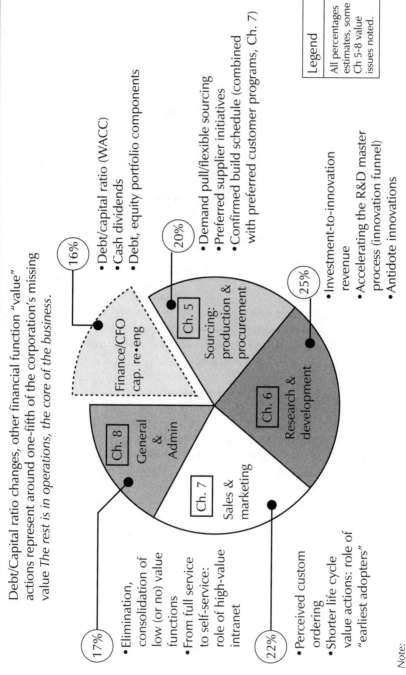

Debt/Capital ratio changes, other financial function "value" actions represent around one-fifth of the corporation's missing value *The rest is in operations, the core of the business.*

16%
- Debt/capital ratio (WACC)
- Cash dividends
- Debt, equity portfolio components

20%
- Demand pull/flexible sourcing
- Preferred supplier initiatives
- Confirmed build schedule (combined with preferred customer programs, Ch. 7)

25%
- Investment-to-innovation revenue
- Accelerating the R&D master process (innovation funnel)
- Antidote innovations

Ch. 5
Sourcing; production & procurement

Ch. 6
Research & development

Finance/CFO cap. re•eng

General & Admin
Ch. 8

Ch. 7
Sales & marketing

17%
- Elimination, consolidation of low (or no) value functions
- From full service to self-service: role of high-value intranet

22%
- Perceived custom ordering
- Shorter life cycle value actions: role of "earliest adopters"

Legend

All percentages estimates, some Ch 5–8 value issues noted.

Note:
*Percentage for financial reorganization plus other chart elements developed from Figure 6-1, Peter J. Clark, *Beyond the Deal: Optimizing Merger and Acquisition Value* (New York: HarperBusiness, 1991), page 183.

Value is created one specific action at a time—with the emphasis on "specific." The broad-brush procedural modifications that seem adequate when first announced are notorious for only working on the whiteboards in headquarters, but nowhere else.

Management pronounces new resource allocation policies: 5 percent is taken from headquarters pencil-pushers and shifted over to researchers striving to find the next stellar innovation.

Does this create new value? Truth is, no one can tell. If the HQ expense reductions are actually deferrals instead, the top-heavy administration endures, to suppress corporate value long into the future. If the R&D recipients of the reallocated resources are not focused on key value opportunities in their key science areas, those funds can easily be wasted, becoming unnecessary, unwanted expenditures.

So much for the argument that it is all right to simply add back R&D expenditures to earnings as a lump sum to provide a more accurate perspective on corporate value generation.

Value metrics do have a place. Timothy A. Luehrman's Adjusted Present Value methodology, introduced in the *Harvard Business Review* in 1997, is included in Appendix A of this book. But the appropriate place for value models is after the new wealth has already been developed. By managers operating in the guts of the corporation.

Manipulating the variables in generic valuation models to show an apparent increase in value is easy. It is far, far more difficult to devise and implement the decisive actions that give those statistics with any credibility.

Merely pursuing a few of the well-known customary value-enhancement tactics is scarcely better than doing nothing. If your corporation's value increases by 10 percent but your competitor's worth improves by 30 percent on a comparable basis, the market's sense is that you've lost 20 points' value.

A couple of the specific value opportunities are identified for each of the four key nonfinancial value sectors in Figure P-1. These and others principal value sources are addressed in Chapters 5–8.

Test of Time

In the face of fad-of-the-month management principles and arm-waving presentation gurus, it is reassuring to find something that endures the test of time.

Value-based management is no flash, heralded as the next great thing one month and disintegrating the next. It has been more than fifty-five years since John Burr Williams stated, in the Theory of Investment Value, that the value of any business is determined by cash inflows and outflows, discounted at the appropriate discount rate. The essential principles of Professors Miller and Modigliani's Capital Asset Pricing Model go back to their 1958 and 1961 articles.[2]

And yet, value-based management has been underutilized for years, limited to an underweight agenda, within the chief financial officer's domain, where the quickest nominal improvement to corporate worth can be achieved.

Value-directed capital changes are important for generating initial momentum, but what about the corporation's missing 80 + percent value? Left to little more than computer simulation, actions to extract value from the non-financial areas of the corporation are too little, too late.

Too little to substantiate management's claim that "we are maximizing value for you, our shareholders." And too late to be used as an acquisition defense during the M&A feeding frenzy in the first years of the new millennium.

Incremental cash flow improvements are already reflected in a company's current value under efficient market assumptions, so there's no positive value impact from just a bit more, a bit better. CEOs who want their corporations and themselves to be applauded as value outperformers—as meeting the value mandate—must discover the significant value opportunities. The specific campaigns need to alter company economics by at least five margin points each, with corporate value moving higher in concert.

A key purpose of this book is to help the reader identify and begin to pursue several of those specific major value opportunities. A related goal is to introduce a continuing framework for measuring and monitoring the corporation's progress toward its maximum shareholder value goal. That framework is referred to herein as the Value Opportunity Gap. VOG represents the continuing difference between potential company value and current, actual worth. The investigation that helps close the Gap through specific priority actions is referred to here as the Value Opportunity Audit.

Who Should Read This Book

This book is for everyone who aspires to achieve a corporation's Value Mandate to achieve maximum shareholder value.

Chief Executive Officers

The Value Mandate is for the chief executive who knows deep down that creating and sustaining value means far more than just manipulating some financial ratios. Who knows that push-button "value" formulas are simulations at best, but that no formula ever created one dollar of additional corporate value all on its own. The CEO who requires a systematic approach for extending new value creation deep into the organization—along with the CFO, who made value "work" first. Who realizes that the combination of balance sheet tweaks plus perhaps a few scattered incentives scarcely scratches the surface when it comes to maximum value in the corporation at large.

Board of Directors

This book is for directors and representatives of active shareholder groups seeking to maximize their total shareholder return. In relative terms, as well as absolute numbers. If the general market index rises by 50 percent but their company's value increases by only 30 percent on a comparable basis, the judgment is that value is destroyed, on a relative basis. These are the representatives for the owners who will no longer accept "trust me" bromides that maximum shareholder value will be achieved at some magical date in the future. Who insist on practical, effective value-creation actions.

Executives, Managers, Others Who Wish to Be Part of the Full Value Solution

Or else, they may be seen as part of the value underachievement problem. These are the managers who want to ensure that they are indispensable in pursuing maximum value. Who seek the professional freedom and rewards of being designated as individual key value generators: Corporate Key (Value) Contributors as introduced in Chapter 3.

If No One Acts to Maximize Value, the Raiders Will Act

Then there are the active acquirers trawling for value-underperforming corporations as takeover targets. The independent and aligned acquisition groups amassing unprecedented war chests in anticipation of the 2000–2004 merger boom period. If management fails to secure a large portion of the missing 80 + percent value, outsiders have the incentive and now the funds to take advantage.[3]

SECTION I
Value Foundations

1

Your Corporation Is Underperforming by 50 Percent

Your corporation is underperforming by 50 percent. In value terms, on a continuing basis.

Such words have the sound of an anguished workout manager ready to give up all hope on a fast-failing company. Certainly such strident warnings don't have anything to do with an effective, well-managed corporation. Such as yours.

Wrong. Even well-managed corporations leave significant value on the table. Unrealized and unachieved. Ripe to be plucked by rivals with the speed and tenacity to take advantage.

Value unavailable to shareholders, who own the corporation and provide the sustaining capital. When management leaves significant value behind, all of those proclamations about "maximizing shareholder value" (MSV) *really* mean "we only capture a small portion of the total value available to the corporation—but that minor detail won't prevent us from proclaiming maximum value development, in any event."

This smokescreen might even work, for a while at least. The chief executive points out that the corporation's stock price has dou-

3

bled over the past two years as evidence that your management is maximizing value for shareholders. It is only later, following an unsolicited and unwanted takeover bid at 40 percent over today's market value (stock price times shares outstanding), that the propaganda is revealed as a lie.

The more placid the shareholder group, the longer this smokescreen endures. But increasingly, the corporation's shareholder-owners have minds of their own. They are not easily led by the slick financial PR phrases alone. And they are increasingly motivated and willing to raise uncomfortable questions about the adequacy of the corporation's value creation efforts.

A shareholder might well ask: "If the stock price doubled over two years, yet industry leaders' stock prices tripled over the same period and on a comparable basis, wouldn't that indicate destruction of 50 percent of achievable value? And if the bid from an acquirer 'does not maximize wealth for shareholders' as you describe, then why is it that accepting that bid makes us rich while standing pat leaves us with little more than Trust Me excuses?"

At the center of these questions is rediscovery of what *maximizing shareholder value* actually means. And what it does not.

MSV should not be some bolt-on, all-purpose embellishment for use by the corporation's financial spin doctors. It is a phrase conveniently vague enough to prevent the manager from being pinned down yet still conveys a favorable future for all. MSV is often used by spin doctors to mollify shareholders enough to discourage challenge, or even follow-up questions.

But examine each word carefully, and the true, full implications of maximizing shareholder value emerge:

- *Maximum.* This means that no value opportunity is knowingly missed. That nothing is permitted to continue within the corporation that suppresses value. Management that destroys value by missing the critical product launch and/or by sustaining zero-contribution deadwood managers can and will declare they are "maximizing shareholder value" despite evidence to the contrary. But such statements swiftly unravel when it becomes apparent that value is missed. Or even worse, actively destroyed.

The word maximum begs a reference point. Maximum compared to what? Yesterday's performance? Tomorrow's results? An unsolicited bid from outside? Choose a deliberately modest point of comparison, and management only delays the day of reckoning. "We've increased current value 25 percent since the time of the last measurement."

But what if even present performance is only half of the achievable potential? Spinners' slick words are no defense against the acquirer with too much cash, trawling for target opportunities.

Without some form of systematic, consistent method for capturing full value, a company might achieve, say, only 35 percent of total available value. But that improvement won't hold water if the industry's average improvement is 45 percent and a few well-funded predators harbor suspicions that full value management can get that figure up to 60 + percent.

• *Shareholder.* Total shareholder return (TSR) is the owners' ultimate method of evaluating management's value creation performance to date and into the future. It matters little that the company's market value has increased 20 percent to date. Unless there is clear evidence that future TSR will do just as well or better, the owners will probably follow the path of their self-interest and look elsewhere. All capital has alternative uses. So a complete and objective performance assessment requires comparison of expected future returns from this corporation contrasted with the best of the alternatives.

Three of those best alternatives are: (1) non-risk returns (e.g., from 30-year long-term government bonds); (2) top TSR levels within the same industry; or (3) the corporation's own return under optimal value performance.[1]

The CEO of a $20 billion global technology corporation in 1999 suggested that his company's TSR should be assessed by shareholders compared only to returns from risk-free bonds (alternative 1, above). But without both of the other two comparisons, alternatives (2) and (3), the comparison is flawed. The target has been set too low.[2]

• *Value.* The overwhelming empirical evidence confirms that the corporation's market value (stock price) varies most directly with that corporation's projected net cash flows, discounted at weighted average cost of capital over that analysis period.[3]

Such a definition means gnashing of teeth by those purely interested in the PR potential of the phrase "maximizing shareholder value." These are the spin doctors who far prefer the advantages of a phrase that sounds favorable but lacks precise definition to the reality of tough, continuing effort to chase a continuously improving goal. Do you believe that your company's top five overall major action sets for creating new value have been identified? The true value maximizer is open to the stark reality that half of the more important value priorities have been missed or underdeveloped or both. Or that new opportunities to improve corporate value still more have emerged just recently, raising the MSV bar still higher.

Do you believe that maximizing shareholder value is a general-purpose spinner phrase? Think again. Maximizing shareholder value is the *purpose of the corporation.* The singular objective of impor-tance, because without achievement of that goal first, nothing else matters.

The chief executive of the corporation mired in the middle ranks of his industry tries out the MSV phrase in its old role as perceptions-bender, only to find that there's no reaction at all. Nothing. For in its financial PR shadow form, the MSV phrase is banal and simple to ignore. The phrase takes on life only when applied in a competitive sense. Are we creating more value than our competition? Are we cre-ating enough value to discourage unwanted predator interest? How are we doing competing against *ourselves*—by striving to capture all of the corporation's missing value?

When a company comes "in play" because of an unwelcome ac-quisition bid at, say, 40 percent over stock price, the chief executive will face some tough questions by shareholders about what he plans to do to increase value by that premium percentage or more. If the answers are unsatisfactory, management is history, and acquisition is imminent. Even if this CEO acts immediately, the tough truth is that it may already be too late. Extraordinary value creation must occur before the raiders come to break down the door. Value discover-ies made after that point are seen as frantic desperation measures. Too little. Way, way too late.

The leader of the rental company whose stock has risen mini-mally during the unprecedented boom decade of the 1990s might try to proclaim that MSV is being achieved, but such words are now to-tally unconvincing. With their downloadable comparative stock charts, it takes institutional investors about five seconds to figure out their relative TSR losses from choosing this company instead of the top value performer.

Doubt that there's such a thing as a double-digit Value Opportu-nity Gap (VOG) separating the corporation's current value from its full potential worth? Better hope that acquirers in the post-millen-nium acquisition boom trawling for new targets buy your reasoning and not your corporation.

The extended 1990s economic expansion is entering its third phase in 1999–2003. In past cycles, this third phase has been characterized by the highest levels of merger and acquisition activity, both in terms of deal volume and percentages of acquisition premiums paid, relative to pre-bid market value.

Management that leaves 40–50 percent value on the table effectively hangs a ten-foot-high "For Sale" sign on their own corporations. Acquirers look first at those deals that exploit the value gap themselves to pay for all or part of the deal premium, describing those companies as "undervalued." The truth is even worse: the targets are undermanaged and undeveloped, in value terms.[4]

Curiously, it is the chief executives of the corporations with the highest current analyzed valuation and market value who tend to be among the first to comprehend the essence of managing the corporation according to Value Opportunity Gap (VOG). These executives manage the business through a never-ending process of taking key actions to close the difference between value today and full, potential value tomorrow. Maximum value.

Don't make the mistake of confusing VOG management with mere "value based management." The first applies to a fully robust, continuous approach that combines both analysis and actions—directed to capturing all of the company's missing value, not just some of its worth. By contrast, value based management is the standard label for the consultant-statistician's theoretical models that prescribe some value creation and its effects, but little more. More value-based management is a partial effort that applauds the creation of $200 million in added value, even when another $800 million is left behind, undiscovered and unrealized.

Those who are obsessed with maximum shareholder value as contrasted with partial value are the first to understand the multiple advantages of achieving MSV for real. The immediate benefits of capturing all the value are immediately understood by all. Lower capital costs, today and probably tomorrow. More wealth for the owners of the business. Increased access to capital markets, as past owners have been well-rewarded for providing capital to date. Increased TSRs along with an increased chance that shareholders assess management's performance as creating maximum value. The shareholders are the only group with a right to proclaim true MSV; only they have the perspective to make that determination.

The secondary benefits of achieving full, maximum value may be less apparent, but are no less important. These benefits include:

- Increased shareholder wealth for each increment of new cash flow, as reflected by a superior market value (price)/cash flow ratio (P/CF).

- Greater protection from unwanted acquisition interest.
- Increased opportunity to act as acquirer during the 2000–2003 merger and acquisition boom, facilitated by low-cost equity for use as deal currency.
- Advantages in attracting Corporate Key Contributor people: the walking, talking sources of new value creation who will make all the difference in the future. These top employees are already calculating how much money they lost by their mistake of accepting last year's offer with share options. They want to help build more value in the future.[5]

Vague best-efforts corporate resolutions to merely "improve shareholder value" are never good enough for the pragmatic CEO who's heard it all and knows the difference between results and hollow rhetoric. All the three-letter-acronym statistical valuation models together never created one dollar of corporate value all by themselves (including APV, Appendix A). Maximum value is achieved through action only. Especially the top initiatives that elude the budgeteers and value statisticians, who treat MSV only as a number-crunching exercise.

How much improvement is enough to reach maximum? There is never enough, as the full potential value (Vp) bar is always being raised.

Any manager seeking an instant accolade that they are "maximizing shareholder value" is sure to be disappointed by the reality of continually increasing Vp. Even if management takes exhaustive actions and closes the Vp-Vn gap to almost nothing, accelerating change and other factors mean that bar will be raised: next week, next month, next quarter. Stand pat, even for just a moment, and the corporation falls back, in relative value terms.

There is no rest for the corporation that achieves maximum value for real. None.

In sometimes significant, other times subtle ways, corporations that perform well nonetheless leave substantial shareholder value on the table. This can happen in the form of a capital structure that boosts value some, yet fails to optimize shareholder wealth. Or value can be lost through delays in eliminating the lower rung salesperson presently subsidized by the others who are functioning closer to maximum value level. Value is also destroyed when research and development budgets are based on yesterday's rule-of-thumb ratios instead of tomorrow's competitive requirements. Finally, shareholders lose when ponderous, bureaucracy-intensive corporate capital expenditure (CAPEX) decision systems react so slowly that key business opportunities are missed.

For the chief executive with a resolve to meet The Value Mandate to maximize shareholder value—all the time and for real—the challenge is to embark on a major, sustainable value agenda and program. This program is a continually updated process capable of achieving the full operating and value potential of the corporation. The alternative to meeting the Mandate? Chapter 4 states that the average American or British CEO now lasts less than four years in office. The CEO on the wrong side of those comparative market value trend line charts makes a case for shortening that time frame still further.

This chapter starts the journey for those managers obsessed with fully meeting the shareholders' Value Mandate. This book is for those seeking to maximize shareholder value for real, because nothing less is acceptable on either a professional or personal basis.

1.1 The Case for 50 Percent Value Underperformance

Defining the difference between the company's potential value (Vp) and present worth (Vn)—that is, defining the Value Opportunity Gap—is far more important to accomplish in general terms than pursuing false precision.

The future cannot be precisely measured. So it is far better to direct most of the corporation's value program resources and people toward finding those few, key value initiatives that make all the difference. Far better to be aware that the Value Opportunity Gap is presently in a 50 to 57 percent range and to know the critical actions necessary to close that Gap, than to waste time trying to pinpoint the exact underperformance amount. An insecure CEO might be impressed by an unnecessarily complex valuation model. For the rest, the dazzle connotes paralysis by analysis, not progress. Precise future estimates exist only in economists' dreams. Pragmatic, outperforming top managers emphasize the key actions to narrow the VOG.[6]

Leaping Ahead in the Marketplace: or, When Not Keeping Up Means Chronic Value Underperformance

The Jack Welchism, "Number-One-Or-Number-Two," communicates the GE chairman's no-nonsense perspective on the performance required for the corporation to remain in control of its own destiny.[7] Unless the company dominates its group or is a relentless contender for the top, probabilities are high that the same corporation will not show up on two Standard & Poor's 500 lists in a row, compiled five years apart. At least not in the same form and under the same name and ownership.

Industries of twelve competitors shrink down to just six continuing rivals. Segments comprised of six implode to two competitors. In both instances, mandatory increases in investment combined with continuously accelerating speed-to-market requirements force out the laggards.

Disruptive new market entrants perform a dynamic role in these industries, far beyond their early cash flow impact. Examples are FedEx in overnight package express; Southwest Airlines in discount air travel; and Schwab in retail securities brokerage (and again, later, in retail online securities brokerage). Each of these new irritant-entrant introduces its own "impossible" (as seen by rivals) new performance threshold. And yet that new higher level rapidly becomes the industry's new standard.

This new order involves not just changes in cost and revenue elements, but also radical rearrangement of the industry's entire profit, cash flow, and value creation structures. All aspects of how wealth is created within that industry are revolutionized: what is sold, how customers use the product, the basis for competition, the pace and pattern of product and service migration.

It used to be that the new entrant's limited-risk, market-entry tactic called for displacing an existing, mid-level participant. Slow to react and quick to choose the wrong response, the target laggard was pushed far deeper into the ranks of that industry's also-rans, with the new kid taking its place.

This displacement tactic worked because market cycles were still slow enough and predictable enough for me-too imitation to work. A company could wait to see what another is doing, copy the essence, and then adjust terms in order to present a proposition that the marketplace could not refuse. Services were even easier: The key resource to grab walked out of the target laggard's door at night.

This combination of a me-too product with a 25–30 percent reduction in pricing and a momentum-setting initial ad blitz resulted in the capture of the middle rung participant's customers. The middle-rung company then became a lower rung, often just before disappearing completely.[8]

Today, faster-paced times and shrinking life cycles have eliminated the middle competitive tier of companies altogether. Figure 1-1 shows the pattern of shrinking economic life cycles over fifty years, in five different industries. Other data show that the market rental life of personal computers shrinks each year. PCs' rental lives are among the most sensitive indicators of life cycle changes in technology industries, as the pattern of shrinkage reflects both new changes in economic obsolescence and utility. In 1994, PCs based on the Intel 486 chip had a United Kingdom rental life of around 17 months. Three years later, the market life of next-generation PCs with Intel 166 chips was down to 11 months, a shrinkage of 35 percent.

In some high-technology industries, watershed changes in market conditions occur as rapidly as every six to nine months, with each change potentially involving a switch in product direction. It isn't a coincidence that you find most of the content in your physical or on-line database has become stale after six months or so. By 2003, you'll be regarding as ancient intelligence that is only one quarter old.

Faster times mean soaring investment burdens for all continuing participants, thus encouraging industry consolidation and explo-

Figure 1-1. Shrinking economic life cycles: some examples.

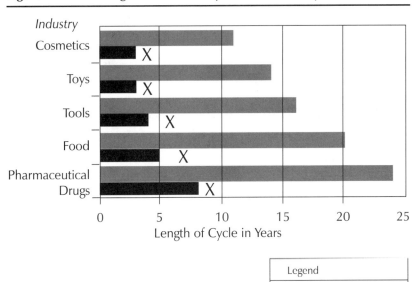

Source: A. D. Little, from Christopher-Friedrich von Braun, *The Innovation War* (Englewood Cliffs, N.J., Prentice-Hall PTR, 1997), page 10. Reprinted with permission from A. D. Little.

ration of unconventional leap-ahead shortcuts to market that companies previously rejected outright.

The investment dollars necessary to bring each new product or service from the point of initial inspiration all the way to viable commercial offering remain relatively unchanged. But radically shrinking life cycles mean that the number of new launches per year doubles or triples. It isn't just that new products are arriving to market faster, its also that there are far more of them. As an example, competition in the Internet-business-to-consumer (B2C) search engines segment seems to follow a geometric population curve that looks like something from Malthus: First there are two companies, then twenty, then two hundred in just a couple years. As more and more businesses become Net businesses—in one form or another—the growth pace soars.

Whether the company is a new entrant scrambling for survival market presence or an old hand trying to command its market role rather than be bent by it, time must be invented, somehow. Time is value, after all (a slight twist on your mother's parable). So the company that somehow discovers new time sources that others miss is also the company with a value-creation edge. The development double leap is one of time and value technique: deliberately skipping every other product/service generation in order to establish a minimum 50 percent performance/features/price advantage over key rivals, continually. Some other techniques for translating time into value are addressed elsewhere in the book.

Internal Value Development Opportunities

The value outperformer chief executive recalls other, past instances when internal cost-reduction initiatives or new product launches achieved a 50 percent or greater improvement in cash flow, the principal determinant of value.

Those precedents suggest to him or her that other improvements of comparable scale are also achievable elsewhere, in other parts of the corporation. Numerous value building blocks of this scale are described in Section II in this book, Chapters 5–8. The improvement opportunities also suggest the extent of the difference between present value and potential value—The Value Opportunity Gap.

Examples include changing to a progressive commission schedule for the sales force, continually updated on a ninety-day moving average basis. Combined with annual cropping of the bottom 10–20 percent of the sales force each year. Straightforward action to extract the most value from the sales force, on a continuing basis.

Other 50 + percent value improvement actions include: a change from manufacturing products from parts for finished goods inventory to module assembly of products built on a confirmed advance-order basis only (hence no finished goods inventory). Another value improvement strategy: replace field pricing by sales representatives with a central, but responsive, analyzed approach led by a professional pricing manager who is pursuing maximum return.[9]

Each company's list of key value improvement opportunities is different. That list can only be developed from investigation of that corporation's specific circumstances. No number-crunch valuation formula can guide management to these opportunities—at best, value statistics only help make the right decision once the value opportunity has already been identified and developed. Trickle-up suggestions from employee ranks may miss the most important opportunities for the simple reason that what's best for the corporation is not necessarily best for each employee. Consultants describe grand plans to capture the intellectual property of the corporation and encourage employees to describe the secrets of their success. But some are hesitant to share, reasoning that if they give away their competitive edge, they are more likely to disappear in the next downsizing move.

Similar considerations prevents the minor trickle-up suggestion from being of much value help. Some value is always suggested—insistence that things are good as they can be and cannot be improved at all merely puts a harsh spotlight on that operation. What are they hiding? An employee might fear that significant changes in process or implementation could affect how he does his job. Sometimes even threaten that job itself.

Figure 1-2 illustrates how some of the more significant value opportunities are only uncovered when *how* things are done and even *who* conducts those activities are subject to challenge and possible reform (B and C).

Budget adjustments (A) generate minimal new value through incremental changes in costs and/or productivity goals. Structural adaptations (B) alter the approach to the function. Fundamental changes in the activity (C) involve changes in use and timing; sometimes this also involves changes in provider if that means an improvement in value.[10]

The revenue side project in Figure 1-2 involves bid preparation by international consulting engineers with offices worldwide, headquartered outside the U.S. (circumstances adjusted and name changed here to "Grommark-X"). The expense side activity in Figure

Figure 1-2. Fifty percent value underperformance.

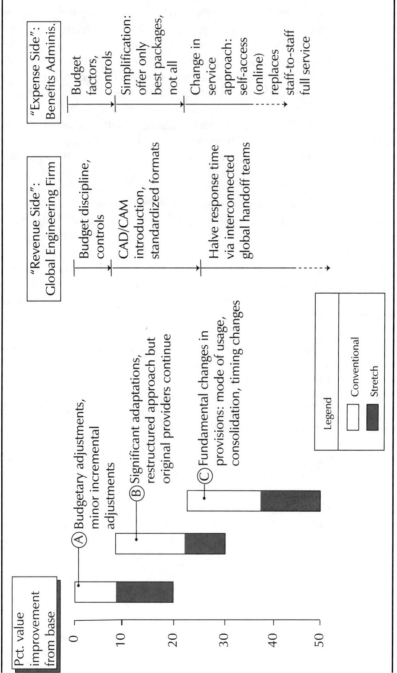

Source: VBM Consulting (www.vbm-consulting.com).

1-2 involves changes in the corporation's internal provision of benefits data for company employees, based on the experience of several companies.

Creating Value by Changing How the Corporation Wins New Business

Grommark-X management achieves minor value improvement of around 8 percent from limited cost changes (Figure 1-2[A]). Replacing manual drawing and a one-off design approach with computer aided design/computer aided manufacturing (CAD/CAM) and standardized tools (B) increases new value by a further 17 percent, which combined with (A) adds up to a 25 percent overall value improvement. Questioning incumbent practices about how and where bids are prepared adds another 15 percent, and Grommark-X's total value improvement surges lurches toward the 40 percent mark (C).

Instead of preparation by one team in one city, the design bid is prepared by pass-off teams located approximately eight time zones apart around the globe—for example, Paris, Singapore, Chicago. The three teams exchange progress drawings and bid estimations via videoconferencing and/or officing via the company's global intranet, enabling the corporation to respond in a fraction of its previous time. The sun never sets on the Grommark-X Request for Proposals (RFP) response process: Work goes on 24 hours a day, every day. But each separate team of engineers stays fresh by working normal hours.

Faster response time means that more bids can be pursued, and more bids are won due to the advantage of being the first with a fully complete package. Customers respond with "Hey, these guys really have their act together. No need to look at anyone else." Even if a second round is necessary, however, Grommark's odds of winning the business are still far greater than before. Faster response speed in the follow-up round means more time for extra questions and test scenarios to refine the winning bid.[11]

Grommark-X's value soars as (1) more RFPs can be handled per period, with (2) increased success probability on each RFP. Management figures that the company can now handle more than twice the number of RFPs compared to before, within the same time period. In the era of Internet time, time is value. By spreading staff throughout the world and hiring locally, average cost-per-engineer decreases significantly. Fresh perspectives are introduced to the corporation. New business development is enhanced, as each separate location in the global pass-off chain acts as an active listening post for new RFP opportunities originating from each office's region. Intradepartmental political cliques are disabled. No longer is it possible for one self-important group located at headquarters to dictate to others despite superior contribution and insight elsewhere. For at the department level, global pass-off means there is no longer a headquarters, practically speaking.

Goodbye to the meeting mavens and all the value-destroying, forgettable intrigue they foment. Global pass-off returns the central focus of the business back where it belongs, to the actual work conducted for clients. The slick coaster who once hid effortlessly behind the accomplishments of others now stands out like a bad penny in the harsh light of internal competition between different, compact pass-off teams. Each team can only keep up with the pace set by others when every member is a full and significant contributor. No team can afford to ever be viewed as the corporate weak link; that designation threatens everyone. So the value-destroying individual coaster is quickly discovered and jettisoned for the good of the whole. The whole team, the whole corporation. The whole of shareholders' value.

Flexible Menu Benefits: When the User Would Rather Do It for Himself

The benefits administrative example in Figure 1-2 is a composite, reflecting what can sometimes be achieved when assumptions regarding staff-to-staff services are challenged in pursuit of something better. These new approaches change how things are done and, as a result, lower significantly the cost per internal transaction.

Value is *added* in the sense that the situation is better than if nothing was done at all. But value is *destroyed* in the sense that the *optimal* value has not yet been implemented.

Management introduces a menu-style flexible benefits, providing employees with new flexibility to adapt their benefits package to personal needs, rather than a take-it-or-leave-it dictated package. But this greater flexibility must be carefully implemented. If uncontrolled, this greater flexibility can add extra layers of value-destroying bureaucracies. New staff mini-fiefdoms can pop up to drain corporate cash flow and diminish value as extra fixed cost burdens on the corporation.

Initially, all questions concerning the corporation's new array of benefits are channeled through one of these bureaucracies. By necessity, rather than choice: it seems that those staff are the only ones fully versed in the arcane but mostly meaningless detail of special terms, tracking numbers, and forms required for even the simplest of program revisions.

For department heads looking for a soft featherbed to park a coaster with more pals than ability, the result of this unnecessary complexity is the equivalent of a full employment act. This illustrates suboptimalization at its worst, as narrow individual interests are allowed to destroy corporate value. At some point it becomes apparent that a key competitor has established a cost advantage, including an enduring edge in general and administrative (G&A) expenses. The need for face-to-face services has been justified to date on the basis of service. It will take forever if the beneficiary has to investigate these matters himself. No company officer will put up with performing his own benefits analysis. Convincing arguments, at least until the rising mountain of complaints about surly, lackluster results makes a bad joke of the word "service." Management's reluctant conclusion is that they might as well explore radical non-staff alternatives, as there's no personal service to speak of now.

But new, dual goals emerge: to simultaneously reduce ongoing costs while improving service. Budget veterans who know the horse-trading game of swapping budget for commitments respond with the bureaucrat's automatic response: "Yes, you can have that extra speed and simplicity, but it will cost xx amount more to get it done . . ."

At one point in time, management might have played this bluff game—not because it efficiently allocates resources, but because there was no other alternative. No longer. Shocked bureaucrat-negotiators are informed that not only is their trade-off rejected, but that there's no longer any debate. The company will pursue a radical/pragmatic alternative that liberates company value by changing how things are done.

The key is to simplify and standardize the base services to permit the broadest number and range of alternative, qualified providers, wherever the best exists, either within or outside the company. A major aspect is deliberate reduction in the number of benefits-menu line items. The seemingly endless number of possible benefits combinations are cut down drastically by limiting the options to those covering the greatest majority of requests. Exceptions are discouraged, but when accepted they are handled on an exception basis with that department absorbing the additional cost.

Such simplification is also a precondition to converting the service approach from expensive full service to more affordable user self-access, with requests made directly on the corporation's intranet. The individual becomes responsible for accessing data and making changes himself. The service survives, but not necessarily the corporation's internal middlemen.[12]

Acquisition Bids as Indicators of Value Underperformance

> Ultimate arbiter of value is the price at which an enterprise itself actually changes hands. That's why investors normally pay close heed to the valuations of mergers and acquisitions.
> —David Simons, *The Industry Standard*[13]

> Either the acquirer develops additional sources of corporate value and makes up the (value) gap—and succeeds, or it does not.
> —*Beyond the Deal*, p. 23

According to efficient market theory, the publicly traded corporation's full value is already reflected in the company's share price. All intelligence and rumors about possibilities, opportunities, threats, costs, and competitive data are instantly assimilated by the financial community and brought to bear on that company's market value.

The predatory acquiring group's management knows that even though the present stock price is "full," an even greater value must be paid to acquire that company. The minimum practical bid premium is around 20–25 percent in the two phases of the economic expansion. But this deal premium tends to expand to 30–35 + percent during the third, concluding, merger- and acquisition-intensive phase of the expansion (Figure 1-3).[14]

Implications: Every Company Is Now in Play, All the Time

"Today, any company can be put in play." This acquirer's claim sounds like bravado, but it isn't. Management's lowest risk assumption is to presume that the corporation will be bid upon. Which means that every manager must be concerned about the adequacy of their value development programs.

Whether the acquirer's bid is a bottom-trawling 12 percent over

Figure 1-3. U.S. acquirers' offer prices vs. share prices one year prior to bid announcement.

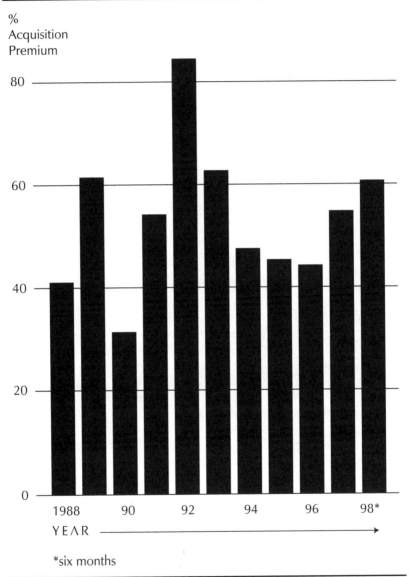

%
Acquisition
Premium

*six months

Source: J. P. Morgan study of 1,200 transactions cited in Daniel Bögler, "U.S. Investors Grow Wary of Merger Fever," *The Financial Times,* August 5, 1998, page 29. Reprinted with permission from *The Financial Times.*

prevailing full market price or a breathtaking 50 percent, the standard response from target management is predictable: "This offer is not in the best interest of our company's shareholders." Guess they mean top management who are shareholders, those who stand to lose their jobs in any takeover. Because shareholders at large benefit far more by taking up the outsider's deal than wondering if incumbent management can or will make good on their value promises.

A scarcely disguised plea to major shareholders is implicit in management's first response: "Please give us another chance to develop value we've missed to date, and we pledge to do an even better value-creation job than represented by this outside bid." Prospects that such a plea works depends largely on value-creating progress to date. Management that has taken substantive actions to identify and reduce their corporation's Value Opportunity Gap through specific key campaigns probably get their wish—for now. But if the pledge for action dissolves into reliance on half-measures such as trickle-up suggestions from the field or balance sheet reengineering alone, time quickly runs out. Major investors—and more importantly, potential acquirers—know that much of the corporation's missing value remains uncaptured.

Major investor groups, still wincing from disappointing relative TSR results from investing in this incumbent management, ask the embattled CEO: "If you say that you can increase value more than outsiders, why have you waited until now?" Polite words for a far tougher question: "Why should we believe that you can or will meet The Value Mandate now, when you have not done so to date?"

Truth is, there are no good reasons to delay substantive value creation until the company is put in play. There are, in fact, many reasons not to wait. The corporate value agenda implemented under duress of an outsider's acquisition offer shouts management self-interest to all: suboptimal actions that places a few careers ahead of overall shareholder value. Expenditures are slashed without careful consideration of value effect—just cut the costs, any costs, so that tomorrow's planted headline can shout "value improvement." Prime assets of the company are dumped at fire sale prices to remove them from the predator's clutches.

At best these frantic too-little, too-late actions spotlight areas for attention by predators.

It is apparent that holdover management does not command a workable program for major new value progress. It is apparent that incumbents lack a systematic program necessary to deflect acquisition bids at prices up to 50 percent above present market value.

It becomes increasingly evident that beleaguered management doesn't know where to look to create value beyond surface balance sheet cosmetics, and confuses minor tweaking of the debt/capital ratio with an adequate value creation agenda. Or, management confuses incidental changes to the business—price, product, and resource allocation adjustments— with substantive new value creation. But the market does not make the same mistake. Incidental actions fall far short of maximum value, and are already "in the market" and part of current stock price. Or, that the value opportunities investigation fails to probe deep enough into the right sector's base business where most of the operations value opportunities reside.

Hard-hitting value-creation programs rarely bubble up from the staff ranks, for the reason that some of the more comprehensive value reforms mean uncomfortable changes in present ways of doing things. Sometimes, value reforms mean the loss of jobs. Maximizing shareholder value may be the driving interest of those with a significant equity stake in the company. But for employees with nominal or no share ownership, *first* priority is self-preservation—regardless of any lip service to maximizing shareholder value. Some of the changes in process, channel, incentives, and focus with the greatest value development potential also pose the most threat to the existing order. Something has to give.

The value improvement program that sacrifices the other guy's position or rank is a tough but necessary value improvement. But the action that sacrifices *my* position, rank, or role is immediately seen as "cutting the meat not the fat." Everyone moans about the $15 in office supplies that cost the company $150 when processed via the corporation's procurement labyrinth. But don't hold your breath waiting for the purchasing department to commit budget suicide by voluntarily suggesting radical value reforms, which involve staff losses.[15]

Maximum value must be implemented while it is still effective. Late, careless, and extreme actions implemented only after the company is put "in play" is an effective admission of management's value development failure.[16]

Acquiring Group Guesses about Missing Value in the Target: The Acquisition Bid Range

The acquiring group's CEO justifies a bid in excess of present (full) market value based on the reasoning that he or she has knowledge of and access to additional value sources not presently in the market: sources not known in the efficient marketplace.

Different sources of out-of-market hidden value are sought and proclaimed. In the early 1980s, leveraged buyout proponents declared "undervalued assets," epitomized by WesRay Capital's purchase and subsequent round turn sale of Gibson Greeting Cards in 1983. But such value windfall gains are exceedingly rare. "Untapped value" may make good spin-rhetoric, but efficient markets assure that prices quickly adjust, removing most windfall opportunities.

Alternatively, there's the dealmakers' bread-and-butter ratio-nale: out of market, post-transaction synergies. The argument: Elim-inating expense overlaps in back office, advertising, and other administrative functions liberates value to help make the transaction more affordable. Again, spin-rhetoric: May sound okay in the evening biz-press, but it doesn't work. The majority of synergies are openly debated in the financial press, particularly during merger and acqui-sition high season, which confirms that such adjustments are usually already "in the market," at least in part. Thus, no such value cre-ation is available to offset the typical 30–45 + percent acquisition premium necessary to close the deal.[17]

After such undervalued-assets illusions and double-counted syn-ergies are crossed off, where else does the acquisitive CEO look to cover the deal premium? To the operations of the target company itself—those fundamental changes in core operations that have prob-ably never been discovered by predecessor management. Or if they have been discovered, never enacted.

Proclamations come fast and furious from the acquiring group's spin doctors. New, superior management will find and secure the value that the others could not. Although it is important that share-holders be convinced, a second audience also needs to approve of the acquisition: the acquiring company's own Board. Approval may stall unless the acquirer-CEO can convince his Board on two points. First, that there is sufficient untapped, but realizable, new value in the tar-get to cover the bid premium. Second, that his team is uniquely capa-ble of extracting that extra worth, not an outside acquirer or replacement management team.

Thus, the acquirer's bid premium takes on special significance as an indication of estimated missing value (Figure 1-4). Acquirers who bid, say, 37 percent over pre-bid market value in effect communi-cate that they believe that they can extract that amount of extra value in the acquired corporation.

Figure 1-4 illustrates three bid ranges. Range A refers to a bid

Figure 1-4. Expansion cycle third phase: acquisition bids as trailing indicators of underdeveloped value.

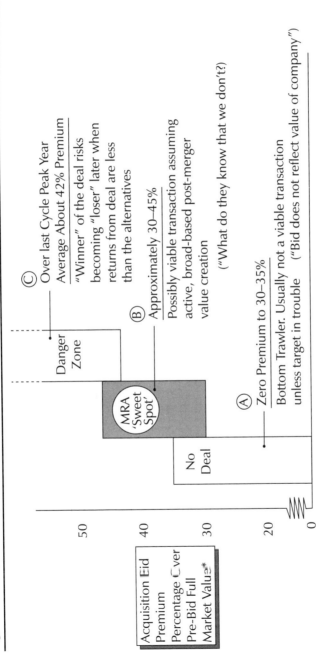

Ⓒ Over last Cycle Peak Year
Average About 42% Premium

"Winner" of the deal risks
becoming "loser" later when
returns from deal are less
than the alternatives

Ⓑ Approximately 30–45%

Possibly viable transaction assuming
active, broad-based post-merger
value creation

("What do they know that we don't?)

Danger
Zone

MRA
'Sweet
Spot'

No
Deal

Ⓐ Zero Premium to 30–35%

Bottom Trawler. Usually not a viable transaction
unless target in trouble   ("Bid does not reflect value of company")

50

40

30

20

0

Acquisition Bid
Premium
Percentage Over
Pre-Bid Full
Market Value*

*Based on stock prices five trading days
before acquisition announcement.

Source: Beyond the Deal: Optimizing Merger and Acquisition Value (New York: HarperBusiness, 1996), pages 11, 25, 37, and 77.

premium of less than 30–35 percent. This is a null set, as deals below that level cannot be closed at least not during the merger- and acquisition-intensive third phase of the economic cycle.

Range B is the acquisition sweet spot: a premium around 30 percent above pre-bid market, into the low 40s. Rich enough to close the deal, yet not out of reach in terms of additional value to cover the acquisition premium.

Range C is *beyond* the predator's grasp. Excessive bids raise immediate suspicions that pricing is dictated solely by the resolve not to be outbid, regardless of spin to the contrary. The new acquirer better enjoy his press description as a winner now; the praise may be short-lived. Deals in 45 + percent premium range were among the first to collapse in the brief but severe 1990–1992 U.S. economic downdraft.

1.2 Relative Value, the Backward Valuation Illusion, Value Types

Three issues emerge that are central to achieving maximum shareholder value. The first involves separating true maximum shareholder value programs from impostors. The second issue is how to achieve future cash flows that correspond to present value.

The third issue involves the origins of value. The complete MSV agenda includes value from both revenue and expense sides. No corporation ever shrank its way to industry dominance and value leadership.

Relative Value

Any unilateral proclamation from management that "we are maximizing shareholder value" should ring alarm bells. Maximum value implies a systematic, robust, continuing program that identifies and captures all the possible value, coupled with priority lists of actions aimed at closing this Value Opportunity Gap (VOG).

When Top Management Tries to Have It Both Ways

The chief executive of hypothetical "Striver Corp." states that he aspires to maximum value for his company. The words flow easily, but he's far less eager to take the full actions necessary to reach that objective. Not just because of the temporary disruptions that come whenever value-destroying actions are removed, but also because of the time and effort mandated by a serious MSV program.

Striver Corp.'s CEO would much rather take partial actions and try to convince outsiders that they are "maximum." Say, bump up debt as a percentage of capital, from 40 to 60 percent, then declare an increase in *allocated* (but not necessarily financed) research and development spending. And then leave it to others to spin those actions into a press-friendly blurb about how well management is doing in maximizing shareholder value.

But achieving MSV for real takes the time and effort to develop and implement a thorough program. Sooner or later, Striver's CEO comes to understand that no one ever believes the ruse. That disbelief is underscored by a market price-to-cash flow (PCF) multiple that is well below that of the industry's leaders. If Striver is the leader of an underperforming industry, the PCF is still far below what it should be. Management of the corporation closest to closing its VOG is the first to acknowledge that total potential (maximum) value can never actually be reached.

Closing the VOG takes time. Management needs to take the time to construct a company-wide mechanism to pursue MSV on a continuing basis; to distinguish between the apparent and actual major value thresholds; and to review and augment incomplete value actions already enacted, such as a tweak to financial ratio that falls far short of a comprehensive Value-Optimal Capital Structure.[18]

Closing the VOG takes effort. Effort must be made to sustain pursuit of maximum value as an essential corporate activity. Value opportunities are continually changing, as is the corporation's full potential value—that is, its maximum value. The one-off value event is as incomplete as the effort that reduces sales costs by two points when eight are available for the taking.

Some of the loyal cronies of Striver Corp.'s CEO shudder when they realize that they might become expendable if an objective assessment of value contribution is enacted for real, not just for show. Passive supervision was once celebrated as an essential business role. But when technology and expertise advances to the point that the generalist supervisor depends on his direct reports to inform *him* about the issues to be raising in managing *them,* supervision becomes a farce.

There are more shocks to come. Maximizing shareholder value for real probably means the beginning of the end for the oversized

suburban headquarters. These headquarters can no longer be justified as a sales showcase now that most major contract sales are made
in the client's office. No more trendy doorknobs emblazoned with the
company's logo.

If door knobs give pause for thought, you can imagine the quick
intake of breath when confronted with the next challenge—to double
innovation investment and yield while halving general and administrative expenses as a percentage of revenue. All at the same time.
Such action must become a priority because competitors are either
doing that now, or will be doing it soon.

Striver Corp.'s chief executive officer notes with pride that the
company's stock price has doubled over the last two years. Stock price
movements generally coincide with these changes in value for
Striver. The press release barks that "hundreds of millions of dollars
of value have been created for Striver Corp.'s shareholders." It is, of
course, just a coincidence that the CEO is planning to introduce a
new, revised executive incentive package based on broad interpretation of value "created" in the days ahead. His hope is that Board
members will remember the "hundreds of millions of dollars of value
created" part and respond with suitable gratitude.

And luckily for Striver's senior executives, responsibility for apparent value seems to apply only if the stock price *increases*. Even if
Striver's stock price plunges because of a management misstep—a
slow innovation pace or enduring fat or fundamental sales channels
errors—the CEO can count on being able to blame it on "unavoidable
market conditions" assuming a broad-based market slump, regardless of the truth.

Striver management rests easy, confident that there will be no
headlines the next morning that "Striver Management Is Destroying
Billions in Shareholder Value."[19] But they are.

The Rising Tide, which Lifts All Ships

By itself, Striver's doubling of share price over two years tells nothing
about management's true effectiveness at value creation. Only by
contrasting value and value surrogate results with results of other
corporations is the value star distinguished from the bluff.

When it appears that the Dow Jones Industrial Average (DJIA)
index moves in concert with the company's stock price, observers
have a new perspective about whether management is actively creating value, or merely being carried by supportive general market conditions.

Total Shareholder Return (TSR) represents the performance measure of choice, within companies and among investors. TSR in its simplest form calls for measurement on the basis of appreciation in stock price plus cash dividends.[20] As is the case with market value (stock price), indications of stellar performance in TSR terms sometimes dissolve when the basis of reference is expanded. The company's indicated performance is broadened to include reference to: (1) key same-industry competitors; (2) that industry's index; and (3) broad market indexes.

An irritating questioner at Striver's annual meeting notes the corporation's recent 40 percent TSR decline. He asks (only partially tongue-in-cheek) whether the corporation's new executive bonus means that some of the past payouts to top executives for "value created" will now have to be paid back.

Dead microphone. "How'd that guy get in here?" But the question isn't from some professional meetings disrupter, but rather a leading institutional investor in the corporation who happens to equate loss of corporate value as money extracted from his company's pockets.

British Airways Flies Too Low

Microphones can easily be shut off, but tough questions about performance relative to others cannot be quashed as easily. Any sustained slump in value relative to comparable companies suggests that the corporation's value engine is malfunctioning.

Figure 1-5 shows the relative market value (stock price times shares outstanding) indexes for five major airlines from the beginning of 1996 to late August 1999. British Airways (BA) led the group in comparative market value until about the middle of 1997. Then chief executive Robert Airing's sensible objective of liberating BA away from the industry's debilitating boom-bust pattern made great sense on paper, as did stories about rooting out underproductive meetings managers who do little beyond generating internal corporate chatter.

Then something happened. Most eyes focused on headline developments, including friction with unions and the stalled alliance with American Airlines. But those are the side issues compared to the actual value crisis: losing command of the airline's value engine with nothing developed to replace it. Business class passengers were treated as if they were costs rather than resources, leaving BA stuck with the worst of both worlds. Curtailed potential revenue seat miles

Figure 1-5. Quarterly stock price indexes: four airlines, January 1, 1996–August 24, 1999.

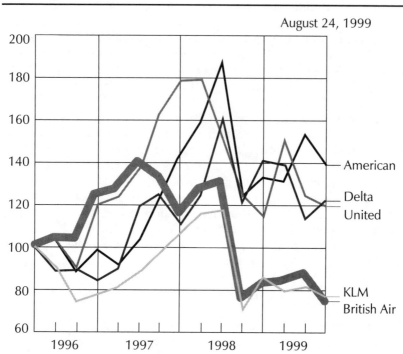

Source: Janet Guyon, "British Airways Takes a Flier," *Fortune,* September 27, 1999, page 90. Reprinted with permission from Time, Inc.

(RSM) as capacity was controlled tightly. A sense of alienation arose among some of those passengers who pay the most per RSM, as evidenced by capture results of arch-rival Virgin Airlines and others.

Few actions are as potentially damaging to a corporation's ongoing value than losing control of its preferred customers. Because even when corrective actions are taken, the costs of reversing the decision can be prohibitive. At times these corrections can be so expensive that management faces a Catch-22 dilemma: preferred customers are required to sustain the business, but paying the extra costs to pull them back from the competition mean that those accounts are now only marginally profitable or even unprofitable.

Avoiding the Backward Valuation Illusion

Followers of Professors Miller and Modillion (M&M) and their 1958 and 1961 articles cited in the Preface quickly realized that their discounted cash flow model is reversible. The more familiar application is to estimate corporate value "forward"; that is, deriving an indication of current value based on the level, timing, and composition of *projected* future cash flows and investment.

Reversing that order means starting with the company's current value, then inserting assumptions about analysis period, present and future capital costs, risk, terminal value, and other components. The solution is then in the form of the future cash flow streams that correspond to today's corporate worth.[21]

Future cash flows correspond to current analyzed value. But that schedule of increasing cash flows is merely the equivalent of today's indicated value: standing pat. The increasing cash flows may appear to be future goals, but such a perception is wrong.

Standing pat is never acceptable—at least not by the corporation that expects to remain a going concern. Not in evolutionary times past, and certainly not in the future. Net-speed markets mean that it takes only a few years for stand-pat coasters to be run out of the industries they once dominated.

In Figure 1-6, cash flow trend line AB corresponds to the corporation's current value: standing pat. Only by advancing beyond present value does improvement occur. Cash flow line CD increases value, but by how much? Management first proclaims CD as maximum shareholder value. Truth is, the trend line reflects only partial value. Partial value means that much of the corporation's worth is left achieved.

Value Types

Types of value refers to how the corporation builds future worth. Revenue-side value initiatives aim at generating incremental revenues in excess of related expenses and investment. Expense-side initiatives focus on decreased costs and/or improved efficiencies not later offset by new costs or reduced revenues or both.[22]

Both expense-driven and revenue-driven types of value improvement initiatives are essential, in balance. At one extreme, no corporation ever shrank its way to industry dominance or full value. The corporation that focuses on expense cuts and efficiency improvements to the exclusion of revenue-driven value finds the average age of its products and services slipping behind competitors', an increasingly dangerous tactic as product cycles shrink.

The corporation that only pursues growth while disregarding ex-

Figure 1-6. *New value creation is all that matters.*

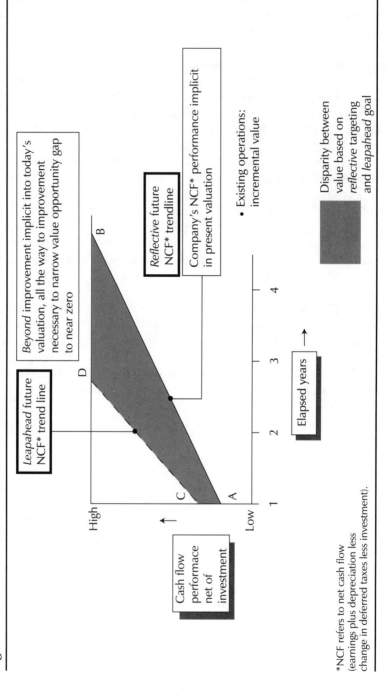

*NCF refers to net cash flow
(earnings plus depreciation less
change in deferred taxes less investment).

pense controls quickly becomes unwieldy as profits plunge. Cash flow to revenue (CFR) overall margins decline, with the result that the corporation becomes progressively more dependent on success with the highest risk form of new innovation: the once-a-generation blockbuster.

In theory, increases in management's projected cash flow from the two types are immediately discounted and added to present value. Modeling tools make it easy for any budgeteer to churn out the corporation's all-new, positive projections.

But the market doesn't discount management's cash flow projections. Rather, the market discounts analysts' and investors' collective interpretation of those projections. The insightful, probing analyst is continually on the lookout for fantasy projections of low credibility.

The analysts know that on that on the revenue side, only about one out of every ten all-new innovation launches is commercially viable. The rest lose money, reducing company value. On the expense-side, the analyst is wary that some of the efficiencies merely push costs to latter periods, rather than achieving true reductions. The next step is to try to narrow down areas where management's cash flows are not credible. Three points that follow probably explain most of the discount:

1. *Mystical Market Projections.* An international technology company invents a fictitious positioning for itself of "Internet enabler" as a viable position, even though the company has few talents in the strengths, objectively assessed. But pride and some positions are on the line, so management tries to make a convincing pitch anyhow that: (1) the obtuse segment actually exists and has demand; and (2) the company will dominate that segment. The adept analyst quickly debunks the implausible market with critical questions, such as: Do major customers seek to buy this product/service in this form and on a completely unsolicited basis? Is the company's toughest competitor also pursuing this opportunity?

2. *Expense Cuts and Projected Efficiencies.* In the summer of 1999, The United Kingdom's NatWest Bank struggled to make a convincing case for synergies from a proposed expansion into the insurance field. Problem was, the bank had demonstrated acute problems with creating value from past non-core acquisitions. The marketplace signals that suggested savings were not believed. Management then misdiagnosed the problem as one of communication rather than credibility.

3. *Time Period.* Perceptions of how long a new product will last in the marketplace tend to be far more optimistic within the organization than outside. If anticipating future shrinkage in market lives, the analyst could be discounting on the basis of two-thirds the term of the company's internal calculations.[23]

Enduring value is built by specific, planned actions—one specific improvement initiative at a time. Value is not derived from any spreadsheet, but rather by effective implementation of key value actions.

1.3 The Old Tools Don't Work: Backward Management, Overreliance on Non-Operations "Value"

Changes in reported earnings per share (EPS) are incidental to value creation. Disregard the business TV talking heads when they attribute a slump in stock price to a missed EPS number. If the market is declining, the response is to adjust interpretations of future cash flows. Current reported results are irrelevant, except where they might be interpreted as incidental indicators of future cash flow generation, net of investment.[24]

Over two-plus decades, the message is well-known: certain financial restructuring tactics can increase nominal corporate value. But it is also now apparent that CFO-initiated value actions are too limited in scope and too overused to serve as the corporation's primary value development base.

Financial restructuring comprises less than a fifth of the corporation's total value development potential. Tactics that increase nominal value—such tactics as capital ratio adjustments—are now widely adopted in some industries, canceling out any particular corporation's advantage.

Updating Perspectives on Management by EPS

Maximizing shareholder value for real is the driving concern of the Value Mandate chief executive, and thus also the driving force of his or her corporation. As noted, market value—stock price—varies primarily with perceived changes in discounted cash flow (DCF). And at best coincidentally with changes in reported earnings per share.

Of course, reported Generally Accepted Accounting Practices (GAAP) earnings per share statistics are not going away. Historical accounting measures continue to be essential to assessing the corporations' liquidity and viability. But in terms of trying to manage the corporation towards maximum value, EPS becomes increasingly unreliable as a guidepost, even dangerous.

One by one, companies that boast of 20+ uninterrupted reported quarterly EPS increases drop by the wayside. Sometimes the departure is because performance slips, such as when U.K. services company Rentokil Initial indicated in 1999 that it would slip from its past pattern of 20 percent annualized EPS growth to a somewhat slower pace.

Other times, myopic management pursues earnings per share but misses maximum shareholder value. Here are two illustrations of how narrow pursuit of EPS can obstruct value development:

1. *Only half the qualifying prospects are pursued (sure hope we guess right)*. With tremendous effort and great expertise, the would-be outperformer corporation develops prototypes of twenty major prospective innovations. Each exceed the Weighted Average Cost of Capital (WACC) hurdle rate by the required amount to proceed, with room to spare. But internal financial analysts warn the CEO to proceed with only half of the projects, or next quarter's EPS number may be missed. The chief executive defers half the projects.

This rigid adherence to EPS destroys value relative to the corporation's potential. All the projects that exceed the corporation's cost of capital should be pursued.

Deferrals dramatically increase the probability that competitors will catch up with their own rival design. Management of the deferring company is voluntarily abandoning something of great worth: its time-to-market edge. In times of accelerating change, success despite late market entry is rare.[25]

2. *Unavoidable in value terms, unaffordable in accounting terms*. The factory's transformation from stack-and-wait assembly to flow promises to double margins. For the interim two years, however, profitability will be shattered, so only the corporation with its back to the wall is normally willing to endure the critical value reform. Corporate value is ultimately generated by a handful of achievers and their teams. Management decides not to proceed on the basis that to do so could mean endangering EPS goals over the near term.[26]

These are just a few examples. Most of the value initiatives described in Part 2 of this book require front-end expenditures. Management who myopically focus solely on "making the (EPS) number" only miss value opportunities and actively reduce the corporation's value.

Backward Management: Driving the Car Forward While Looking Only in the Rear View Mirror

When the industry's success fundamentals change entirely every two to three years (sometimes sooner), the worth of historical information also changes.

The corporation-car speeds ahead into the future on a six-lane superhighway with treacherous curves. Potholes and debris obstruct the road. Other cars (competitors) are continually switching lanes without warning. The pace becomes faster with each mile. The question is not *whether* a major disaster will occur, but *when*.

The CEO/driver's approach for dealing with these challenges? In the EPS world, the response is to stare only in the rear view mirror. The (il)logic: the road behind provides the best indication of what can be expected ahead. Instead, the road behind is history, nothing more. Increasingly irrelevant, even dangerous if responsiveness is slowed by looking for tomorrow's answers in yesterday's issues.

As the CEO/driver shifts his gaze away from the road behind and forward to the road ahead (managing based on forward projections of cash flow), at least the corporation has a fighting chance of success.

Overemphasis on Non-Operations Value Sources: or, Where's the Missing 80+ Percent?

Enduring corporate value emerges from fundamental improvements in the day-to-day operations of the corporation. Which suggests an operations-first approach to comprehensive value creation: first encompassing all four key sectors of value development within the corporation, which is then supplemented by value-optimal capital structure and other financial value improvement actions.

CFO: Critical Early Value Leadership

Early leadership on value issues by the corporation's finance function has been both welcome and necessary. Concepts such as Capital Asset

Pricing Model and NOPAT tend to cause the eyes of some non-financial employees of the corporation to glaze over. Without knowledgeable financial officers to apply value principles and demonstrate that they can work to create value, value management may not have survived to the present.

By linking new value creation to maximizing shareholder value, organizations such as the Financial Executives Institute helped ensure that discounted cash flow (DCF) principles endured, long enough to be effectively applied in the 1980s as a legitimate value source.

Next step: to move value out beyond the CFO's department to broader application in other parts of the corporation. Addressing value management solely as a financial restructuring issue fails to capture much of a corporation's true value.

Value program ownership is not some corporate turf battle. The chief financial officer who for years has been an adamant supporter of new value creation is gratified to see his good judgment confirmed as pursuit of maximum shareholder value grows from a single department focus to a total agenda that extends across the full corporation.

Chances are the knowledgeable financial officers who understand how value is achieved already suspect the situation illustrated in Figure 1-7. Financial restructuring represents less than one fifth of the corporation's total value opportunities.

Where's the missing 80+ percent? Figure 1-7 answers that question from a functional perspective, with marketing and sales and administrative efficiencies highlighted. These source areas of value generation correspond to Chapters 7 and 8 in this book, respectively. But it is also apparent that issues of sourcing (production and/or assembly) and innovation creation, development, and launch are implicit, non-financial sectors. Chapter 5 deals with value from procurement and production; Chapter 6 from research and development.

Where's the missing 80+ percent? Not long ago, compliant directors on insider boards could be counted on to never ask such irritating (to the underperforming chief executive) questions about value development. Not long ago, unless the corporation was staggering toward insolvency, almost any performance could be accepted by the members of the board as MSV. No longer. Now, the burden of proof has shifted to the CEO to demonstrate that maximum shareholder value actions are fully competitive with comparable initiatives being taken or contemplated by industry rivals, present and potential. The CEO must demonstrate that the corporation possesses a clear sense of its ongoing Value Opportunity Gap—the difference between potential value and present worth.

Figure 1-7. New value sources: emphasis on operations.

**Corporate administrative expense and
decision related -42% of total**

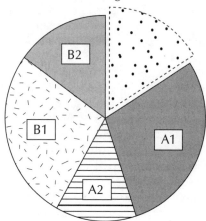

A1 Efficiency and
productivity
improvements in
corporate/division
overhead activities
and functions: 29%

Financial reorganization: 16%

A2 Improved capital
expenditure and
resource allocation
decision making:
13%

**Other value sources-
42% of total**

Operations improvements: 84%

B1 Marketing and sales
improvements, including sale
productivity improvements,
marketing support
efficiencies, and product line
optimization: 27%

B2 Industry concentration
and facilities
consolidations: 15%

Note: Percentages are based on total corporate value enhancement, including both financial
reorganization and operations improvements.

Source: Adapted from Frederick W. Gluck, "The Real Takeover Defense," *The McKinsey
Quarterly,* Winter 1988, pages 7–8, based on analysis of sources of value creation of sixteen
larger transactions involving changes in ownership. Reprinted with permission from *McKinsey
& Co.*
Reprinted from Peter J. Clark, *Beyond the Deal: Optimizing Merger & Acquisition Value* (New
York: HarperBusiness, 1991), Figure 6-1, page 183.

1.4 Chapters of This Book

The other chapters that make up Section 1, "Value Foundations," establish the framework for a true total corporation MSV program.

Chapter 2, "Value Opportunity Gap Explored," examines the development and use of this analytical and action structure. Ultimately, the corporation's key value rival is not another company, but itself. That is, the same corporation performing in a way that achieves maximum continuing value.

Chapter 3, "It's (a Few) People, Stupid," addresses the ultimate font of value creation: a relatively small number of Corporate Key Contributors (CKCs). CKCs are top talent who are effectively indispensable. If no such description applies to anyone in a corporation today, that is not a strength, but rather a weakness. The corporation that lacks CKCs also lacks the critical talent base necessary to achieve maximum wealth.

Chapter 4, "The Value Mandate CEO Acts," establishes some parameters and specific actions for full value program effectiveness. The greater the potential for change, the more important the CEO's active leadership becomes.

Section II, "Value Opportunities," describes value-increasing opportunities in the four key parts of the corporation. The intent is to provide a starting point for development of the company's own specific value development agenda and program.

Chapter 5, "Value's Engine Room," addresses several new value developments in sourcing. Such as how the corporation purchases components and parts (procurement), and integration of flow-type, lean assembly with other parts of the company.

Chapter 6 is titled "Value Lifeblood: The Innovation Research Enigma." How else can one refer to something that is (1) essential to corporate success yet (2) on average, succeeds only one time out of ten? Concentration here is on changing the odds while still pursuing the prospects capable of propelling new value.

Chapter 7, "Outperformer Marketing, Sales," addresses new value creation actions necessary for a revolutionary sales and marketing environment where change is the only constant. The challenge of value creation is made all the more difficult as product and service cycles shrink at a accelerating pace.

Section II's final chapter, "Unwinding the Crony Bureaucracy," focuses on general and administrative (G&A). Those parts of the corporation that contain the largest amounts of discretionary costs attract focused attention when value reform is overdue.

2

Value Opportunity Gap Explored

When Half Empty Means Full Speed Ahead

The Value Opportunity Gap (VOG) serves as the starting point for the systematic, continuing maximum value management effort across the corporation. The VOG acts as the company's blueprint, guiding all company efforts aimed at closing the *full* difference between current value and potential (maximum) worth. VOG represents the difference between the corporation's potential value (Vp) and current value (Vn), as of the analysis date. By itself, no valuation model, formula, or analysis ever generated a dollar of new value. What creates value are the specific actions underlying the models and statistics. A focused value agenda must be directed at the heart of the business. Programs supporting the agenda must be actively led by the chief executive and joined by all others in the organization.[1] Potential value (Vp) represents the upper limit of the company's worth under present circumstances and marketplace conditions, and, as such, Vp is continually changing, as shown in Figure 2-1. Vp, then, represents the value that the company *can* achieve by executing the full agenda of actions that close the VOG range. In the minds of the corporation's shareholders, who are increasingly inclined to view *anything* below maximum value as money out of their pockets, Vp represents the value that management *must* achieve.

Current value (Vn) reflects the market's interpretation of management's projected cash flows.[2] Vn establishes the lower boundary of that company's VOG. It is the beginning point for answering the value mandate CEO's two unrelenting questions:

1. How much new wealth must we develop from operations to reach the point of maximum shareholder value?
2. What actions and programs will close the Gap most quickly and most completely?[3]

The firm's Value Opportunity Gap is characterized less by dollars and percentiles than by the component actions for closing the Vp-to-Vn difference. It matters little whether the exact statistical Gap is 45 or 47 percent. Paying too much attention to devising a precise VOG number can result in a misleading precision. After all, value is based on cash flow future projections (read: informed guesses), and no one has found the infallible crystal ball yet.

What *is* important is that the Value Opportunity Gap is large—too large to be closed by incremental tactics or partial actions such as performance incentives alone. At a corporation with the constructive mind-set that it is underperforming by 50 percent in value terms, management concentrates on major value development opportunities, not on incidentals. For example, management might focus on the specific actions aimed at halving the corporation's general and administrative expenses as a percentage of revenues, as we discuss in Chapter 8, or concentrate on new channel approaches to slashing ten or more margin points from internal costs (Chapter 7).

The VOG needs to be reassessed periodically. Change in opportunities and challenges means that Vp continuously evolves. Actions that were suitable to close the VOG four to six months ago are inadequate now.[4]

The forward direction is clear. First, uncover those value opportunities throughout the organization that promise major reductions in the VOG and then fully achieve that value with implementation as if the corporation's survival depends on it. It does.

Figure 2-1. Value Opportunity Gap (VOG) illustrated over time.

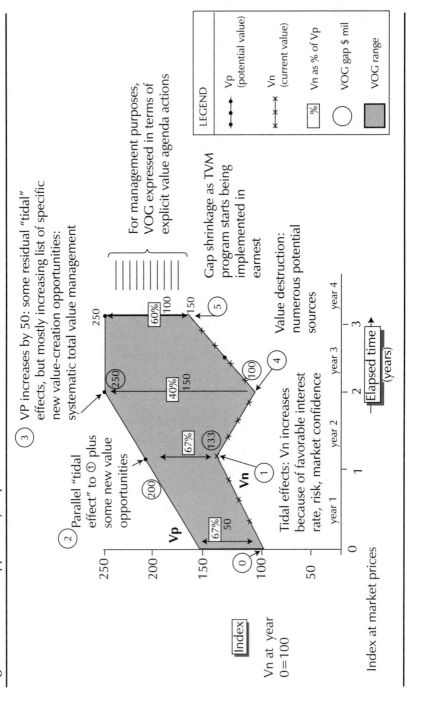

2.1 The Value Opportunity Gap: No, You're *Not* Maximizing Shareholder Value (Not Yet)

Figure 2-1 shows the company's dynamic Value Opportunity Gap pattern over time. The vertical axis shows market value as an index. Beginning point (year 0) for the corporation's current value (Vn), which is the lower boundary of the VOG, is at Point 0 on the vertical axis.

Gap Expressed, Objective in Sight

At the beginning of the period illustrated in Figure 2-1, the aspiring outperformer company shows a current index of 100. The current *potential* value (Vp) is 150. Our assumption is that the corporation is underperforming by 50 percent in VOG terms. The full range of the VOG is depicted by the shaded area between the two boundaries, Vp and Vn.

Expressed another way, current value at year 0 is about 33 percent below the potential of what the company *could* achieve at that point in time [1- (100 / 150) = 33%]. A third from the top or half-empty—no matter how current worth is expressed relative to potential—the company's spin doctors don't like that at all. The form-over-substance advocates argue that admitting a value gap is the same as admitting any weakness—the ultimate business no-no.

But managers who are striving for The Value Mandate know better: What the spin doctors perceive as half empty, they view as half *full* instead. The goal of reaching for full value is not a negative to be avoided, but a challenge to be embraced and pursued.

The Value Opportunity Gap Varies over Time

At Point 1 in Figure 2-1, Vn has increased from a level of 100 to 133. Some managers would be tempted to state that they caused that 33 percent rise. Such an explanation might be convincing were there no contradicting comparison.

But in the real world, current value is continually compared to potential value, which changes as new opportunities become known. At Point 2 in the figure, Vp has increased from 150 to 200. It appears that the "rising tide" of a buoyant overall stock market has lifted the "boat" of the company's current value, as the VOG at the end of year 1 is unchanged at 67 percent, or 33 percent from the goal. In index terms, the Gap has widened from 50 to 67.[5]

By year 2, potential value jumps from 200 to 250, reflecting a competitor's successful conversion to a new Internet-first channel strategy. As of Point 3, the rival's sales force has been scaled back and used only for those sales that are too complex to be closed entirely on the Net. Still, the fact that such an approach works elsewhere suggests the addition to the company's Vp.

But the company cannot deliver; its responding channel strategy is muddled and misfires. Current value slips back to 100 (Point 4), or 40 percent of goal Vp. The company's value "glass" is now *less* than half full.

But by the end of year 3 in the illustration, the major channel problem, which has been suppressing value, has been resolved, while there has been no further increase in potential value. Thus the Gap is narrowed. As of Point 5, current value has rebounded to 60 percent of the maximum value possible.

2.2 Potential Value (Vp) as the Corporation's Performance Obsession

By definition, potential value *is* maximum value and thus serves as the corporation's overriding performance objective. Accordingly, in Figure 2-2, Vp (represented by $\overline{AB}$) is the base against which all company value progress ($\overline{CD}$, $\overline{CE}$, and $\overline{CF}$) is measured.

$\overline{AB}$ is shown as a straight line in the figure. Actual performance, though, varies according to changes in industry-specific and overall market conditions and the emergence of new value opportunities. Initially, the best that management can do is to keep the Value Opportunity Gap from widening further, shown by $\overline{CD}$ remaining parallel to $\overline{AB}$. But when potential value swings up or down, so does current value. Effects on the VOG are minimal as long as no major value initiatives are enacted. At best, the VOG remains unchanged on a percentage basis. But as potential value tends to increase over time as more and more possible value prospects become known and incorporated into Vp, the risk grows that the VOG may widen in future periods (if this occurred, $\overline{CD}$ in Figure 2-2 would *decline*).

This situation usually causes concern at the level of the Board of Directors. The directors would be concerned that a known persistent

Figure 2-2. Toward maximum value management, to close the VOG.

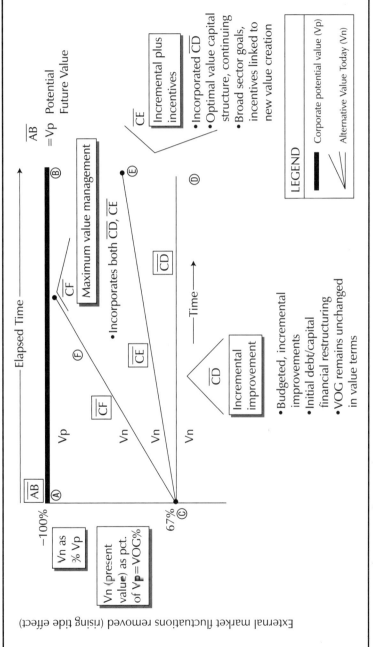

Source: VBM Consulting (www.vbm-consulting.com).

Gap is an invitation to unsolicited suitors and that a chronic Value Opportunity Gap could reflect poorly on the due diligence being exercised by the Board itself. Although VOG analyses do not exist outside the company, what does arise are those charts in the print and online business press showing how much better competitors and the DJIA are doing, comparatively.

The fact that management has not been able to narrow the VOG often means that the Board conducts frank discussions with the management about what must be done to jar the company out of its stagnating value situation.[6]

In response, management implements $\overline{\text{CE}}$ ("Incremental Plus Incentives"), which involves continuing the course ($\overline{\text{CD}}$) while adding incentives to encourage trickle-up value suggestions from other employees. But if $\overline{\text{CD}}$ already involves a 20 percent annual increase in net cash flow, then *extra* value is required to move the slope upward and thereby VOG. Normally, unless the added inducements resemble Executive Incentive Program (EIP) grants and options, the best that can be expected from implementing $\overline{\text{CE}}$ are minimal actions on the order of budget adjustments (recall Point A in Figure 1-2).

Maximizing real shareholder value is the corporation's obsession, which the CEO and other executives in the EIP share. But experience suggests that short of extending EIP to many employees outside top management, the instinct for survival takes precedence, followed closely by the desire to limit the extent of disruptions in how work is conducted at present.

The combination of (1) advance intelligence into the areas where extra value might be found and (2) appropriate spot incentives helps ensure that the VOG is narrowed at this stage. Emphasis is on taking fast, effective actions to credential the overall value efforts quickly.

Management that stops at this point is settling for only part of the value goal. A substantial VOG persists. $\overline{\text{CF}}$ in Figure 2-2 represents maximum value management (MVM). MVM incorporates the minor value-creation actions in $\overline{\text{CD}}$ and $\overline{\text{CE}}$, plus more. In MVM, management aggressively addresses all the specific value actions that comprise the company's potential value (Vp).

These value actions vary by company, according to the resources available to it and the creativity it employs in adapting them. If a rival (Company W) generates significant new value, Company X needs to generate more. So, Company W slashes the square footage of its headquarters and encourages periodic telecommuting and flexible hours. Not to be outdone, Company X splits up time-consuming functions such as bid preparation, software maintenance, software development, and records administration and assigns responsibility for each function to a different team of employees.[7]

Maximum value management here refers to the company's permanent agenda covering finance in addition to the four key value sectors of the corporation (which we'll explore in Section II). This agenda comprises changing value actions whose sole purpose is to completely close that corporation's Value Opportunity Gap. But potential value is continually changing, and thus it can never be fully reached. Note that in Figure 2-2, $\overline{CF}$ never intersects $\overline{AB}$.

Ongoing costs are reduced and responsiveness dramatically accelerated in what has become a 24-hour corporation. Headquarters is now permanently downsized, and you might say that, from now on, headquarters is wherever the chief executive can gain access to the corporation's intranet.

Accelerating speed is not just a time-to-market issue. Intranets and specific-function online systems begin to form the spinal cord of the maximum value corporation. A procurement officer in Dallas can hardly sneeze today without his counterpart in Scotland saying, "God bless you."

Value coordination is key. The Internet purchase site for the new generation of Triumph motorcycles (administration) works only to the extent that the customer spec becomes a confirmed order with a cash commitment (finance). The value in component assembly (sourcing) could be canceled by greatly reduced orders unless the array and combination of components gives the customer a sense of near-custom ordering (marketing).

2.3 Achieving Value Creation, Not Just Measurement: Framework for High-Value Operations Improvements

Valuation metrics should never be confused with value creation. The company that understands this simple but extremely important fact helps ensure that the resources in its value development program emphasize policies and actions that generate the most value, most rapidly. The intent is to maximize shareholder value for real, not merely overstate as "maximum" a partial value, thus avoiding the rather unpleasant consequence resulting when a corporation's value program is incomplete.

Figure 2-3 depicts some key elements in the discounted cash flow formula. The foundation feature of the figure—the split triangle—is the observation that the present value of the total business entity is the sum of its present value and assets in place plus the present value of its future growth.

But the value triangle principles are sterile in the context of discrete value-increasing actions. The company that is committed to pursuing maximum value faces a dilemma when key officers, each counted on for a major contribution to the value program, are on different pages, in value terms.

Imagine the catastrophe if the head of procurement in Des Moines, the chief of research in New Jersey, the CFO at headquarters, and the EVP of marketing all pursued different value approaches.

The left side of the triangle in Figure 2-3 is labeled "Present value of business and assets in place." It addresses the company's present cash flow performance, plus cash flow–generating assets and resources in place. The resulting value stream reflects estimated net operating profits less adjusted taxes (NOPLAT), based on that unit's prevailing weighted average cost of capital (WACC). NOPLAT results from embedded investments in assets of the business adjusted for the rate of return (ROR) achieved on those investments.[8]

The right side of the value triangle, "Present value of future growth," looks to the future. The discounting rate is based on that unit's WACC, adjusted to the amount and timing of future cash flows.[9]

The right side includes one "box" of special note in this era of accelerating change and imploding life cycles (described in Chapter 7). "Period of competitive advantage" refers to that period of time during which the corporation enjoys key cost (price) and performance superiority over alternatives available to customers.

Figure 2-3 illustrates how new value can result from specific improvements, as denoted by the asterisks:

*Changes in Investment Amounts: Assuming constant return rates, an increase in the amount invested boosts total return. The opposite is also true, as when short-sighted management decides to "save" cash today by reducing essential investment. For a while, analysts are none the wiser. Explanations such as "invest smarter but spend less money" might raise suspicions, yet still pass unchallenged. Eventually, though, reductions to the corporation's value investment are manifested in the form of reduced cash flow, thus reduced value.

Figure 2-3. Value triangle: building corporate value through specific operations improvements.

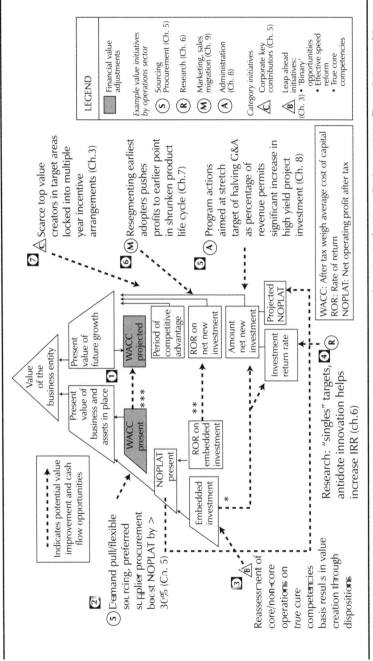

Adapted from Peter J. Clark, *Beyond the Deal: Optimizing Merger & Acquisition Value* (New York: HarperBusiness, 1991), Figure 3-4, page 84.

**Changes in Return on New Investment: Conventional capital expenditure analysis (CAPEX) wisdom suggests that the corporation proceed with all projects that exceed the firm's WACC by the stipulated amount. But if management can increase development funds at the upper end of those projects exceeding WACC, the beneficial spread between IRR and WACC widens, and returns increase, all other factors remaining the same.

***Changes to Cost of Capital: Reductions in WACC, all other things remaining equal, increase corporate value because the rate at which the company's future cash flows are discounted is usually lower. But this tactic has now become standard practice, removing any relative advantage.

Discovering new opportunities for value development begins with those who know the corporate landscape best: the firm's own employees, guided by advance hypotheses of where some the principal opportunities reside.

Internal suggestions often prove to be particularly helpful when it comes to shrinking or eliminating the ponderous twenty-plus-step internal process for which better alternatives can be found. But if the employees rely on internal suggestions alone, they will achieve only partial value. Factors for less-than-complete results range from active resistance to lack of familiarity. Achieving MSV for real requires stretching goals with a commitment to continue until success is reached. That's quite a different mind-set from that which prevails in the risk-averse corporation, where sticking your neck out for any reason is the first step out the door.

Value actions 2 through 7 below are selected, as illustrations, from the various possibilities contained in the latter chapters of this book. No two corporations are the same, so the optimum wealth-development path may differ from company to company as no one-size-fits-all value template exists. But there are some opportunities, such as:

• *Capital Structure Changes: WACC Present to WACC Projected.* The good news is that increasing corporate value by reducing WACC can be done effectively on a unilateral basis. The financial officer can proceed with many changes to capital structure with minimal effect on other parts of the business.

Unfortunately, the "bad" news is that the practice is so well known now that no competitive value advantage may result. Figures

P-1 and 1-7 suggest that financial restructuring represents less than a fifth of a firm's overall value sources.

• *Sourcing Breakthroughs with High-Value Impact: NOPLAT Present to Future.* If conversion from conventional stack-and-wait assembly to demand pull/flexible sourcing does not achieve at least a 30 percent increase in same-period net cash flow, implementation has failed.

• *Core Business Reassessment on True Core Competencies: Investment and Return, Present to Future.* Every company has its pet "core competencies" list: mere characteristics inflated into advantages by internal wordsmiths who underestimate the challenge from others, particularly new entrants.

• *Research Funnel "Singles," Antidote Innovation: Investment Returns Rate, Present to Future.* While executives talk about viable prospects in the company's pre–market launch pipeline, the value creators deep within research & development (R&D) know that the pipeline can be no more prolific than the prospect funnel that precedes that stage. R&D returns increase by (a) eliminating development in non-score technologies and areas, (b) curtailing "gold-plating" and similar unwanted/unneeded effort, and (c) pursuing modest return targets (singles, not home runs). (More in Chapter 6.)

• *Specific Actions Aimed at Halving G&A as Percentage of Revenue: Increasing Amounts Available for Innovation Investment.* In the drug, communications, and intranet technology and controls industries, companies find that they must achieve a quantum increase in effective investment if they are to remain in the industry following consolidation.

But where will this new investment come from? A substantial part must come from within the company itself. Chapter 8 describes a series of specific initiatives for winnowing costs, including "downsizing the deadwood," and changing the overall support approach from full service (by permanent staffs) to user self-access online ("self-service").

• *Resegmenting Earliest Adopters and Increasing Returns on Net New Investment.*

Shrinkage of product/service life cycles bordering on implosion makes it imperative that management change its traditional adoption pattern of cash flow over the cycle. Peak revenue must be achieved far sooner in the cycle to prevent sabotage by competitors.

Resegmenting the earliest adopter (EA) groups represents a central strategy for shifting the demand curve. Instead of treating EAs as an undifferentiated group, key subsets are identified and exploited to establish early inroads in the post-migration cycle marketplace (see Chapter 7).

- *Locking in the Top Individual Value Creators and Extending the Period of Industry Primacy.* The 80/20 Rule applies to top value-generating people, not just to projects (locking in "Next Jordans"— the scarce, highly effective value producers who make all the difference (more on this in the next chapter).

3

It's (a Few) People, Stupid

Ultimately, Corporate Key Contributors Generate Most of the New Value

All new wealth comes from creative engineering types, who are difficult to manage and easy to offend.
—Dan Hutcheson, president of VLSI Research[1]

3.1 The Cost of Market Dominance Is $185 Million
3.2 Key People, Key Value: Issues of Scarcity, Necessity
3.3 The Franchise Value Controversy
3.4 CKC Identification
3.5 Acquiring the Corporate Key Contributor
3.6 Lock In: CKC Retention Challenges

The question: What is the most important resource for generating new shareholder wealth while closing the company's Value Opportunity Gap?

The answer: the few, scarce people referred to in this chapter's title—*Corporate Key Contributors* (CKCs). These are the corporation's highly mobile value stars, its value performance elite. They are the nearly indispensable resources who create and sustain much of

the corporation's new value, assuming the company possesses any at
all (a big if).

Although CKCs are a corporation's value vanguard, they are not
rivals of the other employees. In fact, because CKCs are often involved with novel product development or other innovations, they
help to ensure that those growth-sustaining roles and positions endure. Without a significant, predictable infusion of incoming cash
flow from novel sources, management's value emphasis turns easily
from revenue-side opportunities to the expense side—cuts and re-
trenchment.[2]

There is a saying that a corporation's value walks out the door
at 5:00 p.m. Actually, it's more like 11:00 p.m. The Corporate Key
Contributor contradicts the image of a worker victimized by the relentless march of impersonal technology and speed. Self-actualization means everything to the CKC, and a faster pace means
opportunities to accomplish more, faster, better.

True CKCs are possibly the closest thing in the non-sports and
non-entertainment business world to free agents. CKCs enjoy un-
usual security because of their abilities, and sometimes have the ultimate luxury: to actually say the things that other employees only
think. Corporate Key Contributors care little about the spotlight (except among peers in their field). What they *do* care about—and what
only the chief executive officer can deliver—is an environment in
which they can flourish.

With that in mind, it takes a certain type of chief executive to
get the most out of the Corporate Key Contributor. A CEO with a
massive ego might chafe at the perception that a couple of mere employees are more valuable to a company than its leader. The arbitrary
my-way-or-the-highway manager doesn't have to be concerned about
such matters. The CKCs never come to that manager's company in
the first place.

Similarly, rigid corporations will not attract the CKC. These
companies don't welcome the peg that doesn't fit the hole, especially
when the peg is a mid-level specialist who wields more value impact
in the company than any manager.

When a true Corporate Key Contributor is lost, the corporation
suffers double value damage. First, the corporation is hit with reduced future value. Thus, the corporation faces a riskier future because it is forced to rely on a mix of fast-fading past developments
plus long-shot big bets. The latter is unavoidable: The corporation
limited to a shortened list of viable prospects has no other choice.[3]

The second form of value damage is the prospect that a rival company may hire the departed CKC. Over the near and intermediate term, critical talent is a zero sum resource. The arch competitor's gain is proportional to the original employer's loss.

Occasionally, the CKC starts up a new company that threatens *all* existing competitors. Jeff Hawkins is co-founder, chairman, and chief product officer of the third-generation handheld computer company, Handspring (www.handspring.com). Inventor of the Palm and Palm Pilot, Hawkins and colleagues introduced the compelling Visor model, packed with so many key features that the key problem in Winter 1999–2000 was allocating demand. "We're in demand suppression," says Handspring's head of sales.[4]

What is a true Corporate Key Contributor worth to the corporation? A CKC like David Cote can mean as much as 10 percent of the corporation's market capitalization. Cote was described as "just what the doctor ordered" by several analysts (CNBC, November 12, 1999) when he joined aerospace and automotive components multinational TRW. Cote's hiring caused TRW's sluggish stock price to surge (Figure 3-1), propelling it to a close of $50 per share on massive volume. That's a $5 per share increase from the previous close.

A 25-year General Electric veteran, Cote had been part of the corporate executive council, reporting directly to GE chairman Jack Welch, and CEO of GE Appliances, a $6 billion business by its own right. In the company's announcement, chairman Joseph T. Gorman, Cote's new boss at TRW, describes the financial manager turned operations star as having demonstrated success at some of GE's toughest assignments while not being tied to the past. Gorman's statement echoes that of Reginald Jones, who used similar language to explain the selection of dark horse Jack Welch as GE's CEO-designate in 1980.

Of course, not every CKC-in-waiting exerts such an impact. Many CKCs are invisible except within the boundaries of their company and their field. The smart chief executive knows a good thing when he sees it, and is eager to keep his treasure secret.

3.1 The Cost of Market Dominance Is $185 Million

That's what the fans and owners of the baseball Arizona Diamondbacks figure. The team invested that much and, as a result, the sec-

Figure 3-1. Impact of the perceived CKC: TRW names Cote president.

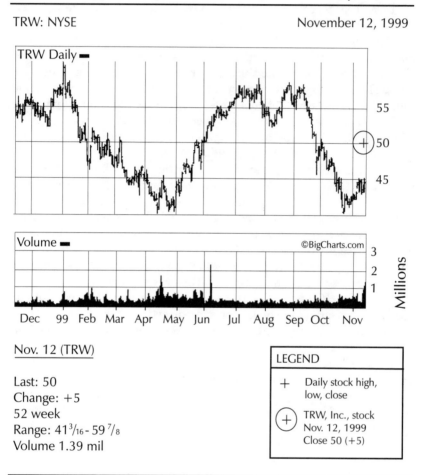

TRW: NYSE   November 12, 1999

Nov. 12 (TRW)

Last: 50
Change: +5
52 week
Range: $41^3/_{16}$ - $59^7/_8$
Volume 1.39 mil

LEGEND

+   Daily stock high, low, close

(+)   TRW, Inc., stock
         Nov. 12, 1999
         Close 50 (+5)

ond-year expansion club won the National League West pennant in 1999.

One hundred eighty-five million dollars is the combined face value of the contracts for several star free agents added in 1998 and 1999. These CKCs were free agent pitchers Randy Johnson and Todd Stottlemyre, and daily players Matt Williams, Steve Finley, and Jay Bell.[5]

Unwilling to tolerate being a doormat for five seasons—the norm for most start-up professional sports expansion teams—CEO Jerry Colangelo opened up his snakeskin wallet for the second-year team.

Colangelo proved that a couple of key additions in the right spots can make all the difference; that is, when those additions are proven contributors. Just by adding Johnson and Stottlemyre, Arizona addressed their most glaring weakness, the starting pitching staff, and bounced back from their dismal inaugural season of 1998.[6]

Arizona had a precedent. The Diamondbacks borrowed their CKC strategy from the Florida Marlins, the 1997 World Series Champions. To position themselves for the 1997 championship, the Marlins applied a simple formula: (1) find the best players at the most important positions for success—the roles that make all the difference; (2) sign 'em up. Arizona's 1999 success means that other teams will now try to duplicate that model.

In the business world, Michael Cassidy, CEO of search engine Direct Hit (www.directhit.com), estimates that each of his developers are worth about $10,000 per day, based on an estimate that comparable companies are "worth" around $100 million, in terms of market capitalization. According to the chief executive's new math, Cassidy figures that each of his top developers is worth $3 million per year to Direct Hit.[7]

But many other executives still shudder at the prospect of even thinking such numbers when it comes to employee worth, much less talking about them. The attitude: If an employee even suspects what he's worth, that's what he will demand. Then it spreads like wildfire throughout the company and *all* employee costs spin wildly out of control.

Sometimes, such concerns may be so great that the CEO deprives his company of the top talent required for success, preferring more pliable (and lower paid) employees who would never even think of asking such an impertinent question. But the price of silence can be high. The overly modest employee may be that way for the simple reason that there isn't much about which to be boastful.

The CKC Is Identified by His Actions

If the pro sports free agent star has a parallel in the corporate world, it is the pivotal corporate employee who addresses a need in the critical development area. Examples include: the Silicon Valley stellar developer who can generate a *series* of "gotta-have" products, and the researcher who is able to beat the long odds associated with bringing a new innovation to the marketplace.

The CKC is a relentless developer of *new* corporate value: Yesterday's closed sales, inventions, innovations, and permanent cost savings are old. Whether the business involves carrying a bat or a briefcase, the implicit question from that organization's owners is "What are you going to do for us next?"

3.2 Key People, Key Value: Issues of Scarcity, Necessity

They're the crown jewels . . . and they know it. Brain power can't be tallied on a ledger sheet, but it's the prime factor driving the New Economy.
—"Ten Driving Principles of the New Economy—No. 4,
People." *Business 2.0*

There's not a shortage of people, but there is a shortage of great people.
—Professor John Sullivan, head of human resources
department at San Francisco State University[8]

The problem with blanket accolades such as "people are our most important resources" (besides the oozing insincerity) is that everyone in the company immediately assumes that the verbal award applies to her or him, specifically. Either out of company belief, or because such posturing is a standard corporate gamesperson's survival tactic.

The Corporate Key Contributor Litmus Test Question

But the litmus test for separating out the true CKC issue involves subtraction. The indispensable contributor leaves a hole by his or her departure:

Often, the most accurate way to assess the value contribution of the employee is by subtraction. Answer the question, "If this manager was no longer here (along with his costs), would the corporation's value decrease or increase?" Loss of the star account developer who draws away a dozen major accounts with him. The loss of an essential developer, with the result that several launches are now a month later than before. Enough difference that a rival company is handed an opportunity to establish an early, unassailable advantage; an opportunity that is eagerly seized.

Eighty percent of the value (or more) generated by 20 percent of the company's staff (or less)? 80/20 turns out to be more like 95/5 in "people are our most important resources" companies.

Which is exactly the point. Invariably, there's that one salesman out of seven who excels spectacularly, while the rest struggle just to scratch out an existence. When a key account relationship is in danger, there's that one individual designated to save the day.

On the championship basketball squad of 12 players total, there are always the two or three stars who are effectively indispensable. Jordan and Pippen of the 1997–1998 Last Champion Chicago Bulls, for example. Whatever the reason, replace that critical mass with merely adequate journeymen, and, well, you have the 1999 Bulls.

The once-excellent company that slips into trouble in just a few years is no longer a chance occurrence. A key is that the championship team/corporation must continually seek to deepen its CKC base or risk slipping back into the pack or lower.

3.3 The Franchise Value Controversy

A key reason the CEO and his HR officer may be inclined to bury their heads in the sand when it comes to dealing with the imperative of Corporate Key Contributors is because of what is referred to here as the Franchise Value Controversy.

CKCs Are the Company

Franchise value is the notion that the company's Corporate Key Contributors *are* the corporation; that a few key employees represent most of the enduring worth of the corporation. CKCs are the essence of what customers appreciate and what today's competitors fear. And what tomorrow's competitor/CKC acquirer covets for itself.

Management sometimes forgets that the CKC's accomplishments can walk out the door with that individual. A recurring base of major account revenues is developed by the CKC salesperson. When the CKC's current employer is acquired by another company, the acquiring CEO boasts that he now possesses a world-class customer base.

The preferred accounts, the innovation function that consistently beats the odds and the competition, even the marketplace reputation for going the extra mile that wins hotly contested bids—all are counted as possessions by the corporation. But all mean nothing without the CKC who made it happen in the first place, who sustains that source of value today.

The corporation that disregards the source risks serious damage. The CKC's contributions may carry over, for a while. But any victory is an illusion. Much of the value created and nurtured by the CKC can revert back to its source if desired.

A further issue associated with The Franchise is that the bureaucrats back at headquarters aren't part of *it*. When the sports team is acquired, front office staff are terrorized while top field talent have their contracts upgraded. The specialized search engine company is acquired, the development talent and key problem spotters are treated as kings. Non–sales support bureaucrats are shown the door, their roles absorbed by the acquirer's staff.

Who They Are: The One(s) Who Makes the Difference

Dr. John Sullivan is professor of human resources management at San Francisco State University, and consults for companies looking to secure their own (nearly) indispensable value contributors.

In this chapter we have used modern sports stars to illustrate the principle that a mere handful of extraordinary value creators make all the difference to the businesses fortunate enough to attract and keep them. In "How to Hire the Next Jordan" Sullivan uses the Michael Jordan/Chicago Bulls illustration to make some points.

First, to illustrate that on some pro sports teams, as well as in industries where speed and effectiveness to market are critical for success, the difference between championship performance and exclusion from the playoffs often comes down to just a handful of key contributors. Success is not a result of senior management leadership, as might be suggested by a fawning leadership writer. Nor does market dominance flow from the financial officer's skills or the general manager's trading acumen.

Second, designating Next Jordans (or, the parallel here, Corporate Key Contributors) is a waste of time and value if done on a ceremonial basis. Mislabel the marginal journeyman as a franchise savior, and credibility is destroyed.

Third, the CKC/Next Jordan knows that he needs a critical mass of other stellar talent to achieve his own goals. Sonny Jurgensen, a quarterback with the 1960s NFL Eagles and Redskins, is a good example. Jurgensen was a franchise player who, in some ways, never achieved his full potential because he lacked a supporting group of comparable contributors. To hire the CKC/Next Jordan, corporations need to be alert to this need for supporting talent. Even the best single performer can't do it in isolation.

More than anything else, the Corporate Key Contributor strives to be *effective*. The true CKC suspects that he can't do it all by himself, all the time. However, he or she may often try to do it all. The laboratory, sales office, or development station manned by a solitary, prolific mad-scientist-type may be a fixture of children's adventure movies, but has no place in the real world.

Thus, even the most earnest CKC can quickly switch from positive value source to negative drain if and when they overreach. The CKC's personal nature and love of a challenge make overreaching, at some point, an almost certainty. In areas beyond his or her expertise, the key contributor in one area relies too much on instinct alone. With few or no true peers, their own mistakes go unchallenged and possibly even unnoticed.

But the worse value impact is yet to come. Discouraged by the lack of fellow top talent to help him develop his own skills base even further, the CKC abruptly quits. Or stays in place as a disgruntled employee, which is probably worse.

Power to the (Most Valuable) People

Vapid prose such as "people are our most important resource" communicates the opposite of management's intent. The true slogan—*we are highly dependent on key value developers and never have enough of them*—never sees the light of day.

Never mind that the stellar team makes all the difference. CKCs can be difficult to handle, and others in the corporation are uncomfortable with the prospect of finding themselves on the wrong side of a new divide between value creation "haves" and value destruction "have nots." Besides, top value talent is far too expensive.[9]

Avoiding the Corporate Beauty Pageant

Raise the issue of a performance and value elite, and the first thought by ambitious executive and manager is "Who within our company

are the top value generators?" The second: "How can I assure that
it's me?" Especially if the CKC designation comes with increased
added internal status, perhaps some extra perquisites.

The beauty contest has started, if permitted. The first hint of a
performance and value elite causes a flurry of activity like Cub Scouts
lining up for cookies. Motivation is not just the internal recognition
and possible perquisites, but, more importantly, avoiding any hint of
being a *non*-contributor.

If Corporate Key Contributors generate value by their own actions and their teams' initiatives, does that imply that everyone else
destroys value? The career bureaucrat whose smoothest skills involve
sliding through the corporation without any marks at all knows exactly where that leads.

But few mistakes can be more devastating to the corporation's
future than allowing the corporation's CKC program to be kidnapped
by the internal games-players. In place of a solid CKC acquisition
effort, management settles for CKC illusions: shadows from within.

3.4 CKC Identification

Spotting the corporation's value-creating elite is a key role of management. Get it wrong and the company quickly slips behind competitors, saddled with lower PE and slower growth than rivals.

The CEO of an underperforming company is hard pressed to
identify why the organization is floundering. CKCs may be the corporation's value engines within the company, but they are often invisible to the outsiders.

But get Corporate Key Contributor identification *right,* and a
series of other value challenges that once seemed arduous suddenly
become easier. Critical choices about people and projects to keep; decisions about critical areas of future corporate emphasis; and future
areas of focus.

Starting Point: Who *Aren't* Corporate Key Contributors?

A practical approach for identifying Corporate Key Contributors
starts from the opposite direction: understanding the characteristics
and other identifiers of those in the company who *are not* CKCs.

Without true CKCs, a company finds itself on the defensive, regardless of past reputation or value. Self-deprived of the ultimate value engine that makes everything else happen, the company struggles mightily to catch up to competitors who always seem to be far ahead.

Reserves are quickly depleted. The longer the CKC deficiency persists, the greater the risk that the corporation will resort to high-risk desperation action—such as an overpriced acquisition in an unrelated field—in an attempt to catch up.

First Indicator: Self-Nomination

"Corporate Key Contributor" threatens to become just another ceremonial designation within the company as nimble managers vie for the title like it is some type of internal trophy. Which explains why the initial working assumption is the corporation possesses no CKCs at all. Better to impose an overly conservative perspective than permit the CKC identification process to be dominated by incumbent managers pursuing their own agendas, rather than the corporation's.

But self-proclamation is helpful in the sense that it provides an early indication of who the CKCs are not. The true CKC is almost never self-nominated. Phrases such as "value added" and "managing for value" dominate the self-nominated statements. Usually there is no attempt to define what value means.

Permitting cronyism to contaminate the CKC process is doubly damaging. First, management gains a false sense of well being, betting the company's future on holdover employees who are at best adequate. Second, any misstep slows the search for *legitimate* value contributors. The corporation with a late start in finding its critical future people never seems to fully recover from its self-inflicted wounds.

Sometimes the Most Reliable CKC Identifiers Aren't within the Corporation

The true CKC is off the chart in terms of self-actualization, and he or she leaves a mark in their field. Hence, the best identifier of the true Corporate Key Contributor is the peer CKC—in the same or a related field, or in the same or another company. This is someone who has actually worked with the individual in question toward a stretch performance goal.

The next best spotter is the probably the competitor who is desperately trying to win the zero sum battle to secure the most and best CKCs first. Of course, the archrival's judgments must be assessed only by actions: he has no interest in tipping his hand.

But the lagging competitor—especially a new CEO—is likely to see new CKCs as a critical part of his corporation's value rebound. "We've got to get some new people here who can build a more competitive company," will be this CEO's common refrain.

3.5 Acquiring the Corporate Key Contributor

> When we acquire a company . . . we're acquiring the next generation of products through its people. If you pay between $500,000 and $3 million per employee, and all you are doing is buying the current research and the current market share, you're making a terrible investment.
>
> —John Chambers, Cisco Systems CEO,
> October 1999 *Business 2.0*[10]

Maximizing shareholder value depends on securing requisite Corporate Key Contributors. Not just spotting the likely candidates, but securing the top talent for some time to come.

The Case for Providing Corporate Key Contributors with Incentive and Bonus Packages Matching the Company's Best

Professor Michael Jensen's research into the actions and motivations of agent-managers points to the importance of limiting eligibility for the corporation's richest incentive programs to those employees who create the most new value.

The half-dozen corporate executives at the top of a company's organization chart are part of the corporation's top-most compensation program, its executive incentive plan (EIP). EIP programs are now widespread, positioned to serve as the principal models for post-millennium compensation arrangements for corporations' leading Corporate Key Contributors. Accordingly, EIPs are addressed in the next chapter, "The Value Mandate CEO Acts."

It becomes clear that major incentives packages (that is, sufficient to cancel Jensen's agent-manager concern) cannot realistically be extended at all levels of the corporation, to all employees. The expense is prohibitive.[11]

That realization leads to the issue of where to focus the corporation's limited bonus and incentives funds to achieve the greatest value benefit. The answer is clear to the CEO who is aware that success depends in large part on attracting and retaining CKCs: Offer major incentives and bonuses competitive with EIP payouts to those few Corporate Key Contributors being counted upon to generate much of the company's new future value.

Fail to extend top incentives to a corporation's top value-producing talent, and the company's overall value program may be jeopardized. Offer second-rank incentives to CKCs, and the risk increases that those employees quickly become ex-CKCs: either by killing their incentive or causing them to join a competitor.

Setting the Maximum Acquisition Price for the Corporate Key Contributor

When it comes to the issue of the maximum to pay in order to secure the proven Corporate Key Contributor for years to come, the presumption up to this point is that there are no set limits. As long as the reasonably expected value performance exceeds the present value of total outflows.

However, this is one of those CKC situations where practices in the sports and entertainment fields do not appear to apply well for businesses back on earth. High-profile media businesses are sometimes deliberately run at a loss by their billionaire owners, who proclaim that "money is no object" and then break their own budgets.

In most major team sports in the U.S., the argument arises that you can't win a championship without going into the red. In order to buy a divisional championship in 1999, Arizona Diamondbacks owner Colangelo extended some contracts for new CKCs well into those players' forties, when performance invariably deteriorates.

But extending contracts past the period of peak usefulness is not an acceptable proposition for other businesses. The CEO finds that some directors seek to cancel contracts already offered to proven CKCs: The costs are known but the full future value of the added employee is always subject to speculation.[12]

When it comes to the maximum offer to the CKC, neither extreme provides a full answer. Companies cannot afford to compensate based on what the market will bear, nor can they afford to rigidly adhere to existing corporate compensation.

Above all, the Corporate Key Contributor is a valued resource. On that basis, the upper limit to any compensation package is realistically determined on an internal rate of return basis, APV, or similar basis of analysis.

Limiting CKC Payout to Conventional Executive Payout Formulas

A decision to limit creators of new value to the corporation's customary bonus structure may save the corporation money over the near term, but at a potentially far greater cost later.

General Electric Capital's GE Equity unit was headed by Jeffrey Coats, who reportedly grew $300 million into around $1 billion in 18 months in the late 1990s, assisted by shrewd selections and a highly supportive equity market.

Despite his extraordinary performance, Coats was limited to conventional GE bonus guidelines, which are based on corporate, not individual, achievement. Coats reportedly suggested a vencap-type participation approach to GE chairman Jack Welch. But compensation arrangements customary for the venture capital industry are foreign at GE. One unverified description has Welch writing "NOT IN MY LIFETIME" across the request.

Coats and several of his team departed. Welch reiterates the importance of everyone in the company having similar goals, and that those goals relate to corporate performance. Thus, no mavericks will be compensated according to individual performance.

But the GE chairman's action and opinion raise broader issues relating to focused incentives for Corporate Key Contributors. The top CKCs are not generalists, but are key experts in their areas. Matching their compensation to their area of contribution appears to make sense. But then that might call for split incentive compensation arrangements, precisely what the GE chairman rejects.[13]

Affording the True Corporate Key Contributor: The Guaranteed Contract

The guaranteed contract for the Corporate Key Contributor appears indefensible at initial and subsequent glances. Yet failure to pursue the true CKC is equally unacceptable.

The chief executive proclaims, "We can't afford the outlandish demands of these so-called 'stars.' " At the time, the expressions of admiration for this bold stance are sincere.

But reality is that without the key value-generating talent, there is no success and sometimes no team/company. The sports team that proclaims that it can do just as well with average players with reasonable salary demands is initially applauded, and then finishes dead last. Examples include both the mid-70s Oakland A's and the late 90s Florida Marlins, after fire sales of top talent.

No responsible manager would knowingly disregard an opportunity to implement the major internal procurement process, cutting overall corporate costs by five points. Nor would she or he miss the opportunity to secure a key stake in an emerging high-margin industry. The CEO who misses value opportunities or even one who destroys value, albeit passively, is marked for swift departure.

And yet, the chief executive who grinds his own company/team into dust by depriving it of skills and talent often lingers for quarters or even years, sometimes praised as a vigilant cost-cutter. This despite the fact that CKC cuts threaten to kill the corporation.

Once it is realized that sitting out the Corporate Key Contributor contest is value destruction, and thus not acceptable, emphasis shifts to how best to package the compensation offer to the CKC. The offer to the CKC must be compelling, yet it must also minimize risk and cost to the corporation.

Limiting the contract term is one obvious safeguard, but that one action provides inadequate protection all on its own. Everyone has war stories about the shining star who quickly fades upon receiving his overly rich, extended contract. And yet the occasional CKC mistake is part of the price of doing business.

3.6 Lock-In: CKC Retention Challenges

Microsoft's bright bulbs have always been the company's greatest asset. But now, the brightest new talent wants to join start-ups where growth potential is greater.
—Rich Karlgaard, Publisher, *Forbes*[14]

In the average acquisition, 40 to 80 percent of the top management and key engineers are gone in two years. By those metrics, most acquisitions fail.
—Cisco Systems CEO John Chambers[15]

Value is squandered when the CKC is identified and acquired, but then not retained. Losing a CKC can be damaging, like giving competitors the company's trade secrets. Which in a manner of speaking is what defines true CKCs.

Corporations that fail to retain CKCs effectively subsidize the rest of the industry. They have to work somewhere, and that place is often at a competitor's.

Everyone in the industry praises the "great to be from" company. That company trains and develops top talent, yet retains few of the stars itself. But the CEO of such a company is dismissed by his rivals as a value-destroying fool. Not to their faces, of course: They might stop what they're doing.

The Long-Term Contract Conundrum

From the corporation's perspective, the best and most direct way to lock in the proven value star is through an extended contract. But legitimate Corporate Key Contributors are not particularly security-oriented, raising the prospect of possible adverse selection. If the prospect seems a bit too eager to sign up for an extended contract, maybe he or she knows something that you should, too.

The precedent of using multiple-year contracts has significant appeal for the company or team that wants to ensure that they secure the scarce talent they need to prevail. Never mind that some of the payouts stretch out over many years. When all the pieces of the multi-year contract are added up, the big numbers all by themselves make for a powerful close.

One risk is that the extended contract outlasts the CKC's contribution period. Deliberate coasting is always a risk, too, as is the possibility that the contributor's area of special expertise becomes irrelevant due to change. Or talents may simply decline, despite the employee's best efforts.

Guarantee a fortune for doing nothing, and that's sometimes exactly what the company will get. Except that the "signee" gets the fortune while the "signor" receives nothing.

But there's an even more basic reason why the long-term contract leaves much to be desired as a solution to CKC retention: The most important employees for the corporation to retain are also those who should be the least interested in securing long-term contracts. Conversely, the employee of any type who energetically seeks the longest contract term possible could be sending a signal of troubles to come.

The true CKC has multiple, alternative sources of demand for his services. Moreover, the CKC may figure that he will be in an even more advantageous position a year from now.

The fallback links shorter-term contracts with specific, performance-based incentives. As much as 50–70 percent of the potential pay-out may hinge on these incentives. Such contracts typically involve too much risk and too little return for everyone except the true Corporate Key Contributor.

Key provisions that help ensure that shorter-term contracts work include: (1) right of last offer by the contracting company; and (2) automatic extension of present terms for another installment unless something else happens.

One legitimate concern is that any benefits from short-term contracts quickly dissolve as CKCs become entangled in seemingly endless employment negotiations. No sooner is the first round completed than preparation for the second begins.

Critical Mass and CKC Retention

Closely related to the long-term contract challenge is the issue of revisions to existing contract terms in accordance with changes in prevailing market conditions for proven CKC talent. The most contentious issue of this type involves the repricing of stock options.

The issue of adjusting contract terms for new market conditions generates deep passions. Contract purists insist that terms of the prevailing arrangement are sacrosanct, and cannot be altered in the slightest. Others on the opposite side of the issue are equally insistent, contending that there is no choice but to "meet the market."

Corporate officers who fail to follow through on commitment to build a CKC critical mass should not count upon contract fine print to fix the critical mass problem. Resorting to "you're under contract" heavy-handedness is a negative threshold to be avoided at all costs. Such tactics will inevitably cause the relationship to unravel.

Sullivan explains how the performance of the NBA's team of the 1990s, the Chicago Bulls, was reinforced by the expectation of all key cogs in the wheel that they would be supplemented by others. Thus, Jordan, Pippin, Coach Phil Jackson, and Rodman became a critical mass. The departure of one undermined the continuity of all (at least with the Bulls after the 1997–1998 season, that is)

Protecting CKC's Interest in the Knowledge Equity that They Help Create

The true Corporate Key Contributor joins the chief executive and the company's chief knowledge officer in appreciating the value of key insights and actionable intelligence. But that also means a possible retention problem. The CEO who runs roughshod over CKCs' interests in their own "knowledge equity" may later discover that critical talent has walked out the door.

The true Corporate Key Contributor exists at an elevated level on Maslow's needs hierarchy, motivated as much by an interest in ensuring that his ideas are realized as in any monetary reward.[16] Sometimes more.

A workable balance must be struck between the corporation's interest in increasing its knowledge-based wealth and the CKCs' sense of equity in their own intellectual property creations. This balancing act never completely ends, regardless of any formal documents dealing with transfer of rights to intellectual property. Right or wrong, the father of the invention never stops being a parent. As the CKC sees it, if he didn't come up with the inspiration and give it life, then no value would exist.

Rather than being at odds with the corporation's knowledge strategy, this sense of continuing involvement can instead be the glue that binds top talent to the company. But if company officers "win" the battle of knowledge equity in the wrong manner, the true war— the contest for scarce, great Corporate Key Contributors—could be lost.

The CEO characterized by an autocratic heads-I-win-tails-you-lose perspective on intellectual property rights is arguably less visible at the millennium than two or three decades ago. But that may merely indicate that tactics have changed, rather than intent.

It may be stylish to speak of specialized knowledge as a "company asset," but if that intelligence is also what ensures demand for that employee, why in the world would he voluntarily give it away for free?

But the spark necessary to move the product from the edges of viability to a major success is missing. No CKC knowingly works under duress; he or she has alternatives. Substitutes might be brought in by the former CEO to try to mop up the job, but the rules of adverse selection apply.

By now, the industry's most valuable employees have branded the company a "Bad Company to Work For," using the criteria most important to them. The lackeys who remain behind have little interest in the knowledge equity issue, for the simple reason that they create none.

4

The Value Mandate
CEO Acts

Establishing, Inspiring, Energizing the Corporation's Maximum Value Management Program

Rewards for *Top* Value Creation Performance?
The chief executive's first priority is survival. Even the chief executive who is achieving The Value Mandate in full may be excused for putting first things first. If the corporation is approaching maximum shareholder value yet the CEO's no longer around, who cares?

Yet the two goals are intertwined. Average CEO duration in office in the United States and the United Kingdom is down to around four years and shrinking.[1] Escalating value expectations are the central issue. Suddenly, CEOs are being fired from profitable corporations. Their companies just aren't profitable *enough* to keep up with competitors that the Board fears are pulling too far ahead.

69

Rakesh Khurana of MIT's Sloan School of Management examines 1,300 CEO dismissals between 1980 and 1996 involving Fortune 500 companies. He concludes that for similar levels of performance, a chief executive appointed after 1985 is *three times* as likely to be sacked as a counterpart appointed before 1985.[2]

A modest annualized EPS growth rate scarcely into double digits used to insulate most leaders, most of the time. But no longer. Those irritating comparative stock price charts such as those in Figure 1-5 and Figure 4-1 tend to be interpreted as indications of relative value performance.

Board members used to be the first to warm to the CEO's maximizing shareholder value (MSV) slogans with few if any awkward follow-up questions. But as of the millennium, every Board seems to have at least one independent member with major share backing who refuses to accept proclamations at face value. Once a pariah, this responsible irritant is now looked to for leadership by other independent board members who are feeling pressure from their constituents to strengthen Total Shareholder Return performance.[3]

Spin doctors' MSV proclamations prepared for the chief executive are greeted by this audience not with applause, but demands for backup analysis and concrete plans. Probers aim at separating out the spurious value improvement initiatives from the few comprehensive action programs capable of driving value forward.[4]

Developing a number for current value is easy enough, and numerous discounted cash flow statistical valuation methods exist (see Appendix A). Far more challenging—and what represents a shortfall of underpowered valuation approaches— is the next step: devising the CEO's value leadership program. This is the CEO's clear plan defining the corporation's six to eight most important comprehensive programs to achieve maximum value and close the Value Opportunity Gap.

The true Value Mandate corporation makes its rivals look like they're standing still. Competitors who are less effective at narrowing their own Value Opportunity Gaps—or who don't even have a workable gap approach yet—face higher comparative capital costs and fewer future value opportunities.

For them, the downward spiral begins. The value laggards generate less internal cash flow and therefore cannot fund as many top-yield innovation investment prospects. They also experience fewer internal efficiency investment opportunities, or at least fewer are apparent. Valued at increasing discounts to industry rivals, these companies must endure relatively higher weighted average costs of equity

Figure 4-1. Somerfield vs. U.K. grocery industry, August 1996–September 1999.

Company-to-industry comparative charts of value surrogates such as this involving embattled U.K. grocery chain Somerfield's cause analysts and other value influencers to consider management's "We create value" claims from a broader perspective.

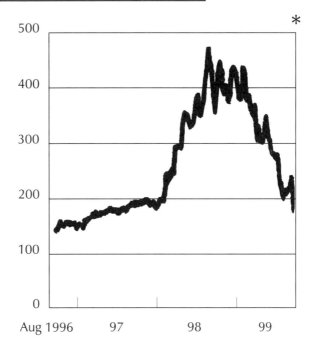

Note:
*Through September 13, 1999.

Chart: Primark Datastream.
From Peggy Hollinger, "Second Warning for Somerfield," *The Financial Times,* September 14, 1999, page 23. Reprinted with permission from *The Financial Times.*

(WACE), which, in turn, can mean higher total capital costs and lower value. Then the spiral starts all over again.

Closing the VOG must be embraced as the CEO's program, not a delegated activity at which the CEO makes a cameo appearance at the beginning and never again. If maximizing shareholder value for real is the corporation's purpose for existence, then it is imperative to involve the corporation's leader as an integral part of that effort.

4.1 The CEO's MSV Pre-Conditions: Implementation and Risk

Two of the advance conditions for success at maximizing shareholder value are highly dependent on a leading role by the chief executive. In most corporations, at most times, implementation and risk-and-reward considerations are afterthoughts, if that. Yet each consideration is critical to the effectiveness of the CEO's MSV program.

CEO's Implementation Follow-Through

"If you can't implement it, don't do it," has the ring of good sense. The chief executive's years of experience suggest that if the proposed initiative is overreaching or poorly planned or both, it is best not to even attempt implementation.

Some CEOs have learned through past pain that the initiative that appears to be unworkable often is. What appear to be long odds of success are often longer than expected because problems not yet imagined crop up: Most of the iceberg is under the surface. Such healthy cynicism should be doubled in the case of the content-free campaign that has lots of style but little more than that. At times, an implementation approach fails simply because there isn't one.[5]

Don't Do It Under Debate

"Don't do it" is not an option when it comes to closing the corporation's VOG. Like it or not, the company is already deeply involved in the battle for value leadership of its industry. The only choice is between robust approaches that succeed in implementing MSV and the others.

Stakes are high. The value leader also becomes its industry's competitive pacesetter, having exploited growth opportunities better than rivals. The value leader is in a commanding position to survive and shape the future direction of the industry to its advantage.

"Don't do it"—choosing not to implement value development programs—does not excuse a company from the risks and losses of failed implementation. The non-participant quits, abandoning the field to the competition without a fight. Then the non-participant watches as rivals surge ahead, securing new value that never advanced beyond slogan stage within her or his company.

Neutralizing Internal Deflection Tactics

The greater the level of new value pursued, the more significant the prospective changes to some parts of the corporation. Achieving further significant revenue-side value hinges on making key changes to entrenched activities and processes. From the CAPEX mechanism to R&D prospect identification, planning for product life cycle shrinkage to tough decisions about which sales channels to develop and which to leave.

Expense-side actions for maximizing shareholder value challenge incumbent operations in one "untouchable" function after another. No matter how efficient that operation is today, the CEO must look ahead to the time when the holdover procurement function will face a competitive burden of twice the unit costs of rivals or time to market grows to double that of competitors who have already converted to new value approaches (preferred supplier programs, component assembly purchasing, online ordering for expendables, among other items, as described in Chapter 5).

The chief executive pursuing the full Value Mandate cannot wait for reactive benchmark indicators to provide the signal to act. This value-maximizing CEO establishes a "stalking horse" procurement function for the company to beat, incorporating new value developments that won't appear on the best-practices benchmarking radar for several quarters yet.

This CEO *assumes the role of* implementation manager for the corporation's Maximum Value Management program. The most agile designated manager is no match for the outperformer CEO who knows what must be done and is sometimes willing to dig into execution detail to get it done. This chief executive converts statements of "might not work here" into "will work here."

Eventually, the chief executive comes to realize that there is no alternative to taking direct ownership of value program implementation. Magically, the top-most officer has a way of making endeavors succeed that would otherwise be ground to dust.

Risk, Reward, and Maximizing Shareholder Value

Closing the Value Opportunity Gap means increasing revenue and projected cash flows from novel (i.e., first introduced to market) innovation. This introduces added risk, usually manifested in the form of increased EPS trend line volatility.

Don't Break the (EPS Quarterly) String: Handcuffing the Value Development Program

"Go ahead and maximize value, but don't jeopardize our string of increasing EPS for eighteen consecutive quarters." Such an instruction from the Board or suggestion from analysts places management in an impossible situation.

Reducing ongoing expenses increases value, but only if offsets don't wipe out the indicated efficiencies. No corporation ever shrank its way to industry prominence, so value growth by expense reductions plus efficiency improvement alone means severe limits to the level of new value that can be achieved.

Some new revenues can be generated from line extensions and imitation products, but as the pace of change accelerates, the once high-margin mature product becomes less and less profitable. New competitors worshipping at the altar of market share slash their margins, providing little or no room for differentiation by lower price.

Focus on Novel Innovation

Increasing corporate value by pursuing novel innovation—all-new products and services that didn't exist in the marketplace a few months ago—also increases business risk.

Pursuing MSV for real virtually guarantees an increase in EPS volatility (forget entirely about the unbroken string of quarterly EPS results). Because even when those novel innovations succeed, timing difference between cash in- and outflows means disruptions to reported results for several quarters.

Company shareholders and other value influencers look for clear confirmation that the CEO is on the same page as them. These value influencers look primarily to future cash flow projections in determining market value (share price), as noted in Chapter 1.[6] The management that still thinks reported earnings matter should consider McKinsey & Co.'s analysis, shown in Figure 4-2. Its examination of

Figure 4-2. Pursuing the wrong measure: lack of correlation between reported earnings growth and market value.

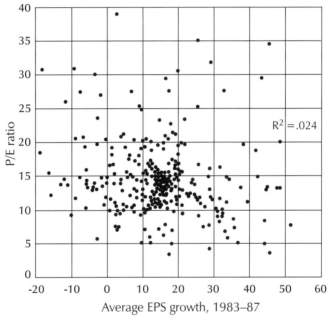

Plotting reported earnings against P/E ratio results in a meaningless scatter diagram and an R^2 of .024 (S&P 400).

EPS = Earnings per share.
P/E = Price-to-earnings multiple.

Source: McKinsey & Co., from *The Independent,* London, February 8, 1997, page 27. Reprinted with permission from *The Independent*/Syndication, London, and McKinsey & Co.

PE ratios versus reported earnings (EPS growth from 1983 to 1987) resulted in an immaterial correlation (r-squared) of .024.

Risk of Stonewalling Must Exceed Risk of Underperformance

How employees respond to early indications of value underperformance is critical to the success of the corporation's value program.

It isn't enough just to demonstrate tolerance of increased, customary business risks by occasionally praising the responsible risk-taker who fails despite his or her best efforts. It is also necessary to ensure that deliberate stonewalling of value destruction becomes immediate grounds for rebuke, followed by dismissal if the situation remains uncorrected.

Why such an extreme stance? Because deliberately hiding evidence of value-reducing practices or sustaining those practices is effectively the same as destroying company assets. The responsive CEO wouldn't hesitate for a second to take decisive action if an R&D scientist sold proprietary trade secrets to a competitor. Permitting value destruction to continue when it could be stopped is no less serious. Consider two examples:

1. The salesperson who won't ever reach quota is deftly hidden through continuing shifts in territory and product assignment (always "getting up to speed"). Who's behind this shell game? Look first to a manager eager to hide a hiring mistake and avoid a black mark on his or her own record.

2. The corporation's system for travel and entertainment reporting and reimbursement is plodding and expensive, with poor controls over disbursements. The original decision-maker is aware of third-party alternatives but, to maintain maximum control, continues with the internal custom arrangement. The reasoning: First the budget goes, then the budget administrator.

4.2 CEO Sets the Corporation's New Value Realities

For the CEO's Maximum Value Management program to achieve expectations, changes in that company's value rules of the game are necessary. This refers to the realities—the assumptions, conditions, and mind-sets—that must be in place before maximum value can be pursued in earnest. Four of these new realities are shown in Table 4-1 and described below.

Two Measurement Approaches, Not One

Backward management metrics are not going away, but neither are forward-facing indications of value performance.

Despite analyses such as that shown in Figure 4-2, managing the company by established historical financial results remains deeply embedded. If the financial market could have only one performance number, that number would be the EPS. At the same time, cash

Table 4-1. Setting the corporation's value realities.

Element	Explanation
Two Measurement Approaches, Not One	Backward management metrics not going away, but neither are forward-facing indications of value performance.
Only Relative Matters	Basis for urgency: If competitor's superior value performance doesn't provide sufficient incentive, your own company's Potential Value (Vp) should.
Specific-Actions Agenda Key to Closing Firm's VOG	Addressing VOG on statistical basis only, inadequate: Value *awareness* not to be confused with value *creation*.
CKC-Centric Corporation	If CKC are central to new value creation, they emerge as a permanent, integrated force within the organization.

flow–based performance measurement is mandatory because of its correlation to market value. The result is that both metrics will continue to co-exist within the corporation for some time. Both must be anticipated in the complete financial communications approach, regulations permitting.[7]

Only Relative Matters

Urgency: If competitors' superior value performance doesn't provide enough incentive, then your own corporation's potential values (Vp) does.

On its own, any stand-alone indication of an increase in "value" is meaningless. Whether expressed in terms of amounts or change, value performance requires context for meaningful interpretation.

Say corporation top management announces that it has "increased value" by $100 million over the past eighteen months, an increase of 10 percent. Internally, the accomplishment is heralded as proof that the CEO's team is maximizing shareholder wealth. But on their own, indications of this "value improvement" are meaningless and possibly misleading. If the $100 million/10 percent value creation "accomplishment" has been caused by the rising-tide effect of an overall market increase, then management may have done nothing

to cause the apparent value increase. (But just try to persuade management that it has no basis for claim "value creation" credit!)

In order to better separate value fact from fiction, outperformer
chief executives and all others who influence the corporation's value
contrast *apparent* value "achievement" against two sets of refer-
ences: equity market and specific companies.

Equity Market References

This reference set assesses value performance against overall market
and specific industry group indices, over a comparable analysis period. If Striver Corp.'s value has increased 10 percent over the past
18 months but the industry value index has increased by 13.5 percent
over that period, Striver's value underperformed in relative terms
rather than outperformed.

Specific Company References

This reference set compares the company's indicated value performance against the "company to beat," present or prospective. This
is a straight value comparison, with the implication that for the corporation to be assured of survival, its only chance is to outperform
the existing value leader.

The CEO of the aspiring outperformer corporation actively pursues such comparisons, even if present performance lags, as shareholders are reassured by a clear understanding of management's
targets and the height of its aspirations.

By contrast, comparing value achievement against a meaningless reference such as an industry or general reference blurs that
understanding. In the past, aiming at the industry mid-point only
assured a mediocre company. Today, with the industry shrinking,
aiming so low may jeopardize the survival of the company.

Specific-Actions Agenda Is Key to Closing Corporation's Value Opportunity Gap

Approaching the VOG on an overall statistical basis alone is inadequate. Value awareness is not to be confused with value creation.

The corporation's VOG is first approximated by estimating adjusted present value (APV) at 50 percent, as we described in Chapter
1. But that's just the start. All that the initial scoping accomplishes

is to roughly approximate the size and direction of the corporation's present VOG target.

Incrementalism: Insufficient to Close the Value Opportunity Gap

Persistence of a sizable Value Opportunity Gap confirm the error of relying on incremental actions to try to close that corporation's VOG. Maximum shareholder value cannot be achieved by such minimal actions as slightly revising sales terms; rebadging, repackaging, and repositioning aging brands; stretching products one more time with yet another type of cosmetic change; redrawing the sales territories and staffing charts; juggling commission rates and advertising spending; and the ultimate fallbacks of hiring freezes and arbitrary across-the-board budget cuts of 10–15 percent.

It isn't just that the value impact from such incremental initiatives is too little to achieve anything more than just a minor dent in the VOG, but that this type of value is already "in the market" and thus not available to close the VOG.

A Third/A Third/A Third

The dilemma that management faces in implementing its value improvement effort in coordination with corporate staff is that only about a third of the actions necessary to close the VOG can possibly "trickle up" from staff ranks. Another third requires significant changes in how that function is conducted. The final third might call for elimination of that function and its budget entirely. Consider the following illustration of operations at a human resources department, reflecting composite precedent.[8]

Initial Third: Business as Usual, Modified Slightly for Some Additional Value Creation

The company's fifty-odd HR staff includes some employees and activities reasonably described as defying justification even in the best of times. Consider the publishing company that maintained a staff to monitor and interview various temp agencies and their placements, when a single master temp contract would do the job just as well or better, slashing ongoing costs and thus increasing value.

To the extent that this kind of incremental change reduces a company's ongoing costs without offsets, corporate value is increased. But a more accurate description is that a weight that has been suppressing the corporation's value for years has been removed.

Middle Third: "But This Isn't the Way We're Used to Doing This"

Suddenly, the way that things have always been done is no longer
good enough. In HR, the once untouchable upper and lower boundaries for total compensation are revealed to obstruct the corporation's pursuit of critical top performer/middle manager talent
(corporate key contributors). From benefits options to flexible hours
scheduling, the HR procedure used to call for appointments and
standing staff. The new lower continuing cost/higher value arrangement calls instead for self-access to the corporation's intranet, with
backup staff on an exception basis only.

Final Third: The Unthinkable Becomes Thinkable

Total outsourcing of the HR function to a third party would be unthinkable. Or how about dramatically narrowing HR's functions to
those activities that impact corporate value the most, e.g., CKC re-
cruitment and development of executive incentives packages for
those value creators. Unthinkable? So was disposing of the corporation's founding account until just two years ago, when that account
was diagnosed as a chronic loss leader.

The CKC–Centric Corporation

If corporate key contributors are central to new value creation, then
CKCs emerge as a new reality for everyone within the corporation.

There are plenty of staff but precious few drivers of corporate
wealth based on significant levels of objective, confirmed value contribution. Each salary dollar wasted on overpayment (relative to value),
or spent anytime for an expendable employee, suppresses corporate
value by at least four to six dollars, based on minimal value-to-cash-
flow relationships we have experienced.

As a result, shareholders become less and less eager to dig deep
into their own pockets in order to subsidize the wasted top 50 percent
compensation for the marginal manager (who raises every issue
imaginable in meetings but solves none) or the expendable employee
(who can be readily replaced at lower cost, presuming the position is
continued at all).

The base presumption, as described in Chapter 3, is that value
ultimately originates with a small number of top contributors. The
physical assets, proprietary processes, trade secrets, and customer
relationships "owned" by the corporation are resources *only* to the

extent that they are activated and developed by the CKCs, assuming that the corporation has any at all.

At the corporation run by a CEO serious about maximizing shareholder value for real, organizational structures, rules, and relationships are adapted to the requirements of these CKCs, rather than the other way around. The result is the start of the CKC-centric organization, which puts value first, by organizing in accordance with the ultimate wealth creators.

This is not new. The corporation *already* breaks some of its own rule on a case-by-case basis to accommodate the occasional star value generator. Acting in its own self-interest, the company bends to the account manager with the Midas touch who asks for special help with support and scheduling in order to make a few extra sales calls per day. Likewise, the CKC-centric company rewards the procurement department star who can effectively implement multiple aspects of optimal value procurement function rather than a counterpart who is familiar with one value program but a novice on all the others. The first officer repays the company many times over while the second manager destroys value compared to potential.[9]

Insulating the Corporate Key Contributor and Team

The bureaucrat who maneuvers to share credit for a promising breakthrough may just be operating on instinct, and the CKC may merely be amused by such presumption. Then again, the CKC's own sense of integrity could cause a top value generator to go over to the competition in disgust. The issue is whether the outperformer CEO is willing to risk double value damage (rival wins, CEO loses) for the sake of protecting a bureaucrat's lies.

Generating Sparks, Intracompany

The deeper the CKC's expertise, the greater the probability that the expertise is also narrow. The millennium renaissance star equally adept at blue lasers and encryption software is the stuff of sci-fi novels. So the CEO who hopes to gain full advantage from cross-pollination of powerful new capabilities must sometimes suspend traditional organizational notions in order to get two CKCs in tangential areas who might *spark* into the same group.

The goal is to cause that combination of expertise and working compatibility that just might yield the next great breakthrough. Presuming no one ever looks at the "Org Chart" anymore anyway, bend-ing the boxes is a small price to pay for a combination that might be explosively productive.

Breaking the Rules about Access to the Top

In the CKC recruiting wars, the outperformer CEO is the corporation's secret weapon—the ultimate closer to secure that rare CKC considered key to the corporation's future. So prior contact between the chief executive and the CKC is not only possible, but likely. This CEO ignores hierarchical order when it comes to getting direct answers to questions and keeping tabs on the corporation's future. First, because the CEO wants to hear from the value instigator, directly. Go-betweens scarcely have a grasp of the salient buzzwords, much less knowledge of the significance of various aspects of the program. The chief executive wants to contact the source to know first-hand what's going on, what's new, what's wrong. Second, the CEO wants to provide the corporation as a whole with some unmistakable signals when it comes to CKCs and the organization structure.

The message emerges: Rules and hierarchy will always be bent as necessary to facilitate value creation. The related message is that the only organizational structures with a chance of survival are those that further the corporation's core purpose of maximizing shareholder value.

The corporation now reorganizes every two years anyway, the chief executive figures. If the structure holds back CKC performance, some career bureaucrats seeking to undermine the growing influence of the CKC may be shocked to discover one day that the CKC *heads* their unit.

4.3 Preparing the Corporation for Value Outperformance

Stop at the point of introducing rules for the new value order, and little happens. Inertia is the true force in many companies, and those unprepared for outperformance in value terms slip back to comfortable practices. That is, unless the outperformer chief executive prepares the company for new value with specific key actions—not just symbolic gestures (see Table 4-2).

Table 4-2. Preparing the corporation for value outperformance.

Element	Explanation
Inevitability of the Value Meritocracy, "Sooner Than You Think"	Never fully achieved, perpetually a goal. Suboptimalizers, noncontributors (coasters), other value destroyers on notice.
VOG "Half Empty" Galvanizes New Value Initiatives Throughout Corporation	Positive use of value gap/shortfall to spur specific value actions and follow-through.
Forget Whatever Happened Yesterday: Moving Forward From Incrementalism	"Killing off" the *past* in order to maximize *future* shareholder wealth.

"Sooner Than You Think": Inevitability of the Value Meritocracy

The value meritocracy is never fully achieved; it is always the goal. Suboptimalizers, coasters, other non-contributors are on notice and ready to act or not act, as they determine the case might be.

Fiefdoms under Threat

Everyone knows that corporate meritocracies exist only in theory. In the real world, *How to Succeed in Business without Really Trying* games players rule. Time and again, the earnest but unpolished solid corporate citizen is lunch for those capable of massive self-promotion and -justification.

This may be so, but today, the outperformer chief executive sees these high-profile, much lower-content games players in a different light. And it is *not* as management depth, but rather as walking, talking sources of value destruction. Remove them (or at least lower their costs to be closer to true, actual value contribution level), and the corporation's current value pops up like a cork released from under water.

The Value Mandate CEO knows that failure to make significant progress in closing the company's Value Opportunity Gap threatens corporate viability. Significant blocks of new value must be captured, if not always through implementation of one value *action* at a time, then by removal of one value *destroyer* at a time.[10]

The value destroyers place their unit's goals ahead of the corporation's key objectives. Forget the prattle about shared visions uniting department and corporate goals. As soon as they understand that MSV means that the department's budget will be halved, or shifted eight time zones away as part of the corporation's 24-hour operations, their true feelings about MSV emerge.

Delaying that day of reckoning calls upon the full complement of a department-fiefdom manager's "skills." Mouthing the MSV line while carefully undermining program effectiveness and fencing in any suspected CKCs, the games players ensure that the star's achievements are counted as their own achievements.

Signaling the New Order

Unless the chief executive lets the rest of the corporation know that such value-destructive games are a thing of the past, the wary CKCs may not even set foot within the corporation. Because, with many other alternatives regarding where to go and whom to enrich, why would the CKC endorse a shark's tank dominated by bureaucrats living by their corporate political wits but nothing else? They go elsewhere, probably to a rival. Or sometimes they create their own rival corporation.

Transition to this new order doesn't happen overnight. With little alternative demand for *their* contributions, the games players fight for the status quo with the ferocity of cornered animals.

The Value Mandate chief executive starts the transition through clear signals that first diminish and then demolish policies that place department concerns ahead of corporate wealth. These signals include fundamentally changing the internal cost structure of the business from fixed to variable costs, lowering expenses throughout,[11] and acting as if doubling the corporation's speed to market and the level of novel innovation investment are tantamount to survival—because they are.

Value Opportunity Gap "Half Empty": Galvanizing New Value Initiatives throughout Corporation

The Value Opportunity Gap is introduced by the CEO with the working assumption that the corporation is underperforming in value terms by 50 percent. This initial assumption is subsequently refined and substantiated by specific value improvement opportunities throughout the corporation.

Instead of a negative (the glass half empty), this shortfall estimate is instead a device the Value Mandate CEO uses to generate the sense of urgency necessary to reach the top and remain there. Coupling the VOG with the realization that corporations with huge value gaps *nominate themselves* as takeover targets (recall Chapter 1) and the CEO has some potent motivational tools available.

Yet the corporations that most require value improvement are often slowest to act. The corporate leader who hopes that an indifferent value performance can slip by unnoticed is quickly brought down by value surrogate comparisons made in the business media, like those demonstrated in Figures 1-5 and 4-1.

Forget Yesterday: Moving Forward from Incrementalism

Only newly created value narrows that company's Value Opportunity Gap, which means that all attention in the corporation—all actions— must be directed to the future and away from prior achievements and characteristics, which are soon irrelevant.

Poison Culture: Yesterday's Attributes Become Today's Albatross

The notion that all answers for dealing with the future are available in the past is comforting. Regardless of the direction or severity of change or how often that industry's business model is turned inside out, there's an answer to be found in the corporation's venerable shared beliefs and behavior. No matter how radical the changes in channels, customers' preferences and profiles, and competitors' tactics, simply revisiting yesterday's stories ensures that the corporation will not only survive, but thrive.

Too bad such fiction is completely groundless. No responsible chief executive knowingly obstructs his or her company's resiliency and responsiveness, yet that's exactly what happens to the company dominated by reverence for the past. Self-delusion may temporarily work within the corporation, but outside, investors prepare their sell orders. Marks & Spencer and Sainsbury, the U.K.'s best-known retailer and its No. 2 grocery chain, respectively, practiced promotion to executive positions from within. The spin doctors' logic: Only those who have operated in these environments for years are capable of guiding the corporation expertly in the future as it encounters new challenges. Both companies appointed new CEOs from within during 1999, but the management shakeouts failed to rally either company's stock price.

But the market is not always appreciative of expertly phrased PR explanations, and stock values remain suppressed. Instead of rewarding the corporation for elevating a new CEO steeped in the old practices and culture, the market instead imposes penalties. That evidence that the past culture is being extended into the new century does not boost value, but rather, somewhat poisons the stock price and company value.

Staring Backward at an Irrelevant Past

Outside accounts don't care about the corporation's culture at all, except as it directly affects product characteristics and supplier performance. The accelerating pace of change affecting their industries means that there's no time available to stare backwards at the past. And no reason: With each increment of acceleration, the road ahead becomes less like the road behind.

The faster industry change occurs, the more likely it is that the past is a value negative, rather than a positive. Even funds managers warn that past performance may not be indicative of future results. Indeed, "may not" is understatement when one of three companies will not even be around five years from now, at least not in the same form, name, and ownership.

Probabilities are high the corporation's cash flow and value (CF& V) model has already been turned upside down in the past five years, reflecting changes in that industry. That CF&V model will be shattered again in less than three years' time, and will need to be reconstructed. And then again eighteen months later, as life cycles shrink.

With each quake, the industry's cost and profit structure changes from the one before. The company's value-sustaining products change, as do value-optimal channels to market and unit costs. Principal customers alter *how* they buy, not just *what* they purchase. The nature of critical talent required for success changes with each transition. Lock in yesterday's deteriorating expertise with a long-term contract, and the corporation ends up eating that contract's cost later. It's called value destruction.

4.4 Making It Work

It is the full and robust corporate value development program, designed to attack the corporation's *entire* Value Opportunity Gap, not just a sliver. (See Table 4-3.) Addressing value in all parts of the corporation where untapped value exists, not just financial operations.[12]

Partial value approaches undermine MSV as the corporation's driving force in the minds of everyone in the corporation. Even if full value is extracted from the limited scope effort, there is ample evidence that far more has been left behind, untouched. Limiting value actions to changes in capital structure, other financial window dressing, and scattered incentives has the advantage that no one within the company objects. No bureaucratic fiefdom is threatened by the balance sheet alchemy, no sacred cow operation is unaffected.

But sacred cows make the sweetest meat. Few of the value opportunities arising in trickle-up fashion from within the corporation reflect full value. Not because staff lack enthusiasm—cooperation is rarely the problem. Self-interest *is* an unavoidable concern. No individual can reasonably be expected to voluntarily nominate a value improvement opportunity that might result in his or her job being

Table 4-3. Making it work.

Element	Explanation
Specific VOG Actions Continuing MVM Program Updates, Adaptations	Progressing from VOG statistical ranges to specific actions, unique for that would-be millennium outperformer corporation.
No Excuses	Acknowledging past value destruction and missed value-creation opportunities represents first step to closing company's VOG.
Preemptive Strikes	Value-relevant changes occur too fast to rely on after-the-fact responses alone.
Some Necessary Separations	Regrettable, also necessary; those who diminish value and cannot/will not adapt to MSV for real.

outsourced or simplified and consolidated to the point of the function and budget disappearing altogether.

At first, access to a robust online risk management service might seem like a great idea to the corporation's senior risk manager, who believes that access to the expertise and analysis not otherwise available will help make the job much easier. But such a comprehensive, simple-to-use service *accessible to others in the company* removes some of the professional armor that protects his or her job.

If the nature of online support available comes to be known, this self-protective risk manager might eventually lose staff and/or his or her own position, in one of two ways. In one way, the risk manager's position is downgraded to a lower expertise and level with reduced salary, and then staffed with a general office manager who also performs other functions. In the second, use of standardized procedures and software associated with the Web site precedes transfer of the company's entire risk management function to a third-party group. Staff are whittled down *after* the absorption, and the manager is the most vulnerable.

Not too surprisingly, the risk manager gets amnesia and "forgets" to raise this possible value opportunity when a voluntary list is solicited. The incumbent's inaction might seem modest, and yet the result is value *destroyed* relative to potential. Unless alternative means exist to ensure that these and similar value opportunities emerge, value is lost.

Specific Value Opportunity Gap Actions

Specific value actions represent the bedrock of the comprehensive value program approach, what we have called Maximum Value Management. Actions specific to that company, changing with industry and company circumstances, encompass all of the principal value sources.

The Value Opportunity Gap Changes: Setting Review/ Reassessment Date Frequency

The first identity of the corporation's Value Opportunity Gap is a statistical estimate of the difference between potential value and current value. VOG's second form is the discrete value projects and initiatives that fully bridge the Vp-Vn gap.

As we illustrated in Figure 2-1, the corporation's VOG changes over time, reflecting (1) changes in the specific *possible* (Vp) and *achieved* (Vn) value opportunities for that company and (2) broad, external market influences (the "tides" that raise or lower all ships).

To ensure that the current value is relevant and powerful, the VOG must be updated on a frequent basis. How frequently? Not any slower than *half* the projected life of that company's *shortest* life cycle of a major product. Company projections of economic lives are notoriously optimistic. Relentless, accelerating change ensures that the product/service life will shrink down to that review date sooner than expected.

As a practical matter, VOG reassessment every six months is about right for most companies outside of Silicon Valley. In the case of the latter, though, if products and value-gap strategies are not fully reviewed and challenged at least quarterly, the risk of solving yesterday's challenges soars. In high-tech and other industries, the VOG review threshold will continue to shrink in the future, in concert with gradually imploding product/service economic lives.

Emphasis on Actions: Setting Review/Reassessment Date Frequency Specific to the Corporation

Management's initial Value Opportunity Gap statistical estimates must be taken to the next level for VOG to be of major use in helping maximum value. The next level is the creation of an action list for closing the full VOG amount, based on the most recent analysis data and covering the full range of legitimate value prospects.

Value Source within the Corporation

This refers to areas/functions of the business where value originates, as illustrated in Figure P-1 and described in Chapters 5–8.

Type of Value Activity

Value activities span revenue-side value initiatives, expense-side hybrids, and cross-organizational prospects, as we discussed in Chapter 1.

There is no such thing as a one size fits all value development template. Each corporation's set of value circumstances is unique. Which means that the same initiative that creates value in one company may destroy it in another.

Replacing all sales channels with online channels only emerges as an optimal value strategy in industries such as consumer software,

plug-in memory components, and travel insurance industries. Wholesale mortgage banking and industrial factoring (purchasing receiv-
ables) aren't far behind.

Yet in such industries as drug stores and high-margin clothing,
"online only" threatens to put the companies in straightjackets. Existing, enduring physical distribution networks mean that the participant that limits itself to a single channel effectively excludes itself
from the most efficient means of getting product from point to point.
Every product may be a bit business, as MIT's Negroponte proclaims,
but you still have to get that bottle of aspirin from Des Moines to
Chicago.

Starting Out: Pick the Low-Hanging Fruit, but Get *All* of It

Financial restructuring is the logical starting point for the corporation's Maximum Value Management program for two reasons: (1) the
chief financial officer is often the company's first missionary for comprehensive, systematic value-based management, applied enterprise-
wide, and (2) many of the value actions that originate within the
CFO's sphere exert little pressure elsewhere in the organization, and
thus face no resistance.

Establishing early value program momentum demonstrates that
value creation is not an infeasible, convoluted idea of the theoretical
economists, but rather, that new corporate wealth *is being* created
within the corporation, every day.

Finance throws down the gauntlet to other parts of the corporation: Match or exceed the value created here, or risk having your
sector designated as underperforming in a value sense. Or worse still,
the sector could be perceived as *destroying* wealth since value opportunities available for the taking are being missed—either undiag-
nosed, pursued by ineffective means, deliberately ignored because of
the change implications, or a combination of the three.

Thus the Value Mandate CEO's first challenge is to extract full
value from finance, lead by the CFO. Without a significant, measur-
able impact on corporate value from this sector, the threat arises that
Maximum Value Management will fail to have gathered enough early
momentum as the value program progresses into the tougher sled-
ding it will experience in the core operations of the business.

It is no secret that value management's roots are in financial
theory. For the program to secure credibility with those in the company who bend metal rather than spreadsheets, the start must dem-

onstrate convincing value impact in finance, value management's traditional "home base."

The fact that the linkage between debt/capital and corporate present value (APV) is already extensively known presents positives and can also pose some negatives for the CEO and CFO in these early stages.

It is a positive that few financial officers argue anymore with the notion that corporate value can be increased by prudent management of the *percentage, mix,* and *type* of capital components. The dinosaur financial VP who insisted that debt must be maintained at levels far below those dictated by minimum debt-servicing capacity was dismissed long ago as other corporations implemented growth-supporting capital structures instead, leaving the dinosaur's company behind.

But knowledge of the capital structure/value relationship may be a negative if minimal increases to the debt/capital ratio are as far as this part of the program goes. If that single capital structure "button" is pushed too tentatively, value is left behind. From our perspective, *value left behind* means *value destroyed,* relative to full potential corporate wealth. If this is the *only* button pushed, then other value opportunities in finance are being missed.[13]

Extracting full value from financial restructuring means expanding the scope beyond debt and capital percentages of corporate capital only, to other areas, such as:

- *Composition of Debt Portfolio.* This refers to the amount, yield, and maturity of specific elements of the corporation's debt portfolio. This directly influences weighted average cost of debt (WACD), thus indirectly affecting weighted average cost of capital (WACC).

- *Possible Changes in Corporate Financial Risk.* Significant changes in debt-servicing coverage (cash flow compared to principal and interest requirements) can and do influence corporate worth. It doesn't take a rating agency downgrade to cause the company's stock price to plunge. Insightful analysts often perceive the signs long before that point.

- *Revised Business Risk.* Financing levels and availability can affect corporate value in other ways, in combination with other developments in the corporation.

Excessive expenses absorb too much of the corporation's combined internal and external funds, with the result that money that would otherwise be invested in high-yield internal projects is instead diverted to pay debt principal and interest.

The consequence is not just reduced corporate income, but also a possible loss of opportunity. If the missed opportunities are critical to the success of the enterprise, stability of the business declines, pulling value down in sympathy.

Reducing the corporation's cash dividend represents a plausible opportunity for further value creation, assuming that funds are instead reinvested at high return. As a practical matter, that opportunity must sometimes be deferred, but it should never be forgotten.

Contrary to the belief of some in the corporation, *all funds incur costs,* including retained earnings. If the company reinvests that money at a return exceeding capital cost, value grows. If it squanders the money by giving it away with nothing in return, value decreases.

Shareholder-owners assess their holdings on a total shareholder return (TSR) basis: the sum of stock price appreciation plus cash dividends received. Thus the initial reaction of the shareholders to a cash dividend cut is probably going to be that they've lost something.

A stickier issue involves the role of the cash dividend as an indirect means of communicating management's level of confidence in its own cash flow projections. If a better means of communicating and confirming projection data is not developed, the knee-jerk reaction of some analysts and others would be to assume that management has abandoned its prior cash flow commitments, on which *their* interpretations are based.[14]

Acknowledging past value destruction and missed value creation opportunities represents the first step to closing that company's Value Opportunity Gap.

How those within the corporation respond to early indications of value underperformance is critical to value program effectiveness. The precondition of severe penalties for the deliberate stonewalling of value destruction is raised in "CEO Sets the Corporation's New Value Realities" earlier in this chapter.

But merely penalizing instances of suppressing value loss is not enough. A "No Excuses" mind-set means *anticipating* the value-loss situation, for immediate correction, and not waiting until the hemorrhage becomes serious, which may be too late.

"Number Corp.": Direct Evidence of Value Underperformance

Direct proof of "Number Corp.'s" disappointing performance in value terms is conspicuous: Number's market price/cash flow multiple (PCF) lags far behind the PCFs of the industry's leaders; Number's share price scarcely budges in buoyant market times, while competitors' share prices are soaring; or, in downtrending markets, Number's stock price seems to fall twice as much, twice as fast.[17]

But Number Corp.'s management still somehow manage to make The Number (quarterly reported EPS), which to it confirms that the corporation is well managed, consistent with the corporate name. But reaching the EPS objective becomes more difficult with each passing quarter until reaching that level depends on deft juggling of aggressive accounting practices plus *deep* cuts to all expenses.

Of course, *all* the expense reductions are described as removing fat, not muscle. But even if that explanation is credible, then Number's reputation as a "well managed" corporation will be the victim. *If those expenses were wasteful, why weren't cuts made long ago?* Either management knew about value-destroying extra costs and did nothing, or it was oblivious to the true situation.

The truth is known within the company. Many of the costs are essential, not fat. Yet they are cut anyway in order to reach the all-important Number. Often, the first cuts eliminate support for several key expansion initiatives, with the result that the market and strategic positioning opportunity is probably lost forever, along with future cash flows and profits.

Second, any efficiency initiative requiring *any* material front-end spending is canceled or "deferred indefinitely," which is effectively the same thing and cancels meaningful efficiency campaigns, especially those involving systems-for-labor substitution. All that remain are lightweight actions, such as entreaties to use less paper—a one-page memo duplicated 10,000 times and sent to all employees.

Other costs are time shifted, pea-and-shell style. Expenses are cut today with a proclaimed "savings" of 100. What company management fails to disclose (and may not even know) is that three years from now, these same costs must be added back plus more. Value has been destroyed, even though the "crunch-'em-out" statistical model indicates the opposite.

Indirect Underperformance Evidence: Don't Ask, Don't Tell

Indirect indications of value underperformance at Number Corp. are equally compelling. Management doesn't even bother to systematically determine the company's Value Opportunity Gap on a periodic basis in terms of size, trend direction, and/or gap-closing actions.

How can the gap be closed without knowing the target, the component actions that comprise Vp-Vn?

This failure even to *try* to assess VOG raises suspicions that the underperformance problem may be even worse than first thought. If management doesn't have a clue about either the scope of the underperformance issue or its possible resolution, there will always be those who prefer the ostrich tactic.

Number Corp. makes its EPS "number" despite flat revenue. How does management achieve this feat? By mortgaging the future. Number Corp.'s CEO slashes growth investment along with essential maintenance expenses in order to ensure that the company achieves this quarter's EPS commitment. But in doing so, management has pillaged the company of the foundations upon which tomorrow's profits are based.

The farmer never, EVER eats his seed corn put aside for planting. Because if he does, there's nothing to plant the next season. End of farm. For the company that "consumes its seed corn," it's the end soon.

Normally, a hiring freeze seems to be a sound, conservative, responsible action to bring personnel costs into line. But unless the corporation has *already* cleared out its value-destroying management deadwood and used the money to acquire some true Corporate Key Contributors to drive future performance, the freeze may destroy value. Deadwood is insulated while the critical talent that makes the difference is described as "unaffordable."

Number Corp.'s once highly touted plan to develop more original products, faster than anyone else in its industry, has been temporarily deferred (read: permanently shelved) because of near-term adverse impact on reported EPS.

Never, Ever Admit to Any Mistake or Shortcoming

Within the corporation, there are the occasional surface indications of a willingness to accept greater risk. At least management is drawn to the prospect of faster growth, until some spoilsport insists that there is no enduring improvement in return without a corresponding increase in potential risk.

So all employees at Number Corp. receive the standard-issue memo about "being entrepreneurial" and—as an addendum— assuming a greater number of suitable project risks. But unless the risk-averse poison culture within the corporation has been neutralized, there will be few takers.

Whatever the reason—arrogance, inertia, belief that spin hype might actually be believed—management denies any and all evidence of a mistake or underperformance, on any basis. The slippery slope beckons. Beleaguered managers fear that admitting to a single pratfall will open the floodgates to a series of criticisms that will force them from office.

U.K. grocery chain laggard Somerfield (see Figure 4-1) announced its second profit warning in two months on September 13, 1999. Problems with postmerger integration caused a startling decline in store-by-store sales. Rather than acknowledge the problems, CEO David Simons instead attributed the disappointments to actions by the competition.[15]

Pre-Emptive Strikes

Value-relevant changes occur too fast to rely on after-the-fact responses alone.

Reorienting the corporation away from value-destructive backward management is a step in the right direction. However, it is a *wasted* step unless it is combined with effective action.

A pre-emptive initiative, which either ensures that the new value is captured or the loss of value is stopped, is such an action. It requires that management be able to anticipate value-diminishing actions (or *in*actions, in some cases) early enough to do something about them. This then must be followed by effective action that either captures the value or at least dramatically slows the pace of deterioration.

This sounds straightforward enough. Yet in practice, attempts to intervene while there is still enough time to do something about the problem prove to be exceedingly difficult to get right.

A key obstacle is the corporation's traditional decision-delegation system. These decision gateways in the vertical hierarchy are generally installed during times of moderate change. They stifle decision speed, and yet they are defended on the basis that the corporation will quickly become strangled if everything must bubble up to the CEO to be resolved.

That explanation, of course, comes from those most susceptible to decision-system reform: the corporate intermediaries in the middle of the complex decision hierarchies. Like intermediaries everywhere, they primarily shuffle products/services/decisions/data from Point A to Point B and are more likely to be seen as interference that adds nothing than as irreplaceable parts of the process. At least the former is the initial assumption, especially when the CEO learns that the corporation's plodding decision pace eliminates many decisions all by itself.

Stopping the Bleeding: Dealing with
Chronic Value Destruction

The comparatively minor stream of value loss is visible, but initially
only scarcely. Management seeks to prevent the loss from becoming
greater. Delegation prevails, with the value losers' explanations and
turnaround plans accepted until management finally loses patience
and pulls the plug.

But a far less visible value-destruction problem occurs when an
optimal approach is missed and a merely adequate approach is substi-
tuted. These hidden value-destruction situations range from the
major to the minor, but all have one thing in common: Left unre-
solved, each situation further widens the Value Opportunity Gap
over time as the difference grows between the best value approach
and the one merely being used by that company. Examples abound:

An international corporation settles for an inexperienced budget
manager to be its pricing manager rather than the professional who
stands to improve net margins each year by up to two full points.
The longer the suboptimal approach persists, the deeper the value
destruction hole becomes.

A corporation subsidizes its internal fleet manager rather than
save money with a third-party alternative (the choice corresponding
to full potential value). The protected manager is one of the gang,
and the shareholders pay in the form of a value "bill" that increases
each year that the suboptimal choice continues to be utilized.

If these corporations were continually reevaluating their value
positions using the VOG, the hidden sources of value destruction
would suddenly become visible. Every difference between the optimal
value approach and what replaces it widens the Value Opportunity
Gap, separating potential value (Vp) from current worth (Vn).

Necessary Separations

This refers to those who diminish value and either will not or cannot
adapt a value-directed mind-set and way of doing business.

The good news is that the corporation that embarks on and suc-
cessfully implements a major program of value development creates
a far more secure environment for all of its remaining employees.

John Costanza of Jc-I-T notes that American Standard, the venerable bathroom fixtures manufacturer, faced bleak prospects, perhaps even departure from its industry. John Tu and David Sun's Kingston Technologies, an add-on memory chip distributor, was and is a commodity business, with another competitor always there to steal customers with lower prices.

In both instances, radical changes to the business model and basic production/fulfillment techniques were necessary to save the companies. The tough medicine included initial staff reductions in a 20–30 percent range to change response time and breakeven point and because the new processes required fewer people.

In part, the personnel cutbacks were necessary to change the economics of the business. A threshold breakthrough in terms of *features & functionality* divided by *price* (cost) is essential to create the compelling market proposition that customers cannot resist. In part, too, the personnel cutbacks were necessary to partially finance other aspects of their high-value profit models. Kingston's business model calls for *ridiculous customer service*—customers can count on near-immediate availability in most instances, compared to the industry standard delivery practice of days, sometimes weeks. But in order to ensure superior availability, Kingston pays its principal suppliers early, deliberately sacrificing trade float.

A third reason for cutbacks is that some employees simply cannot (or do not want to) make the transition to the new order in a way that means enthusiastic, highly productive work.

Employees prosper from the increased value of their corporations, in terms of the shares they own, or in other ways. Kingston is independent once again, but in the late 1990s the company was acquired by Japanese Net conglomerate Softbank. For Christmas in the year of acquisition, Kingston employees received one-time presents amounting to around $75,000 each, as the two top officers shared their good fortune, literally. Not surprisingly, employees at Kingston will run through walls to ensure that Tu and Sun's business model works, spectacularly.

Conversely, the employee who is still wedded to yesterday's lower-value ways of doing things is almost always better off trying something else. Disgruntled acquiescence is as bad as outright, highly vocal opposition, and can be dangerous to the holdout, besides. The true believing one-person/one-machine zealot cannot possibly adapt to a world where he or she must learn the functions of five machines. He is in continual motion, and the mix of functions changes regularly.

4.5 Executive Incentive Packages: Rewards for *Top* Value-Creation Performance?

Generous executive incentive packages are enthusiastically espoused by the CEO as essential to attract the best people—at least the seven to ten top execs who are included in that plan. Highly conspicuous and at times controversial, most of the new plan submissions give lip service to the corporation's value objectives, typically with a TSR goal compared to a reference group of companies.[16]

In the United States, bonuses, perquisites, and stock options compose more than half of the average CEO compensation of $1,072,400. Harvard professors Brian J. Hall and Jeffery B. Leibman, in a study of 478 U.S. companies, suggest that improvements in market capitalization result in changes to CEO compensation more than 50 times greater than increases in salaries.

They suggest that even a small equity stake creates tremendous incentives for the corporation's top officer to further increase company value. "Jack Welch may own less than 0.1 percent of General Electric, but if he were to make changes that raised GE's (market stock price) by just 5 percent, his own net worth would rise by about $8 million."[17]

Broadening the EIP Base to Include Those Who Really Generate the Corporation's Value (Not Just Those at the Top of the Organization Chart)

Eligibility for the top bonus and options package is typically limited to the CEO's inner circle, based on the curious holdover rationale that the value in the corporation all trickles down from headquarters. When it is realized that a person's level in the hierarchy does not always reflect *today's* level of value contribution, eligibility could change.

The issue of who deserves extraordinary bonuses and incentives is of particular interest to the Board and key shareholders. Payments misdirected to negligible or negative-value generators destroy corporate value, regardless of past accomplishments or present elevation in the corporation's hierarchy.

From a corporate value perspective, the most important purpose of the EIP is to ensure that those officers who directly influence corporate value have an incentive to pursue maximum shareholder value, rather than suboptimal personal objectives. To make sure, for instance, that the CFO works toward a maximum APV rather than just a nicer company car and longer vacations.

How much equity is necessary to avoid Jensen's agent-manager effect, that is, tempting an officer to pursue near-term personal wealth rather than corporate wealth? Jensen speaks of the importance of a significant equity stake—something far greater than might be accumulated in the 401K and matching share plans available to most employees in the company—sufficient to meld the individual's interests with those of the corporation. Pirelli's Marco Provera indirectly owns about 12 percent of tire-manufacturer Pirelli's shares, a factor needed to encourage a series of tough-but-necessary value improvement actions.[18]

Heads I Win, Tails I Win

The CEO's challenge is to devise an EIP proposal that appears to support the corporation's MSV statements, and yet is reasonably achievable. If the full EIP payout can only be achieved through performance perceived as nearly unachievable, the chief executive argues that the incentive of the program is lost (and the CEO's wealth is directly affected).

Thus some deft use of terms and comparisons emerge. Choose a broad enough basis of other companies for comparison, then activate performance based on mid-range performance, and the chief executive can at least argue that the incentive is challenging.

The preliminary EIP submitted by Diageo's management in Summer 1998 featured total shareholder returns: growth in share price plus the value of net dividends. That proposal called for a comparison of company performance versus a reference group of nineteen global companies, including Coca-Cola and Gillette.

Vesting of shares in that plan was based on a formula providing for 50 percent bonus shares' vesting once Diageo achieves tenth place in the benchmark order. The vesting percentage increases to 100 percent if Diageo finishes in the top five. That version of the plan did not delight Diageo's major investors. FT's commentary of July 16, 1998, appears to reflect the mood of many investors: "middling performance will be richly rewarded."[19]

Diageo's EIP draft is not alone, according to Pensions Investment Research Consultants, which claims that huge payouts are made for merely mid-range performance in that industry or index group. To further cloud the comparisons, corporations are often hesitant to reveal their specific index base.[20] This better ensures that those in the EIP plan receive a significant payout even with mediocre performance in corporate or individual terms or both. But it is an increasing irritant to activist investors and others who contend that the first objective of any EIP must be to achieve maximum shareholder value and close that company's VOG.

SECTION II
Value Opportunities

5

Value's Engine Room

Outperformance Production, Procurement

Value opportunities take center stage in each of the four chapters in this section. We cover value development in operations (Chapters 5–7) and administrative sectors of the corporation (Chapter 8).

The term *sourcing* encompasses corporate manufacturing, assembly, and procurement functions. Sourcing used to be the last place chief executives looked to secure significant, enduring value advantage; the last place searched in pursuit of that elusive margin improvement that gives rise to superior market value.

Manufacturing management's historical obsession with direct labor costs has meant that, in value terms, most attention tends to be directed toward the areas of least importance. A manufacturing vice president anguishes over where his company's new facility will be located so as to take maximum advantage of changing world labor rates. While he pores over labor numbers, however, 70-year-old assembly practices remain largely untouched. On the production floor, outdated machines paired with stack-and-wait production destroy value.

Procurement, often the corporation's largest bureaucracy, still follows the instructions of a foreman in many companies: "Never permit a stock-out to occur." Woe to any employee (make that ex-employee) who lets the assembly line stop due to a shortage of raw materials and production expendables.

The supreme dictate of "no stock-outs, ever," eventually wanes. At first, the mind-set change occurs only at those corporations that have no other choice. Those are companies with their backs against the wall, facing radical surgery or assured elimination from the marketplace. Someone notes that direct labor accounts for only about 10 percent of total product costs and acts to change the emphasis on this single category.[1] Because there is no other alternative, the company with its back against the wall schedules production of an order only when paid in advance, in whole or part. Speculative production of goods for finished goods inventory disappears.

Demand flow replaces machine location and one man/one machine on the factory floor. Rather than maximizing raw material and work-in-process (WIP) inventories, emphasis shifts toward optimizing both categories. The result—at those companies able to endure the tough transition—is that output increases of 30+ percent per day can be realized, sometimes combined with a 30 percent or more reduction in per unit cost.

Within the procurement function, preferred supplier arrangements expand from promising experiments to company standard practice. The realization spreads like wildfire: Having more suppliers doesn't necessarily improve delivery or even lower costs. The unthinkable happens: No-stock-out policies are retired as the driving force in purchasing.

Combine the cost of running the procurement department with the cost of purchases, and suddenly new perspectives on costs and value emerge. Any cost savings realized from maintaining 15 suppliers, rather than just the five most important ones, are more than wiped out by the cost of additional staff and forms. But if budgets are separate, it is not always evident that the company is gaining a dime in Column A only to throw a dollar away in Column B. But combine operations cost with the purchases cost in a total budget, and such value mistakes become immediately visible.

As the new century gets under way, the revolution will become mainstream, as some insightful corporations actually change before they are forced to do so by the competition. Besides boosting value, a double-digit margin improvement from sourcing helps fund the necessary increase in the corporation's innovation budget.[2]

5.1 Demand Pull/Flexible: Voluntary Adoption Gains Momentum

Transition away from stack-and-wait legacy production is the first of two major manufacturing/procurement developments with tremendous value impact.

Demand pull/flexible refers here to that group of flow production and assembly processes typically characterized by the combination of: (1) production to a daily build schedule based only on advance, confirmed orders; (2) just-in-time inventory practices; and (3) team assembly instead of moving work-in-process to various stationary machine sites.

To the manufacturing lifer—accustomed to the time-honored practice of bringing work to the fast machines and skilled operators—demand pull/flexible often seems like solving a problem by blowing up the plant. The basic change in emphasis, process, and mind-set leaves nothing untouched: Operators, foremen, and manufacturing managers are all significantly affected in ways previously considered off-limits. Demand pull/flexible changes not just what work is to be done, but also how it is done.[3]

Thus, it is not too surprising that demand pull/flexible has historically been treated only as an option of last resort. It has been considered an extreme action undertaken only by those manufacturers that require an immediate reversal of fortune to avoid elimination from the marketplace.

Forced to Rethink Machining: Fixing the Manufacturing Poison Culture

The culture of machining was deeply ingrained for decades at United Technologies' Pratt & Whitney (P&W) aircraft engine unit.

At P&W, the machine shop culture meant fascination with buying faster and faster limited-purpose machines. Different machine speeds, of course, meant wasteful stack-and-wait production, as raw materials and work in process piled up at some points, and shortages occurred elsewhere. The miles-long assembly line meant that the various parts of the line were rarely in synch.

In their book *Lean Thinking,* Womack and Jones described how the ingrained machining ethic at P&W contributed to the division's near-fatal delays in dealing effectively with its competitive threats.[4]

Internal misperceptions about competitive advantage—created when individuals nominate what they do the most as a "competitive advantage"—can prove to be excruciatingly difficult to change.

When this sort of poison culture is too deeply ingrained, the effects are pervasive. Manufacturing may be eliminated from competition even before management wakes up to the reality that their days are numbered.

Shock Therapy

Shock is usually required to open management's eyes to the reality that the entrenched manufacturing culture, the decades-old process revered as the keystone of the company, now instead destroys value. Making a convincing case is difficult. One can cite endless examples of manufacturing operations brought to ruin because of management's inability to change fast enough, but those are invariably rebuffed by the ultimate resistance argument: "Our company is unique." Scare stories are never enough, however. Unless the examples cited are viewed as directly applicable to that corporation's own circumstances, management of the so-very-unique company discovers too late that they are more like others than they care to admit.

Transition from familiar practices, such as stack-and-wait and produce-for-finished-inventory, means a reduction in production workers, at least at the onset. Experienced foremen face an adapt-or-else crisis with the clear message—no matter how carefully stated—that their prior expertise is now considered to be valueless in the new order.

Within the corporation, there are few congratulations for the bold CEO who disbands the tried-and-true manufacturing process for something unfamiliar. Several months of transition losses only increase the grumbles. But to shareholders, there isn't any alternative. Continue in the old direction, and their investment is a throw-away.

Other CEOs look to replace traditional methods with a new sourcing philosophy. Heinrich Fischer, manager of German textile equipment group Sauer, rejects the romance of machining and even the idea that the expert operator is a sacrosanct resource of the corporation. Parts of Sauer's manufacturing operations are outsourced. Special relationships are developed with preferred suppliers. Nothing is off-limits as long as the result is greater value from sourcing—if the assembly can be produced or the part job can be done better outside, so be it.

Accelerating Performance Improvement: The Case for New Order Production

The scenario is familiar: Several producers all hover around the same, low unit-cost level. None holds an advantage in performance or value, and incremental improvements by one company are quickly matched by the others.

Mobilizing Production as a Value Source

In order to break out of this gridlock, management faces the challenge of moving forward to production's new order. This is a transition that few competitors follow, either because they cannot or, more likely, will not. Radical improvement on the order of 30 + percent in terms of both unit costs and speed-to-market doesn't occur without major disruptions. There is no such thing as a graceful transition to demand pull/flexible.

At Pratt & Whitney, American Standard, and Clark's Shoes (U.K.), transitions to the new order required a minimum of a full year. That time was needed to begin unwinding the old "ways-we've-always-done-things" mind-sets. Another year or more is necessary to anchor the new value order.

For Corporations *Not* Facing Imminent Disaster: Three Reasons to Make the Value Transition

The corporation with its back against the wall has no choice but to swallow this bitter medicine and proceed. But with all the transition difficulties and just sheer pain, why in the world would anyone else consider such a transition?

The first reason is that even successful companies easily slip into problems in just a couple of years or so, regardless of government assistance. Stated another way, if things seem too good now to be true, they are. Standing pat means waiting for something to happen. Wait for it, instead of making it happen, and the result is almost always unfavorable.

The second reason is illustrated in Figure 5-1. Transition from old production order to new production cost structure represents a watershed change in product, performance, and features characteristics (horizontal axis) compared to costs (vertical axis).

Figure 5-1. Transition to demand pull/flexible: opening new innovation opportunities.

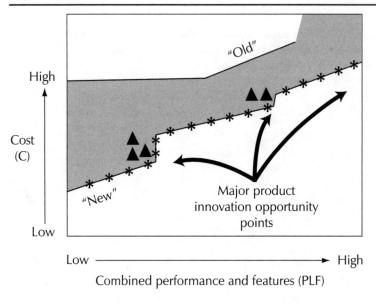

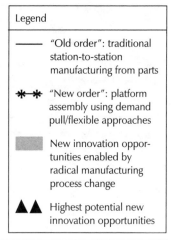

Source: VBM Consulting (www.vbm-consulting.com).

Flexible in demand pull/flexible means that the new order producer covers an extended range of cost/performance characteristics with a single combination of cell stations, adaptive workers, and equipment. In Figure 5-1, EF and GH represent the points where that combination is optimally applied and major innovation opportunity occurs. These are the points immediately preceding significant increase in costs. These are also the points where the new order's value advantage over old practices is the greatest.

The third reason is that the corporation may have no choice except to act because of changes in the competitive landscape. A rival start-up begins with demand pull/flexible operations and economics. The new upstart secures an unassailable advantage unless existing companies meet the challenge. The first company to make the transition is in a position to significantly increase its production volume and range, obliterating rivals' market shares.[5]

5.2 New Order Production: Implementation, Key Aspects

When cost and output advantage are lost, production can quickly slip from a source of value creation to a black hole of value destruction. The amount of value destruction is often invisible except by comparison: either to other companies or the corporation's own optimal value sourcing plan. Even those comparisons reveal little if the peer group is also performing well below their maximum value. The company may be best-of-class yet still performing well below maximum, therefore destroying value.

A theoretical exercise of no practical use? Not when predators assume that any company can be acquired. Acquirers' analysts search continually for value underperformance that they might exploit. That underperformance can arise from any one, or a combination of, value origins within the corporation: finance, sourcing, innovation/R&D, marketing-sales, or administration.

Focus on the Daily Build Schedule

Destruction of value in production starts with the erratic daily build schedule. Without stable advance indication of what is to be built that day, systematic preparation is impossible. Waste soars to deal with contingencies: raw materials, work-in-process (WIP) inventory,

supervision, and direct labor. Rework costs cancel any long production run efficiencies.

Destroying Value by Producing for
Finished Goods Inventory

The day's build schedule has to be torn up and done all over again
because of a new model inventory forecast from managers of the finished goods (FG) warehouse. The warehouse group's revised guesses
in turn force significant changes in that day's production/assembly
mix and amounts, as all output presently goes to FG inventory,
rather than to the customer directly.

The sniping begins. Manufacturing blames warehouse management for the inaccuracy of their initial forecast. Warehousemen respond that the best forecast is never better than an informed guess,
and that the extra costs for more frequent physical counts each day
would wipe out all profits.

But unreliable finished goods forecasts represent a manifesta-
tion of the problem, not the underlying reason. Good money is
thrown, to no good effect, at the symptom while the root cause remains unabated and the pace of value deterioration accelerates.

The real problem is that an embedded approach for producing or
assembling finished goods inventory destroys value by original design. Underlying the build-for-finished-goods-inventory approach is
the field salesperson's insistence that excess product is required, otherwise his revenue commitments cannot be reached. From new car
dealers to sellers of tools, the old-order field salesperson insists that
reaching his quota depends on availability of enough extra finished
goods inventory to meet instant changes in orders. The killer argument: Offering customers anything less means retreat from the corporation's commitment to being a market-driven corporation.

The company that gives into such an interpretation for "customer focus" is effectively capitulating to whatever the sales force
wants, whenever they want it. The salesperson insists on extra finished goods inventory on-site to attract the impulse buyer or the
customer who is reluctant to buy unless his exact preferred configuration is available. If that diversity is missing, manufacturing gets
the blame. "There's no value at all without the sale. If my rival has
a yellow convertible and I don't, then I lose, along with the company," he insists.

To accommodate this sales mind-set, the corporation invests in several finished goods warehouses to provide a buffer between production and customer. The full investment extends far beyond the building alone, and includes the people, systems, and ongoing running costs necessary to sustain the facilities. Plus multiple handling costs, incurred each time the product is moved from one intermediate location to the next.

Within the company, the rhetoric supporting such middleman functions is "added value." But the customer pays only for the value he perceives in the product itself—not the process. One consequence: The producer manufacturing for FG inventory faces massive warehouse write-downs when a competitor that produces to confirmed orders lowers his prices to reflect superior efficiencies.[6]

A comparable dilemma faces companies competing against Internet stand-alone companies. The stand-alones price according to their lower costs. To meet the new, lower price point, traditional competitors are forced to adopt Net efficiencies throughout their companies or be driven from the marketplace.

The turnaround begins the day a manager at headquarters says "no" to the salesperson's request for more and more FG inventory. Yet that same manager still insists that the sales quota is met nonetheless.

Now, the salesperson who depends upon the presence of idle inventory to close his sale risks being perceived as an expendable order taker. Never mind that the company makes an acceptable cash flow/revenue margin on the salesperson's average sale. Include the full burden of extra costs—from multiple handling to warehousing to documentation—and all but the highest margin sales pro suddenly falls from being a source of value to being a recurring source of value destruction.

Value Destruction from Unstable Orders

Back at the traditional manufacturer, the build schedule must be reconfigured a second time after it becomes apparent that a large block of orders, included in the forecast, is false. Some of the changes are because the customer balked when it came to making a firm commitment, including substantial payment. Other orders turn out to be bogus as overly optimistic salespersons double count. There's no penalty for doing so—the salesman can just say that this was one of those "95 percenters" lost because the competition unfairly bought the business.

Another cause of value destruction in the build schedule arises when the sales philosophy is to always make it as easy as possible for the customer to buy (and cancel later), even if that means no deposit and no binding commitment. The sales manager insists that customers are driven away by insistence on large, nonrefundable deposits. The culture is shaken up when someone wakes up and realizes that a close without commitment is not a sale. For production purposes, the easily canceled sale can never be counted on. The value destruction may be reflected in factory numbers, but the origin of the value loss is elsewhere.

The remedy is to make the salesperson personally accountable for all firm build orders submitted to production.[7] The corporation can no longer afford all the extra costs associated with the salesperson who first makes a "soft" close (no commitment) and then insists on nonrefundable payment later. Only the latter is usable for daily build schedule purposes, so why not insist on the single, complete (and committed) sale from the onset?

Creating Value: The Build/Assembly Schedule Is Stabilized

Without a stable schedule, production languishes as a value black hole. The value outperformer manager's top priority emerges: introduce and enforce measures that ensure that once the order is submitted, it remains on the schedule, unchanged.

The objective is to build a schedule that is unalterable for at least three to five days prior to the actual production date. Such a stabilized build schedule permits the types of planning and advance purchasing that can make all the difference between value improvement and value deterioration.

Just-in-Time's potential can be fully achieved only when the build schedule is known and set. Value comes from accurate, advance planning regarding what raw materials and consumables reach which points on the flow process. This is supported by a reliable, detailed plan of action regarding specific processes and component requirements. Management who proceed with JIT without first laying the groundwork for success are quickly disappointed. The pat excuse—"it doesn't work here"—falls flat. JIT does work, but not when supplier and schedule preparations have been missed. [8]

The flexible, multifunction workers who are central to demand pull/flexible's success are used best when they know what they will be doing, on which days. The day of actual production is no time for on-the-job training. Advance scheduling provides sufficient time to address any issues and hone skills prior to the actual run day.

The stabilized build schedule permits common-sense grouping of confirmed orders. Not "long production runs" and old-order manufacturing. This scale is entirely different: Similar orders (by process, materials, the staff involved, or all three) are clustered together for assembly at the same time during the same production run session.

Customer Value and Direct Shipment of Finished Products: Zero or Minimal Finished Goods Warehouse

A related development at the opposite end of the production sequence looms as even more important in terms of new value creation: shipping directly to the customer from the production floor, thereby bypassing that company's own internal network of finished goods warehouses.

The advance confirmed-order customer has already finalized all aspects of his or her purchase. The stage is set for direct-from-factory shipment, avoiding all or most of the value-diminishing costs associated with transfer of goods in and out of the company's various finished goods warehouses.

Today's customers now resist paying for any intermediary costs that they perceive as providing little or no value. Middlemen may self-describe their services as "added value," but they are, in fact, largely irrelevant.[9]

"Getting rid of the middleman" is addressed in Chapter 7. There we discuss in more detail bypassing third-party companies struggling to stay in the commercial chain long after their utility has evaporated. The revolt against internal middlemen in corporations may be less familiar but is actually more promising from a new value creation perspective. The customer who tries to bypass the external middleman often discovers that he underestimated the costs of essential services provided by the third party. But internal budgets are often bloated by allocations and the lack of price-performance discipline because of the absence of competition (more about this in Chapter 8).

In the case of the advance order purchases, the internal bypass alternative to warehouse—internal or external—is no warehouse at all. For years before the commercial Internet arrived, retail car buyers in Japan bought their new cars from catalogues, at home. No more buying something that you don't really want just because it's on the lot. Buyers can specify make, model, features, and colors and then specify the date of production and delivery.

Financing is committed at this point. A firm order is made, permitting inclusion in a specific day's build schedule. The car is then shipped from the factory directly to the customer at the end of that agreed production date.

No showrooms. No warehouses. No car lots stretching as far as the eye can see with acres of cash-absorbing, value-reducing finished vehicle inventories. For the manufacturer, the essential mind-set change is that the product is the customer's property and responsibility immediately upon production. Which means that the customer pays for everything after that point in time, including deferred delivery charges or other requested post-production modifications. In return, the customer comes to expect that pricing excludes charges for the company's unused infrastructure.[10]

But zero warehouse operations represent the ideal. The reality is that corporations are striving for minimum warehouse operations. There are still some situations—prior to an initial product launch, seasonal patterns, and expanding into new territories—when accumulating sizable inventories of finished goods in advance performs an important corporate value support role. Prior to an initial launch, finished inventory is required to fill the initial distribution system and to provide extra stock for trials and samples.

Both seasonal patterns and expanding territories require standing finished goods inventories, available in advance. When a seasonal pattern becomes apparent, some level of production helps ensure that the company benefits fully from its period of greatest demand. New territories are essentially new launches, and thus issues of pipeline fill and extra units for trials and samples reemerge.

Role of Perceived Custom Production and Marketing Knowledge Assets in Creating Future Value

The precondition behind the set daily build schedule is the non-cancelable order. And the precondition behind that set order, in turn, is something referred to here as *perceived custom*.

Practically speaking, the customer perceives that he can specify whatever he wants. *Perceives* is the key word here. Full, true custom is often unaffordable for both buyer and seller alike. The challenge, then, is to offer enough range and diversity to sustain the perception of a custom order, but without bankrupting the seller-manufacturer.

Five years ago, if you told most U.S. auto buyers they must commit, right now, to buying a car that will be built for them over the next two weeks, they would just walk across the street to another lot. That no longer holds true today. Customers will use advance order if it includes a price break that reflects the efficiencies of demand pull/ flexible production. An advance order is even more attractive if customers believe that they can get exactly what they want.

This is the artistry of perceived custom; [11] the customer as *perceiver*. The key is to combine a limited number of central components with a sufficiently flexible assembly process in order to create the largest range and number of alluring, distinctive models.

The customer's perception that there are no limits to what he can specify is an illusion. In reality he or she is actually severely restricted to only those combinations of 8–11 core assembly components. At American Standard's Stevenson furnace subsidiary in Trenton, New Jersey, operators switch and combine only nine different parts. But from those nine, the company can create 202 different "made-to-order" furnace models. Before American Standard implemented John Costanza's Demand Flow Technology™ approach, the company was capable of producing only a few models. [12]

Advertisements support the custom illusion: "Build your own (Triumph motorcycle, Dell computer)." Actual custom is usually unaffordable. This has the look and feel of custom to the customer, but the economics of a stripped model for the producer-seller.

The successful perceived custom formula is a highly valuable, if intangible, corporate asset. Include just a few components, or the wrong ones, and customers will perceive the offering range as too narrow. Permit too many components, however, and the company risks slipping into the value-destruction trap of charging relatively low assembly line prices for a one-off special model.

Consider the fate of the old Indian motorcycle company. Before World War II, Indians were immensely popular. But there were so many separate parts and different combinations that every bike made was essentially a separate, hand-crafted custom model. The bottom line: The manufacturer could not charge a viable price and survive. They didn't.

Platform Assembly

Platform assembly provides one new value answer for the decades-old manufacturing dilemma: how best to meet customers' demands for finished product diversity while at the same time minimizing unit costs. Limiting the number of base product designs—or platforms—emerges as an integral part of high value demand pull/flexible new order sourcing.

This major transition—from manufacturing of parts to platform assembly—has major value implications for value-creation-oriented management. The value comes from the realization that creating multiple models directly from separate parts is both too expensive and too slow.

Moreover, manufacture from parts causes value destruction elsewhere in the corporation, especially procurement. Instead of concentrating on high-value activities such as negotiating key preferred supplier arrangements or creating the next generation of subassembly components, manufacturing from parts forces corporations to carry extra staff and adds documentation costs on the back of procurement. The department must add staff who become mired in dead-end jobs such as tracking and monitoring a mind-boggling array of different parts records and vendor relationships.

Platform assembly helps dramatically reduce the number of stock-keeping units (SKUs). Multiple part subassemblies are affixed directly to the chassis. Platforms are compatible with cell assembly and permit short-path assembly by a few stations, instead of the miles-long labyrinths needed for manufacturing from parts.

One argument against platform assembly is that it appears to limit the full range of possible customer choice. Platform assembly does use fewer total parts and leads to a somewhat narrower product range. But as described above in the instance of Stevenson Furnace, selection of the right components can mean a huge increase in perceived model diversity, despite a dramatic reduction in the number of distinct components.

The platform's value contribution plunges if too few distinctive new models are supported by that base. If less than, say, six separate models are supported by each platform, then the true value of platform assembly is lost.

In early 1998, production cost considerations resulted in an announcement by struggling Mitsubishi Motors that it would halve its number of platforms from twelve to just six. Later that year, Nissan announced its intent to slash "platforms" from an unmanageable twenty-four to only five by 2005.

The quotes apply in Nissan's case because each "platform" supports only a few distinct models. In this case, even if the model is successful, excessive support and production costs narrow margins.

This contrasts with Volkswagen's core Golf platform, which supports both multiple nameplates (Audi, Skoda, VW) and multiple models (Golf and Beetle).

Platform development eclipses individual model development as a core value development activity. If the platform supports multiple models as well as pivotal design and performance characteristics, the separate designs can wait.

For the platform-dominated industry, the issue becomes less when to retire aging individual models than when to replace the entire platform because too many models in the mix are dragging.

Chrysler's value dilemma in the late 1980s with its aging K-car platform is revisited a decade later in Wolfsburg. As more old models dominate the Golf platform, the question becomes: Should management stretch out that base a few years longer to sustain still-promising, newer models (e.g., the new Beetle)? Or should all emphasis be shifted into a new platform capable of supporting a new generation of high-appeal market offerings?

5.3 Procurement: Beyond Stock-Out

Revolutionizing the corporation's procurement function has emerged as one of the fastest, most effective ways to generate new corporate value, both in terms of the total cost of purchases made and the cost of operating what is often the corporation's largest bureaucracy.

Procurement's potential for value destruction is equally formidable. JIT's Costanza estimates that materials represent about 70 percent of the typical manufactured product's finished product costs.[13] A mere 10 percent adverse variance in materials costs can immediately wipe out a full quarter's profits.

Delays in implementing *any* key procurement development—component purchasing, online ordering, systematic parts reduction, or preferred supplier program—threaten the corporation overall, its competitiveness, and value performance.

Overcoming Stock-Out Panic

The VP of manufacturing screams that it "must never happen again!" *It* is the dreaded stock-out. Missing materials cause the production line to shut down.

The assembly line is down for a full shift. Factory workers stand around chatting. Meanwhile, frantic expediters try furiously to reach contingency suppliers, asking about their sources. The VP of manufacturing explodes, "Do you realize how much money we lose when workers are doing nothing?" The order is set in stone. The stock-out must *never* happen again.

Performance and value penalties caused by additional inventory (raw materials, work in process, expendables) aimed at preventing the *next* stock-out are exaggerated in the legacy production order. The assembly line is already highly dependent on excess inventory as the grease that enables a creaking system to operate at all. More is on the way. Piles of over-ordered raw material crowd the production floor so that any gaps in the line can be filled quickly. Work in process accumulates at key points.

The driving conviction behind the no-stock-out order is that continuous, uninterrupted production rules above all else. Yet if one checks the historical pattern of old-order assembly line production, it is evident that uninterrupted operation occurs only a fraction of the total time.

No-stock-out cannot provide the absolute assurance that the shrieking VP of manufacturing requires. The legacy manufacture-from-parts arrangement may involve 1,000 separate parts, with 950 of those double or even triple stocked. But there is no guarantee that an item in those remaining 50 that are single stocked will not be among the ones to fail or go missing.

Other value-destroying costs associated with the no-stock-out inventory bulge are less apparent, but no less destructive in value terms. Double and triple handling costs are incurred as inventory is shuffled from one part of the corporation to another. The procurement department must hire additional staff in order to handle the increased activity caused by more purchase order documentation, more backup suppliers, and greater coordination needed to implement no-stock-out.

Value from Preferred Supplier Programs

Preferred supplier initiatives affect both parts of the procurement department's total costs. The first objective is to lower the cost of specific purchased items in trade for a higher level of guaranteed annual purchases. The second objective is to reduce procurement department internal staff and costs by reducing the number of suppliers, using only those that are the most reliable and most important.

A 20+ percent cost reduction is not unheard of when both factors are included. That's recurring, annual savings not already incorporated in management's cash flow projections. That's new value creation, available to help close that company's Value Opportunity Gap.

More Reliable, Less Expensive Supply from Fewer Separate Sources

Over the years, supplier reliability and quality patterns become well-known. Corporations turn first to the sources with the best access to their own supplies, with the best internal operations, and—most importantly—which value the buyer. Unless the procurement officer is an empire builder who measures his power in terms of the number of people in his department, he thinks at some point: "Give me just a few of the top sources and I could cover almost all of our purchase needs."

Ideally, the streamlined function assumes a new dynamism, attracting top performers interested in developing even more incremental value. Once a corporate career graveyard, there is little room in the procurement department for cronies who seek payment for little more than filling out forms. Fewer suppliers mean fewer forms, simpler operations, and less monitoring. Even before online ordering, single data input, and other efficiencies are added, there is less value-destroying waste.

The preferred supplier program does not eliminate the need for some multiple supply sources. This is especially true for critical items and when prior experience suggests a pattern of recurring shortages. At issue is the degree of such contingency arrangements. It is far better to have three key suppliers that, because each receives enough volume, treats the company as a best customer than to have six suppliers that view the company as a marginal customer.

Structuring the Preferred Supplier Relationship

Careful structuring of the preferred supplier relationship helps ensure that the value omote for real and not just on paper. There are three prime considerations:

1. *Workable Master Agreements.* Fewer suppliers and more efficient transaction volume often means fewer deliveries. But that may

conflict with the production manager's just-in-time inventory goals. JIT requires frequent deliveries of exact amounts to specified production floor cells.

A workable master contract structure is required to permit frequent deliveries of small volumes, while still assuring the benefits from volume terms.

Pre-set delivery volumes represent one approach, with the supplier automatically delivering the same amount to each cell unless notified otherwise.

2. *Systematic Selection of Preferred Supply Companies: Adding Fresh Blood.* Mutual dependency creates an ideal circumstance. Supplier and buyer view each other as a key to their own success. Sometimes this means downgrading the major supplier known to spread its own sourcing arrangements too thin. That supplier can only provide extraordinary service to a few key accounts. Adding a couple of emerging suppliers (read not yet dominant, but leaders fear them anyway) to the shortlist serves two purposes.

First, because his or her orders comprise the lion's share of a small supplier's business, the procurement department buyer is assured of having at least a few suppliers who are ferociously loyal and responsive.

Second, it serves a subtle but clear warning to historical suppliers—you too can be replaced.

3. *Preferred Supplier Programs Entering the Procurement Mainstream.* Preferred supplier programs are no longer limited to a few opportunistic major industrial companies such as major airlines, GE, and Big Seven world auto producers. Such initiatives are now part of the purchasing mainstream.

Gradually, procurement officers come to understand that the venerable Request For Proposal (RFP) system is no longer necessarily the best approach—not in terms of cost to operate and, perhaps, purchase terms.

The ongoing savings are not just to increase some statistical measurement of value, but to fuel investment where it counts. Eli Lilly management estimates that it costs $350 million to develop a single new drug compound. In 1997, Lilly management established as a future goal to slash continuing costs by $230 million. New order procurement performs a key role in helping support this cost by:

Reduction in Number of Suppliers

Management seeks reduction in the number of suppliers of maintenance and repair items. Before preferred supplier program implementation, Lilly managers had to coordinate 1,500 separate supply sources. Afterward, it had twenty sources.

Creating More Clout

Supplier reductions and volume consolidation provide Lilly with more clout. The drug manufacturer capitalized on its additional market power by insisting that slaughterhouses ship carcasses containing less fat. Preferred suppliers complied, significantly reducing costs associated with one of Lilly's leading product categories, insulin.

5.4 Outperformer Production/ Procurement Integration

Integration of production and procurement introduces new, higher value opportunities for those corporations up to the challenge. Experimental at first, some of these surviving hybrids later establish the performance and value baselines for their industries.

If the existing, installed production and/or purchasing approach would not be chosen today, then what is the justification for continuing with that approach into the future? Answer: There is none.

Externally, standing pat on a process or approach may create the appearance that decisions are being avoided. That's incorrect. Inertia means active choice of yesterday's answers. For both the corporation and its management, rechoosing yesterday's approach for no better reason than incumbency becomes increasingly dangerous. Accelerating change multiplies the number of higher value, higher performance alternatives to yesterday's "solution."

Management that cannot or will not act to keep pace actively destroys value on a relative basis, the only evaluative assessment that counts in competitive, fast-paced markets. Absent outright market leadership, or at least close contention, the company's competitive orientation shifts to the defensive. More and more time that could be directed to closing the Value Opportunity Gap is instead misdirected to defending "stand pat" decisions, starting with those in sourcing. Such diversions are themselves destructive in value terms.

Production and Procurement Integration: Value Creation Rewards

C&J Clark, a leading U.K. shoe manufacturer, implemented its own version of demand pull/flexible production in 1995. Tim Parker, CEO, states that the more efficient factories were largely responsible for the marked improvement in reported results.

Clark announces a £4 million improvement in pre-tax profits for comparable half-year periods after demand pull/flexible–type production was implemented. Simpler processes, shorter process paths, and drastic reductions in ramp-up time mean more output per specified build period. Demand pull/flexible–type production worked equally well in the automotive industry. Introduced in mid-1997, demand pull/flexible production is credited with reducing by one third the assembly time for Volkswagen's new Golf model.

At American Standard's U.K. bathroom fixtures plant, output that once took three weeks to complete now requires four days. At American Standard's Stevenson subsidiary, it once (1991) took workers 15 days to build a new furnace from scratch. After fully implementing Jc-I-T's DFT™ approach, management cites production time of 2.5 hours.

Furthermore, effective implementation of demand pull/flexible can mean access to previously unreachable market segments. At Germany's Porsche AG, management faced exclusion from the popular U.S. $30,000–$80,000 mid-range sports car category. High production costs—associated with its unbending quality convictions—were largely responsible. Incremental changes to traditional production methods didn't help much. The maximum price point corresponding to Porsche's unit production costs for the new model were still well above the market ceiling.

To break through the logjam, a flexible manufacturing approach was implemented for a new model, which is today known as the Boxster. Applying flow assembly techniques, the teams met or exceeded all production parameters, including the all-important price to market. The novel $40,000 model is an immediate hit, as evidenced by massive back orders.

Anticipating that the Value-Creating Faction Will Slip to Value Destruction Far Sooner than You Think

Maximum value sourcing is no longer a matter of making one infallible decision about the type and location of a factory, then doing little more than incremental adjustments until economic obsolescence forces a change. The reactive approach is bankrupt, literally: always one step behind the market, with dire consequences for competitiveness and value.

Optimal Sourcing Combinations Change over Time

The full spectrum of options for making the product range from one extreme, outright purchase and rebadging, to the other, piecemeal manufacture from hundreds, sometimes thousands, of discrete parts. There are numerous options in between, characterized both by the methods used and the group that applies them.

The job shop foreman wouldn't hesitate for a second to obtain a machine capable of twice the present output, at half the running costs, but only small extra investment. Yet that foreman's corporation sticks to its sputtering stack-and-wait production approach to finished goods inventories. Higher-performance, higher-value alternatives are available, but are avoided out of hand as the standard inertia apologies are cited.

How can the two opposite performance orientations be reconciled? They can't. Just as the foreman saddled with an underperforming machine quickly falls behind his rival, so it is that the corporation that places itself in leg irons by continuing with an underperforming approach for no better reason than inertia soon fades away.

A full range of excuses are presented to defend the do-little/do-nothing approach that destroys value. These include: threat of accounting write-offs; lack of familiarity with the new approaches; the prospect of elimination of supervisory jobs (as prior expertise becomes irrelevant); and job losses for some workers as a consequence of the transition to a higher performance level.[14]

Providers of capital to the corporation observe the various excuses, and wonder how much longer the now-defensive corporation can survive. The excuses are irrelevant to the marketplace. It takes only one major competitor armed with a disruptive 30 percent output and 30 percent unit cost advantage, led by aggressive management, to bankrupt the underperforming factory and perhaps also its owner.

An Alternative to the Single Decision: Changing Total Sourcing Solution

The only escape from the single decision destruction is to adopt the opposite strategy and anticipate that the corporation faces an imperative every few years to significantly alter its total sourcing solution.[15]

Incremental tweaks to the existing process are insufficient; a few more margin points do little more than buy time. Such incremental actions are readily canceled by competitors' matching responses and are already in the (current) market for valuation purposes.

Corporation U, a composite hypothetical company, has developed an electronic test device with robust market potential and a projected economic life of about seven years. To maximize cash flow and value, management must periodically reexamine their total sourcing solution, placing the incumbent arrangement on level ground with all others. Over the life of the device, various combinations are deployed.

Year One: Internal Manufacture from Hundreds of Separate Parts

Starting in its first year, the testing device is manufactured from hundreds of separate parts bought through the purchasing department. Production occurs only at Corporation U's major factory, which produces to inventory based on traditional stack-and-wait processes.

Year Three: Shift to On-Site Alternative Manufacture (Captive Factory)

A few years pass. Management discovers a more efficient and effective alternative to internal manufacture from parts. Production is contracted to a third party producer that rents space at Corporation U's site. U's internal purchasing continues to buy as many parts as possible from as many suppliers as possible, in the belief that this is the best way to protect against stock-out.

One result is that Corporation U faces opposition to the move from some worker groups, concerned that this is the first step down the slippery slope to outsourcing of *all* production.

In the interim, however, some competitors have already moved up to platform assembly/modular manufacturing, outflanking U's move and exceeding its advantage.

Year Four: Radical Product Relaunch, Parallel Change in Production to Component Assemblies

The captive factory stopgap measure doesn't help much, or for long. There was no change in the process, only a shift in labor and costs, which eventually backfired as captive company employees hired by their company at lower rates soon came to resent their pay. Productivity gains were far less than anticipated.

Following a major inventory write-down, Corporation U implements a radical relaunch of its product in the marketplace, with all-new features and dramatically enhanced performance.

The only cost-effective alternative is component assembly, with a few master suppliers providing multiple part assemblies. The number of parts involved decreases by 70 percent. The old stack-and-wait production line is replaced by demand pull/ flexible.

Now, orders are accepted only with significant advance payment or deposit. Other competitors are also considering such arrangements after observing U's problem with excess finished goods inventories.

Year Six: Preparing for Life Cycle End

The product is being terminated about a year earlier than expected. With 20/20 hindsight, Corporation U management concede that nearly everyone in their industry tended to overestimate product lives and underestimate the pace of accelerating change.

After considering several alternatives, U's management decides that the highest value course calls for licensing the now fully mature product to a third party. The licensee produces the device, affixes U's logo and other identification, then ships the finished goods via its own distribution network.

Co-Location: Redefining Modular Flow Assembly Performance

The central principle to both demand pull/flexible production and just-in-time is that all resources are brought to the assembly flow, rather than the other way around.

Mobile teams swing over to the next station to affix and test two components at the same time, in sharp contrast to the hard-times image of Charlie Chaplin waiting for parts to come to him on a conveyor belt. As the final assembly plant's cell pattern changes, so do the points and timing for JIT in-plant delivery.

Under workable JIT, the supplier comes right into the factory, onto the assembly floor. To do otherwise is to cancel most of the advantages of the process by adding handling and one more place for excess inventory to accumulate.

So locating primary sub-manufacturers on the same site is only a logical half step further. No more wondering if the modular assembly will arrive on time: The door to that supplier's assembly floor opens onto your own. No need for inspectors to travel to the suppliers to check for potential problems. Inspection is a matter of walking down the hall.[16]

The good news is that the common sense logic of shortening supply paths holds considerable promise as a major value and performance step improvement. Co-location is not without difficulties, however.

Major sub-assembly suppliers are located on-site at Fiat's Melfi final assembly plant in Italy. Volkswagen Group's Skoda unit uses a supplier co-location approach at its Mlada Boleslav assembly plant in the Czech Republic. But one of the most aggressive co-location initiatives involves Micro Compact Car's (MCC) plant in France.

Micro Compact Car (MCC) is the original name of the Swatch Smart Car venture dominated by DaimlerChrysler and involving Swiss watchmaker SMH, owner of the Gen X–popular "Swatch" trademark. Daimler's expanded role at MCC was dictated by the same elk test that raised questions about the stability of the Mercedes A series sedans. DaimlerChrysler management invests millions in the Smart Car venture, substantially redesigning the city car to improve its stability.

MCC management estimates that their platform assembly approach means production in about 7.5 hours per vehicle, or 25 percent below 1996's best levels for the industry. Reduced total production time and fewer parts mean reduced fixed costs and labor hours. The assembler locates its major component suppliers in buildings in a star configuration around the central, final assembly floor.

Bosch's building is at one point of the star, adjacent to the MCC floor. The company produces and then affixes the car's front module. Sub-assembly of engine mountings and mechanical parts are produced by Krupp-Hoesch, in another building. Cockpit installations are sub-manufactured by supplier VDO Corp. Other suppliers provide co-located operations on-site: plastic panels, doors, body welding, and vehicle exterior painting. In addition to virtually guaranteeing that suppliers meet MCC's tough JIT requirements, co-location brings other potential advantages, including:

Quality Inspections

Examination of the sub-assembler's operation is easier to conduct, as the supplier is literally next door. Communications are virtually instantaneous. The consequence is that if problems arise, corrective actions can start almost immediately.

Extension of Process Flow Intelligence

The final assembler helps itself by encouraging its major suppliers to adopt high-performance demand pull/flexible approaches, including JIT, within their own manufacturing operations. With supplier and customer located at the same address, exchange of intelligence is fast and clear. Suppliers are able to observe what works—and what doesn't—firsthand, rather than take their cue from some how-to manual.

Challenging the Holy Grail of Manufacturing Final Assembly

The overlap of procurement and production extends further and further. But the manufacturing VP is adamant about one thing. The nameplate company—the company that places its name and reputation on the finished product—must always maintain full control over every aspect of final assembly. No exceptions.

Simply bolting on yet another approach without coordination probably makes matters worse, even if the individual approach is promising in value terms. Horror stories emerge of finish and quality lapses where differing approaches were permitted to co-exist on the same floor. The issue is less a matter of corporate turf than performance. Stop-start rework literally ends the flow and destroys its economics, pulling down corporate value.

And yet, suppliers of major components are being brought closer and closer to direct involvement in operations on the final assembly floor. Final assembly appears more and more like a simple bolt-on and ship-out proposition. The apparent simplification raises the prospect of whether this is a further advance in production output and cost performance, raising corporate value.

Ford followed in the steps of the Daimler-MCC Smart car and Volkswagen's earlier experimentation when it announced in August

1999 that there would be supplier active management of some aspects of final assembly at its new Bahia, Brazil, facility. A major supplier describes the Ford Amazon as the model of how the car giant will proceed in the future. Ford officials say nothing to contradict the remark.[17]

Components from sub-manufacturers can be bolted onto the master platform. On occasion, some suppliers might even be co-located at the nameplate manufacturer's site, such as in the case of MCC. But permitting outside suppliers to actually take command of part or all of the production sequence?

"The jury's still out," cautions Lean Enterprise Research Center (LERC) director Professor Daniel T. Jones. Supplier-assembly schemes such as those emerging in Brazil and France are yet to be fully tested. The Cardiff Business School professor and lean manufacturing authority cautions that even minor departures from exacting flow production final assembly can result in massive disappointments.[18]

Getting the flow process right is challenging enough when one party has total control. Jones and Womack cited the multiple ramp-up challenges encountered at Pratt & Whitney even with iron authority to implement the new order. But when a clear action plan is clouded by the involvement of several suppliers, the Single Best Solution suddenly becomes a matter of interpretation.

Even assuming that final assembly at plants such as Ford Amazon might eventually reach a bolt-on, ship-out ideal, that only means that the challenge of carefully calibrated final assembly in a demand pull/flexible operating environment is backed up a stage in the overall sequence. That is, demand pull/flexible is backed up to suppliers for whom exacting management of the flow production process is at best a second interest, not their first passion.

Challenges of precision final assembly are multiplied, where seven-plus subsidiary final assembly processes must occur, perfectly, rather than just one.

A new source of incremental value from manufacturing? As of the new millennium, Jones's caution is conspicuous. But LERC continues to monitor developments. And, after all, the first lean manufacturing breakthrough, Taiichi Ohno's original Toyota Production System, represented an unthinkable, dangerous departure in the 1950s and later.

6

Value Lifeblood: The Innovation Research Enigma

When Internal Development Is Both Mandatory and "Unaffordable"

R&D executives estimate that they can improve the value creation potential of R&D by 20% to more than 200% with better strategic decision making.
—David and Jim Matheson, Strategic Decisions Group[1]

If production and procurement are the Value Mandate corporation's engine, research and development (R&D) are its value lifeblood. R&D are irreplaceable for closing a company's Value Opportunity Gap, and are key to maximizing shareholder value.

Value from R&D isn't just about increasing research and development scale—a passion underlying the research-driven merger activity in the late 1990s. It is also about increasing development's investment-to-innovation yield.

The corporation that excels in transforming its innovation investment into more market-viable launches, sooner, surges ahead of rivals. This outperformer secures the superior price-to-cash-flow (PCF) multiple and gains recognition as the industry pacesetter. To compete, other companies are put on the defensive and forced to fragment development resources between original inventions and me-too catch-up efforts. The rich get richer, as the emergent top Corporate Key Contributor research talent (Chapter 3) flows first and most to those operations that demonstrate the ability to make invention dreams real.

But is development of novel innovation affordable? In a strict reported earnings sense, the answer is often "no." The company's accountants grimace at the reality that only one of ten innovations grows into commercial success.[2] The accountants wince again at the massive continuing investment, high running costs, and overhead burden.

But the backward-managing chief executive described in the first chapter looks no further than the next quarter. Pursuing earnings per share (EPS) first and foremost, this manager thinks nothing of arbitrarily slashing tens of millions of dollars previously committed to R&D spending.

His reasoning is deceptively simple: No one can tell whether today's extra $50 million in R&D spending will return twice that amount in five years or nothing at all. So forget about achieving maximum value for real and just waft some spinner-speak (e.g., "invest wiser, not more money"). Then plow the R&D funds right back to reported earnings where they can hype EPS. Expenses are reduced. The EPS number is reached, possibly exceeded.

But as the market's valuation is shaped by interpretations of the CEO's cash flow projections rather than unilateral proclamation, this CEO's assault on the R&D budget can easily backfire.

If management's proclamation that R&D cuts have no effect on competitiveness is doubted, market value plunges. Treating the R&D budget as a slush fund to shore up the EPS number is management short-termism at its worst; it is a retreat from revenue-growth sources of value. In this situation, the CEO is seen as pursuing the wrong target. The market expresses its concerns by savaging the company's share price, as a reflection of value.[3]

The corporation's innovation enigma is inescapable. On the one hand, innovation success is critical to the corporation's future value growth. The company without solid future prospects eventually implodes, relying too much on expense cuts and extended cash flow from mature products. Now, both disappear far sooner than expected in this, the era of accelerating change.

And yet, to the EPS-myopic CEO, the R&D looms as an expensive black hole. Even when the innovation program succeeds, results can be so long in coming that original management is long gone.[4]

6.1 Research Spending and Corporate Revenue Levels: An Overview

Not innovating yet? Get going. Already innovating? Double the effective effort—"effective" referring to the real dollar expenditures directed to tomorrow's new market offerings.

Innovation emerged as the management consultants' new theme-of-the-month in the late 1990s. While the ashes of corporate reengineering and contrarian strategy were still smoldering, innovation emerged as yet another "can't-miss" theme to flog. But "innovation is important" presentations merely state the obvious without coming to grips with the reality of R&D as a critical—yet often also unaffordable—mandate.

With one R&D success in ten, sometimes less, it is not enough to merely foment enthusiasm for increased innovation. Everyone already agrees that innovation is "important."[5] Restating the obvious is for also-rans; the Value Mandate corporation creates a concrete plan for increased R&D that balances today's costs and tomorrow's value objectives.

The high-value innovation leader is not always the first one to market. In Internet, biotech, and other key areas of innovation spending, it is clear that being the first to market is critical only if an unassailable commercial market position comes with the invention.

When browsers were perceived as a distinct, key Internet segment, conventional wisdom was that Netscape had developed a key new innovation. But as browsers slipped to the stature of a mere add-on service—following late entrant Microsoft's controversial (to the U.S. government) pricing and positioning actions—the browser's innovation importance slipped. By contrast, the major drug introduction is considered a success because the formula quickly comes to dominate a specific, acute-need market. When the existence of the formula means that an instant market is met, first-to-market innovation speed is essential to survival.

Investing in Innovation

Spending for innovation assumes paramount importance when management realizes that both customers and investors revere their relationships with an industry's undisputed innovation leader.

Customers. The preferred customer—the one your corporation wants—is continually striving to transform its too-long list of mere vendors to a shorter list of true commercial and development partners.[6] The clear innovation leader usually makes it to the final group, even with somewhat higher prices, because it possesses that something extra. The customer's management reasons that they cannot afford to be excluded from new innovations that might provide scarce advantage in their markets.

Investors/Capital Providers. No business endures for long by just purchasing another's initiative and then hoping to prosper on razor-thin remerchandising margins. Management knows that, and those who provide a company with sustaining capital know it even better. The corporation with a reasonably predicable innovation stream controls its destiny. The remerchandiser eventually loses capital support, as there are too many attractive alternatives.

For those CEOs who anguish over their corporation's present levels of innovation spending, the future indications are hardly reassuring. Innovation spending is one of the primary bases for marketplace advantage, a situation that shows no signs of changing in the new millennium.

In some industries, companies face the prospect of sharply higher innovation investment just to keep up. Companies in innovation-intensive industries—from pharmaceuticals to telecommunications, from Net infrastructure to biotech—must pursue consolidation to finance their futures. Now, those futures are together—not always by choice but rather necessity as go-it-alone R&D budgets slip from adequate to inadequate in industry after industry.

Thus emerges a practice of pursuing the highest common denominator. Companies, and sometimes even whole sectors, with comparatively low R&D spending face tough questions about whether their levels of innovation spending is sufficient.

Some Corporate R&D Spend/Revenue Patterns, by Industry

Table 6-1 illustrates the wide disparity in spending levels in selected world industries, with R&D spending expressed both in financial terms and as a percentage of revenues in that year. The table indicates that, in 1997, 300 corporations spent $216 billion on R&D, 12.8 percent more than in 1996.

As a percentage of sales, the 1997 R&D spending level represents 4.58 percent of sales. The overall percent-of-sales statistic is dampened somewhat by industries such as general engineering and vehicle engineering (primarily car manufacturers). Companies with huge R&D budgets in dollar terms, but modest when expressed as a percentage of revenues.

Within an industry, the corporation with a conspicuously low ratio of R&D spending to revenue faces pressure to increase its research expenditures. It is not enough, however, to increase spending up to the industry average. R&D should be funded to match the level of the industry's leader. Aim at the top, and you might contend. But aim at the middle, and it might not be there anymore; it will certainly disappear with the next wave of industry consolidation.

In 1997, the date of the analysis shown in Table 6-1, Merck (pharmaceuticals), Volkswagenwerk (cars), and Nortel (telecommunications) all faced consistent comment from analysts that their level of innovation spending was low relative to the pacesetters in that industry.

Does high R&D/revenue spending mean higher sales? Exclude du Pont at the top of the list of 35 (based on same-year sales) in Table 6-2 and related Figure 6-1, and a pattern emerges. This despite the fact that (1) R&D expenditures today do not become sales or value for several years and (2) revenues include both recent innovation and older sources.[7]

6.2 "Managing the R&D Manager" and Other Expedients

Managers and their budgeteers at corporate HQ would just as soon treat R&D as a conventional corporate function, capable of being as-

(text continues on page 137)

Table 6-1. R&D expenditures: selected sector and company information.

Companies	Sector	1997 R&D Spend BPS Mil.	Increase From 1996-Pct.	1997 Sales BPS Mil.	1997 R&D Spend Pct. Sales
Overall: 300 Companies		131.067	12.60%	2,860	4.58%
	Chemicals	18.991	16%	303.669	6.25%
	Distribution	2.82	17%	48.014	5.87%
	Electronics & Electricals	41.555	18%	641.165	6.48%
	Engineering, Vehicles	23.303	4%	560.135	4.16%
	Health Care Products	3.551	19%	30.815	11.52%
	Pharmaceuticals	9.578	11%	74.771	12.81%
	Telecommunications Serv Prov	7.246	9%	184.92	3.92%
Ericsson (Swe)	Electronics & Electricals	1.856	39%	12.849	14.44%
Cisco Syst (US)	Electronics & Electricals	0.733	202%	3.914	18.73%
Nortel (Cdn)	Telecommunications Serv Prov	1.305	18%	9.389	13.90%
Nokia (Fin)	Electronics & Electricals	0.612	56%	5.872	10.42%
General Motors (US)	Engineering, Vehicles	4.983	–8%	101.158	4.93%
Volkswagen (Ger)	Engineering, Vehicles	1.487	10%	38.278	3.88%
Pfizer (US)	Pharmaceuticals	1.172	14%	7.401	15.84%
Merck (US)	Pharmaceuticals	1.023	13%	14.366	7.12%
Astra (Swe)	Pharmaceuticals	0.67	24%	3.44	19.48%

Source: U.K. Department of Trade with Company Reporting.
Referenced in Clive Cookson, "Advantage to the Scientists," *The Financial Times*, June 25, 1998, page 11. Reprinted with permission from *The Financial Times*.

Table 6-2. Sales vs. R&D spending, 1997.

Rank, Sales, BPS Mil	Rank, Spending BPS	Corporation	Sales, BPS Mil	Spend BPS Bil	R&D Pct Sls
1	1	General Motors	101.16	4.98	4.90
2	2	Ford Motor	93.37	3.85	4.10
3	6	Toyota	57.23	2.11	3.70
4	4	IBM	47.71	2.62	5.50
5	8	Daimler-Benz	41.93	1.91	4.60
6	18	NTT	41.24	1.54	3.70
7	5	Hitachi	39.84	2.35	5.90
8	19	Volkswagen	38.28	1.49	3.90
9	3	Siemens	36.14	2.75	7.60
10	7	Matsushita Elec	35.89	2.03	5.70
11	32	Boeing	27.84	1.17	4.20
12	15	duPont	27.24	1.58	5.80
13	9	Hewlett-Packard	26.07	1.87	7.20
14	16	Toshiba	25.48	1.56	6.10
15	23	Sony	25.17	1.32	5.20
16	29	Honda Motor	24.74	1.17	4.70
17	13	NEC	23.13	1.63	7.00
18	27	Philips	22.92	1.22	5.30
19	14	ABB	19	1.61	8.50
20	22	Bayer	18.59	1.34	7.20
21	12	Motorola	18.11	1.67	9.20
22	21	Hoechst	17.61	1.35	7.70
23	34	Alcatel Alstrom	16.38	1.11	6.80
24	11	Lucent Tech	16.02	1.84	11.50
25	35	Robert Bosch	15.84	1.10	7.00
26	20	Intel	15.24	1.43	9.40
27	26	Bell Canada	14.1	1.24	8.80
28	25	Johnson & Johnson	13.75	1.30	9.50
29	17	Novartis	12.99	1.54	11.80
30	10	Ericsson	12.85	1.86	14.50
31	24	Nortel	9.39	1.30	13.90
32	33	Glaxo Wellcome	7.98	1.15	14.40
33	28	Roche	7.82	1.21	15.50
34	30	Pfizer	7.41	1.17	15.80
35	31	Microsoft	6.9	1.17	16.90

Source: U.K. Department of Trade with Company Reporting.
Referenced in Cookson, C., "Advantage to the Scientists," *The Financial Times,* June 25, 1998, page 11. Reprinted with permission from *The Financial Times.*

Figure 6-1. Sales vs. spending (re: Table 6-2).

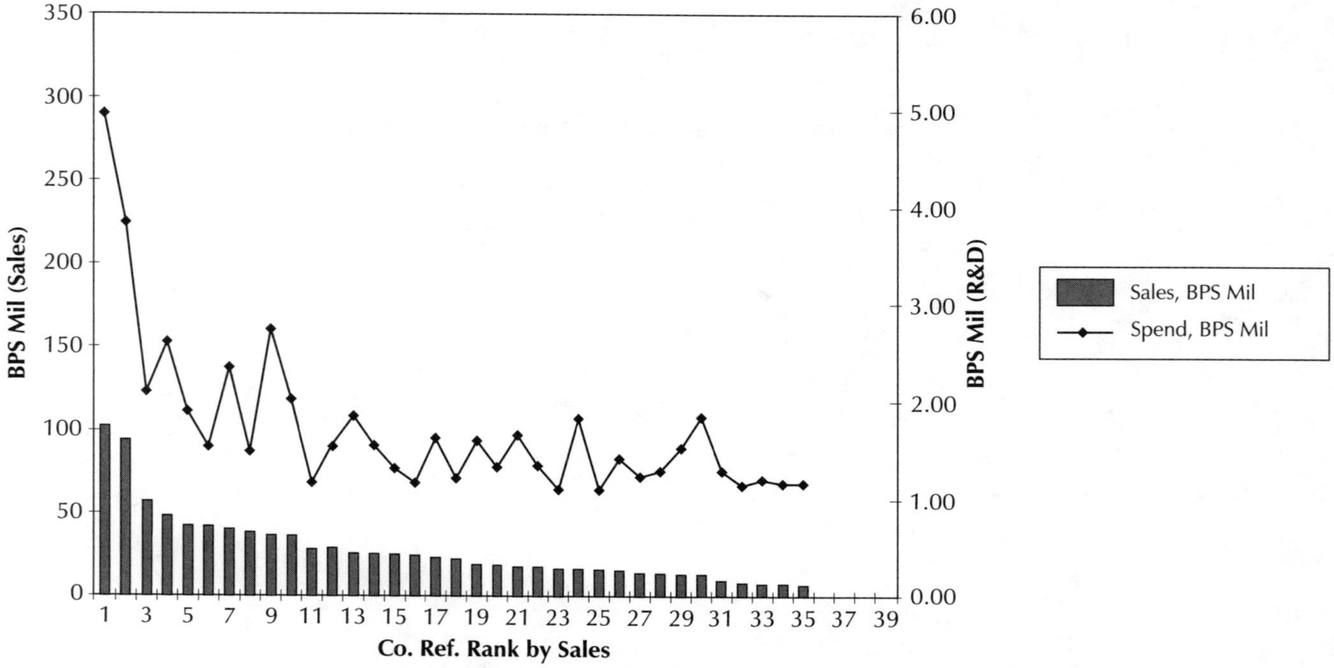

sessed on a straight cost-versus-revenue basis using same-year data. And they sometimes do, despite the fact that such methods have little or nothing to do with the dynamics of how R&D is conducted.

Shooting an Arrow at a Moving Target

Conducting costs-versus-revenue analysis on R&D project expenditures is like shooting an arrow at a moving target; a target positioned three years in the future. That's closer to reality than a conventional view based on same-period costs versus revenues.[8] Expenditures must be made now. Return, if any, cannot be assessed until after several years, at the earliest.

Any such future evaluation happens only if the structure and content of R&D project data facilitate such analyses. The head of R&D, however, is usually motivated to gently obscure any view of true returns. For if the one-in-ten new innovation success ratio holds, R&D management knows that many of the initiatives approved years ago will disappoint today on a returns basis.

The R&D manager knows from past experience that he faces the toughest budget battles when someone demonstrates that a high percentage of past R&D projects failed to exceed the company's minimum weighted average cost of capital (WACC) hurdle rate for authorization. Someone will inevitably go one step farther and point out that many projects lost money. Not only do such findings make future funding difficult, but there's the problem of dealing with aggravating questions, like "Why not just pick winners?"

Observing that, out of 20 projects, only five are highly successful, the simplistic solution is to just delete the 15 losers. Unfortunately, time travel is impossible. Also, any patterns of what succeeds often changes. The 15 "losers" were all funded at least three years ago. So any cutback decision today is ineffective and irrelevant.

But cutting out the disappointing initiatives does have a responsive ring to it, and management might just be tempted if they suspect there will be few challenging questions. Spinners' artistry—such as, "from now on, we'll only be investing in winners"—provides a forceful, although not particularly believable, reassurance that innovation performance will continue at present levels despite management's deep cuts to the R&D budget.

Adding Back R&D Expenses for Value Measurement Purposes: Imperative for a Comprehensive Approach

The corporate measurer-manager seeks a single lever for generating new value from research and development. This helps explain the administrator's early enthusiasm for top-down adjustments and similar, broad-based measures for R&D monitoring. His actions may include adjustments to period cash flow data. His objective is to adjust corporate cash flow to better reflect true value-relevant period performance.

One apparent answer calls for adding back all or most (based on a preset percentage) of the R&D amounts that have been expensed. It is a simple answer, but it is also misleading. The resulting post-adjustment sum is distorted by two factors:

The resulting amount is total R&D expenses less overhead and support (above). Out of this result, the only costs that are defensible as period add-backs for value purposes pertain to novel—that is, all-new—innovations that have not yet been introduced to the marketplace.

This means removal of R&D costs for maintaining past innovations. These extra costs include everything from the unnecessary extra testing of the company formulas to goldplating engineers who add unwanted features and alternative solutions to existing products. These engineers may amuse themselves and create an illusion of usefulness, but unless the customer demands those specific improvements, the misguided effort destroys value.[9]

There is no alternative to a comprehensive, operations-oriented approach to carefully define the amounts and types of R&D expenses added back for value-based performance assessment purposes. Better to spend the time on a brief but effective examination of the elements that lie below the total R&D number than possibly undermine the overall value program by a crude add-back approach easily punctured as indefensible. R&D managers need to probe beyond the numbers to get an understanding of what those costs represent.

When There Is No Value Lever, Delegate

Eventually, the value-destructive R&D manager gets frustrated over the lack of easy levers for generating value from R&D and starts experimenting with an alluring non-answer: delegation. At first, delegation sounds like a solution to the CEO desperate for *any* workable answers to the R&D enigma. It is only later that the non-research chief executive discovers that the only predictable result is value *destruction*, instead.

The organizational theorists argue that even the most obtuse functions can be through a combination of clear lines of authority, delegation, mutual goal-setting, and subsequent monitoring of performance. Whether that theory holds water or not is less important to the non-research CEO than the fact that such a command-control approach is familiar to him or her.

Tired of past R&D performance promises made and missed, the non-research CEO simply says that it's time to do it his way. The people involved with innovation performance will be held responsible, with no more "It is 95 percent complete" migraines.

This strategy—Managing the R&D Manager—gathers even more momentum when the prospective candidate for research department head knows how to play the game and even has command of some the prevailing management guru-speak. The articulate candidate is welcomed with relief that is palpable. "Hey, this is someone we can work with, someone who speaks our language." Literally. If that candidate's track record includes key innovation success at previous companies, then enthusiasm soars.[10]

But a complete approach includes managing both the R&D manager *and* the function. Managing the R&D manager alone means abandoning responsible oversight. The fact that research is something of an enigma to those in HQ trying to manage it doesn't justify inadequate controls. The CEO would never accept such lightweight monitoring in more familiar parts of the business. If anything, research's mystery points demand more comprehensive control measures.

The chief executive wouldn't dream of relying on the production manager's "trust me" statements as the only assurance that maximum value will be created on the factory floor. The responsive CEO insists on developing an independent perspective to supplement such commitments.

Time is a key consideration. By the time the manager's extended string of excuses and delays finally run out and management realizes that it *must* act, the opportunity for effective action may have already passed.

Moreover, managing the R&D manager leaves the chief executive with only one action possible if results disappoint—fire and replace the manager. It is an unsatisfactory answer. Like the football team owner who changes coaches every three years only be to disappointed one more time, dismissal often provides no assurance that the successor will do any better.

In his heart of hearts, this CEO knows that simply shifting bodies around does nothing. But the hiring-firing cycle—at least the first few times—appears to be decisive action to outside observers. After a few of these cycles, however, value-influencers on the outside have serious concerns. "Does management have a clue about how to set this right?"[11]

In retrospect, the CEO observes that managing the manager results in a recurring cycle of unrealistic enthusiasm followed by disillusionment and replacement.

The Managing the Manager Cycle

Stretch Goals Envisioned

Corporate management sets targets for R&D performance based on statistical examples from leaders in the industry and other, comparable companies. The "best of the best" benchmarking practice is justified in corporate management's minds by the great importance to future value of new innovation. Aim at the mid-point or lower, and that's the best you can achieve.[12]

Early Discussions

The newly appointed research leader—enjoying the honeymoon period—nods his head dutifully as corporate officers explain their expectations for R&D. Headquarters generalists see their actions as positive control of a field that they do not understand, and the new head of R&D buys time by agreeing to broad parameters.

Assessment by the Metrics Introduced

Headquarters staff devise several metrics consistent with the chief executive's innovation goals. The metrics cover innovations to market, costs, and indicated returns based on market results to date. HQ managers may have no idea about how to make the goals work, but by Managing the Manager, they can delegate that role.

Results Disappoint

Assessment is made in the second or third year as targets are missed. Because the hiring decision was made on a "trust me" basis, failure to achieve the goals brings a sense of deception that spins the cycle faster. The anguished CEO asks of the (soon to be ex-) R&D, "Didn't you hear us when we described the goals?"

The inadequacy of the Managing the Manager approach becomes apparent to outside observers as the cycle of one department head replacing the next is repeated, again and again. Some of these observers influence the corporation's value. Once established, it is hard to shake the sense that the company's research function is adrift, with value-diminishing consequences for the corporation overall.

Acquiring the Innovation-Intensive Corporation as Development Alternative

No corporation ever has enough high-return innovation prospects, just as no corporation ever has enough Corporate Key Contributors (Chapter 3). Which means that every corporation is both CKC- and innovation-deficient. Or, at least, every corporation should act that way.

As with other key elements of value, if management expresses satisfaction with their level of new innovation prospects, that's the moment that analysts and other value-influencers rush to "Sell! Sell!" depressing stock price and corporate value. The satisfied corporation signals that maybe pursuit of maximum shareholder value isn't so important after all.

But for the others that aren't satisfied, the search for new innovation is never-ending. Even assuming a robust capability for generating new prospects internally, acquisitions may provide an opportunity to complement or extend internal new technologies.

For the corporation with a sputtering innovation engine and empty pipeline, a major innovation-related acquisition may mean survival. The corporation with little or nothing in its development pipeline does not have the five-plus years necessary to both establish a new internal innovation structure from scratch and then make it productive. That corporation is already dead, twice over.[13]

The innovation acquirer's reasoning is that, in place of enduring the long odds and long time associated with internal innovation development, why not just acquire another corporation's innovation stream; along with the accompanying future value, of course.

But if there is no such thing as a free lunch, there certainly isn't any such thing as free value. To the contrary, the proven innovation commands the maximum pre-acquisition price to cash flow (PCF) ratio *and* the maximum acquisition premium. The stratospheric price necessary to close the deal offsets the future value that the acquirer can realize in later years.[14]

Even if a company is prepared to spend top dollar, the can't-miss, proven innovation may not be available at all. The innovation-hungry acquirer is looking for a blockbuster class innovation, that once-a-decade discovery that results in creation of a whole new, major product or service category. Innovations that meet those criteria are exceedingly rare.

To make such an acquisition even more difficult, the knowledgeable seller is least eager to unload proven or promising innovations. The proven innovation or the corporation possessing it is usually effectively removed from the market. If a price is cited at all, levels are deliberately set so high that overpayment is assured. Instead of gaining an advantage, the acquirer instead struggles for years just to dig out of its self-imposed value hole.

So sights are ratcheted down a notch, maybe two or three. Sights are set toward lower return, higher risk targets involving far greater chances of adverse selection. The innovation-poor acquirer is anxious to get some deal closed, and it shows. The commercial potential of the tepid prospect is exaggerated, risks are understated. At most, this surface actions buys time to develop a serious value development approach.

6.3 Establishing and Accelerating the R&D "Funnel"

R&D requires a development mechanism equal to the task of becoming and remaining an industry innovation leader. Absent such a systematic approach, value creation from R&D is left to chance.

The long odds of innovation success argue for a series of progressive screens and assessments. The R&D "funnel" is illustrated in Figure 6-2. Figure 6-2(A) shows the largest number of qualifying prospects entering the pipeline at early stages, with cutdowns and combinations after that point. Figure 6-2(B) demonstrates how market indications, demand patterns, and trends provide the basis for modifying the funnel. In turn, those insights suggest new prospects for initial examination.

Retreat from Choosing Winners, Swinging Only for Home Runs

The wide-to-narrow approach clashes with the non-research administrator's directive to "just choose winners." Such prattle is valueless,

Figure 6–2. R&D "funnel": value development through systematic analysis of innovation prospects.

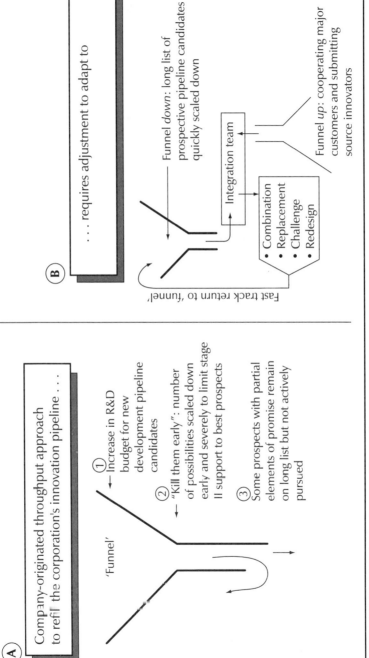

A

Company-originated throughput approach to refill the corporation's innovation pipeline . . .

'Funnel'

① Increase in R&D budget for new development pipeline candidates

② "Kill them early": number of possibilities scaled down early and severely to limit stage II support to best prospects

③ Some prospects with partial elements of promise remain on long list but not actively pursued

B

. . . requires adjustment to adapt to

Funnel *down*: long list of prospective pipeline candidates quickly scaled down

Integration team

Funnel *up*: cooperating major customers and submitting source innovators

Fast track return to 'funnel'

- Combination
- Replacement
- Challenge
- Redesign

Source: VBM Consulting (www.vbm-consulting.com).

or even value-destructive, as the department lurches from one impossible long shot winner to the next.

The apparent logic of restricting development emphasis to major innovation prospects is alluring—deceptively so. The home run innovations—such as the internal combustion engine or the Internet server—are later viewed as revolutionizing the entire competitive structure of their industries. In their wake, these creations generate tremendous wealth in the form of new leader companies, led by managers who recognized opportunities early.

With 20/20 hindsight, the non-research administrator insists that this is where the corporation's emphasis must be directed, rather than diffusing efforts on minor prospects that at most supplement the home runs.

Compelling, but Unfeasible, Goal

The non-research administrator's logic is simple and appealing. His logic is also massively destructive in value terms. The home run prospect never comes with a clear label affixed, otherwise every R&D program would immediately focus on such targets to the exclusion of all else. Both bubble memories and fuel cells have either failed to become the home runs once envisioned or their commercial heyday is still so far in the future that companies can twice go bankrupt waiting for the market promise to be realized.

Choosing winners sounds as if it is a straightforward selection process. And to the non-research administrator, that may well be the perception. But if conventional innovations follow a one-in-ten success profile, huge commercial successes are far, far more difficult to anticipate. For practical purposes, the odds of the home run are so remote that management cannot base any innovation development course on choosing winners. The choice is closer to a wild guess. An extremely high-cost wild guess, which accelerates the corporation's forced exit from the industry if it doesn't pan out. Betting the company, literally.

Moreover, direct pursuit of the home run innovation doesn't seem to reduce the long odds. The miracle breakthroughs that result from laboratory serendipity cannot be replicated.[13]

Many major innovations result not from pursuit of grand designs, but rather from combinations of intermediate step innovations that may have limited market potential on their own. Internet voice and data transmission picked up momentum only after growth of data traffic began to displace voice. Spyglass emerged as the first provider of commercial browser technology only after invention of the World Wide Web.

Scoring Protocols

Priority-setting approaches typically rely on scoring algorithms, with points assigned according to functionality, performance, market potential, and feasibility of the design for volume production at the targeted unit cost levels. The original intent is, of course, to help identify the highest promise potential candidates and put them on the fast track to development.

Instead, the scoring protocols are more likely to be used as a screen for early elimination of the commercially unfeasible prospects. One reason is because few initial innovations survive as stand-alone market introductions, at least not in their original intended use. Particularly if the innovation involves a basic new technology, initial uses do not necessarily correspond to greatest market potential.

Micropower impulse radar (MIR) uses low power and works on distances of 150 feet or less. Originally envisioned as a "cool burglar alarm" by its inventor, Thomas McEwan of the Lawrence Livermore Laboratory, MIR's uses include maintaining distance between cars on a highway, or use as a parking lot car locator that rings louder the closer the searcher.

MIR's greatest potential, however, appears to be something quite different from McEwan's original intent. It turns out that MIR excels at non-destructive testing. It can be used to locate leaks in pipes, flaws in wire arrays, even studs behind obstructions, with significant prospective savings in both labor and materials.[16] The second use, with potentially far greater market potential, emerged only with the parallel development of low-cost sensors that enable broad field use.

When Choosing Winners Is Mandatory

Sometimes there isn't a choice except to try to select specific, winning prospects well in advance and hope that the long odds bet comes through this once. The longer a corporation goes with a depleted innovation pipeline, the greater the probability of having to reach for long shots. To outsiders, the action may appear to be reckless. To management, the word is survival.

In 1990, Warner-Lambert's Parke-Davis (P-D) pharmaceuticals division appeared to be on its last legs, with its product about to go off-patent. The company bet on Lipitor, which reduces dangerous forms of cholesterol, and Rezulin, a fast-growing diabetes compound. The results were that P-D dramatically reversed course by 1997. Warner-Lambert's CEO Melvin Goodes admits that if the bet had failed, his corporation would probably have become some else's acquisition target.

Hitting Singles

Deliberately pursuing major blockbuster innovations—home runs—means unacceptable risks for most companies, most times. The opposing approach calls for pursuit of multiple innovation targets of moderate profitability as an interim development step. Hitting singles calls for a focus on several moderately profitable targets in the target technology sector.

Developing the Long List of Possible Prospects

Not knowing which commercial application and related version of their discovery will catch fire in the marketplace, the development group hedges by examining multiple variants of the base discoveries. In the cases of MIR (described above) and long-life PC battery technology, for example, multiple alternatives exist, but no single approach yet commands the market. Thus, all alternative approaches for that technology are treated as initial prospects.

Killing Off the Losers Early

The research department's funds are quickly depleted if marginal prospects are permitted to remain on the active list too long. Expenditures and staff time continue to be spent on the prospect until it is finally deleted.

Vikay Jolly refers to Myers and Sweezy's investigation of 200 failed innovations. Seventy-five percent of the failures were stopped at the advanced pilot test stage. But a full 20 percent were allowed to linger until the final stage of product preparation, depleting corporate cash flow and destroying value as a consequence.[17]

Delayed termination of the marginal innovation prospect is particularly costly as double expenses are involved. First, the company continues to throw scarce funds away on prospects without a future. Second, the non-viable innovations absorb resources that might otherwise be directed to top candidates.

Internal obstacles sometimes contribute to the inability or unwillingness of section leaders to kill off the losers early enough to preclude value destruction:

Personal Favorite of Scientist/Researcher

Researchers sometimes fail to eliminate several prospects despite low external demand because that would mean eliminating work in their area of professional concentration. As research backgrounds become increasingly specialized, the likelihood of such acts of self-preservation become increasingly likely.

Untouchable: Favorite of Leader

Unpromising prospects can also linger as favorites of the R&D head or another executive. The result is that deletion is slowed, even when well-deserved.

Accelerating the Funnel

Effective development is means throughput: both output and speed, together. The low-demand prospect list generated at lightning speed is as worthless as the mountain of great prospects generated a year too late to be enacted.

Which raises the matter of operating the R&D funnel in practice. The funnel needs to be operated as a consistent, viable approach for dealing with large numbers of low-probability prospects. The funnel's offsetting disadvantage is its sheer magnitude. Ensure sufficient coverage of possible "singles" prospects, and threat of yet another unwieldy bureaucratic process arises.

Thus, the need arises for some means to facilitate the funnel's operation. A company need not develop alternatives to the funnel, but rather accelerators that make it easier to extract the highest promise prospects earlier. Three are suggested in the pages that follow:

Accelerator 1: "Singles" Recombined

Mid-level risk and return prospects—'singles' from the R&D funnel—are recast. Instead of being the intermediate result of prior development activity, the singles instead serve as the raw source materials for a second, higher return R&D investigation.

By definition, these prospects are at least already moderately successful. But when a critical mass of singles are accumulated, the development possibilities shift to a higher plane. Combine software that allows any cellular phone to operate like a global position system (GPS) device (but without the transmitter) with a new blocking device for muffling mobile phone signals, and a whole range of monitoring and stealth applications emerge.

But first, the developer has to have access to compatible singles technologies. For all the excitement about on-screen simulation, there's nothing like physical proximity to generate the spark for a new product that no one even thought about before.

Thus, 3M management assigned some of its microreplication engineers to its signs division and stands back to observe what happens next. Microreplication involves tiny pyramid-type structures that reflect and refract light, creating brilliant effects. Combine the "pyramids" with road signs, and you have a stop sign that can be seen from twice as far away at night, compared to its predecessor.

Accelerator 2: Encouraging Faster Feedback

Great thing about doing business on the Web is that you get so much feedback from your customers so quickly.
—Michael Cassidy, CEO, Direct Hit Technologies, Inc., one of the new generation of Internet specialized search engines.[18]

In theory, seeking knowledgeable customer input makes obvious sense when it comes to introducing the next product generation. Practical application is sometimes another matter. The headstrong development engineer who blames low demand on the "fact" that salesmen "have not done a good job educating customers" is not likely to welcome the prospect of raw key customer input.

"Terrestrial" product businesses still suffer from the problem of introducing meaningful customer response early enough in the development process to make a difference. Enter the saturation responses provided by the Web. The nanosecond attention spans of Netheads also means fast response when things are amiss.

Under conventional serial development of new software, the best prospect is released to market and then incrementally adjusted over two, three, or more rounds of critical comments. Each cycle of release-comment-adjustment requires weeks. But that's time that today's developer just doesn't have.

The alternative is to combine Web response with multiple version release, such as the practice at Direct Hit. Cassidy releases eight alternative permutations all at once, with inducements to online users to try and comment. Criticism is welcomed as part of essential development input, unlike the defensive engineer described above.

An approach applicable only to Net-based software and some services? Initially, yes. But as more services go online and as even physical products are showcased with online representations, further extensions into so-called box (physical) product segment is inevitable. One example: abandonment of one-off concept show cars as a means of testing regional appeal of exotic new design concepts. Ten times as many images can be placed online instead, limiting physical mockups to only those models with proven appeal.

Accelerator 3: Antidote Innovations

Force and counterforce. Each new major innovation brings the possibility of an offsetting counter-product designed to neutralize, modify, manage, and sometimes even cancel the effects of the earlier innovation. These are referred to in the part that follows as *antidotes*.

Cellular phones have become so widely used that theaters are routinely interrupted by nuisance calls. So a Japanese manufacturer developed a network block that effectively quiets all signals into areas where silence is mandatory. Concerns about possible cell phone radiation prompted development of alternative designs with new shielding and antennae placement, actively marketed as an antidote design.

6.4 Antidote Innovations

Antidote innovations have emerged as a new major category of high value development, and hence deserve further discussion. There are no shortcuts, no instant answers for new innovation development. But as the number and diversity of prior innovations accumulate along with related issues, antidote innovations take on enormous importance.

As used here, "antidote" refers to the novel product or service

designed as a counter-innovation to an existing innovation of importance. The antidote may be a device that eliminates or obstructs some
of the functions of the original innovation; car radar sensors, for example. The antidote may also overcome apparent disadvantages of
the earlier innovation, as perceived by groups of key buyers; alternative prescription drug designs that reduce adverse side effects, for
example.

In antidote innovation development, the existing innovations are
the roots of the next wave of novel developments. Antidotes are not
extensions and minor modifications designed to extend a tired product's life a few more months. Instead, antidotes are all-new products
or services.

There are similarities, of course, between the extension and the
antidote innovation. As with the extension, the beginning point is
demand for yesterday's successful, effective innovation. But that's
where the similarity ends. For while the motivation behind the product-service extension is to stretch the past, the underlying motivation
for the antidote innovation is to introduce different, useful functionality. Sometimes radically different.

Problems as Innovation Opportunities

A product with a persistent problem may be a headache for some, but
it also represents a potential innovation opportunity, too. That is, an
opportunity exists as long as those inconvenienced are willing to pay
for an answer (this also assumes that the nature of the problem lends
itself to a profitable solution).

The start point is to understand the different categories of problems associated with past innovations-market introductions, from
the perspective of antidote development:

New Problems

New services and products bring new problems. Side effects that reduce demand until and unless they are resolved, such as in the case
of the promising drug with severe side effects. Pitfalls from unanticipated uses, such as misuse of very high-quality laser copiers by coun-
terfeiters. These are lingering problems that reduce demand unless
resolved. By 1999, for example, concerns about Internet purchasing
security spawned a new series of special purpose, protected Net-only
cards.

Redefine the Problem as a Start to Developing the Solution

James Dyson, inventor of the vacuum cleaner that contains his name, determined that conventional machines merely collected dust while leaving the true problem of continuous suction untouched. His new definition of the problem spawned a relentless search for a different answer, leading to Dyson's patented cyclonic suction design.

The Ongoing (Chronic) Problem as Antidote Innovation Font: Example of Multiple Layer Security Cards

As credit, debit, and personal information cards gradually evolve into multiple function "smart" cards, uses and users expand. Including misuses. Duplicating today's credit and debit cards and emerging smart card versions is a potentially lucrative crime.

Holograms and similar security features at best slow the pace of misuse and theft. Criminals acquire equipment to produce counterfeit holograms. Pictures on the card, mathematical algorithms, complex designs—whatever the nature of the single-barrier security design, the thief knows that there is some way to beat it.

There is no absolute protection. But multiple-layer security presents such overwhelming barriers that few crooks possess the time or resources to overcome all of the interlinked barriers at the same time.

"Coated phase mask" is what Professor Bahram Javidi at University of Connecticut-Storrs calls his combination approach, poised to become one of the leading hybrid security technologies.

At first, Javidi's innovation looks like nothing more than a small clear window cut into the card. But one of the thin transparent veneers contains random scattered laser bits. Diagnostic equipment reads the unique picture of bits and compares against a reference picture for verification. Yet another transparent layer contains biometrics data of the card's authorized user, such as a fingerprint, photograph, retina scan, or a combination.

Combine those two layers, and the challenge to thieves is virtually impossible. As comprehensive solutions such as Javidi's force thieves to pursue less robust barriers, coated phase mask technology faces strong demand from a second wave of card issuers. These are the issuers those who originally turned down the advanced antidote, but now discover that their refusal has been exploited by thieves on the lookout for weakness.

The best antidote innovation can adapt as new flaws emerge or, in the case of credit card fraud, thieves develop more powerful means to undo prevailing barriers. The multiple-veneer window construction allows numerous additional layers, as required.

Correcting the Correction: Traffic Surveillance Camera Systems

Sometimes the need for the new antidote arises from limitations of an earlier solution. Problems that were not fully anticipated in the first generation of antidote innovations establish the basis for a second generation with higher performance and improved functionality.

The original problem was how to reduce highway deaths while deploying manpower more efficiently. Unfortunately, the problem was compounded by pressure on police forces to reduce hiring. Fewer police means fewer speed patrols, as available officers are transferred to current priorities.

The first generation antidote innovation called for speed cameras that automatically record the offender's license plate number, speed, day, and time of day as soon as the offense is detected. Studies confirm that accidents can be reduced up to 70 percent. The stored data is admissible in court as evidence, theoretically permitting officers to be assigned to other work.

But the labor savings attributed to the first generation cameras proved to be overstated when the systems were actually deployed. Film cassettes must be manually changed in the first-generation traffic cameras, sometimes after only 200 photos. As the cameras are deliberately located in inaccessible locations, such as on top of poles, special equipment must be scheduled to reach some of the "eye-in-the-sky" units.

Inevitably, servicing declines and violations are missed because the tapes are not retrieved. As motorists suspect that the camera is disabled, the deterrent effect evaporates. A senior traffic officer in the London metropolitan area stated, "Drivers know more often than not that when they are flashed by a camera they will never get fined."[19]

The problem gave rise to a new antidote, however. The antidote innovation cameras cost a fraction of the £8000 (US $13,200) per year in operating cost required for comparable cartridge-based cameras. Instead of film, electronic images of all traffic—speeders as well as all other traffic—are transmitted in electronic image form to police command rooms. Computers read the plate number and immediately compare it against lists of stolen cars and criminal drivers maintained in department databases. Lower priority crimes can be evaluated later.

The Case for Cluster Development

Contrary to the romanticized images of the researcher toiling over bubbling beakers and chancing upon the major discovery in isolation, lower cost/higher value millennium development involves continual collision of overlapping technologies and applications, all at once. The phrase used here is *cluster development*.

Combine cost considerations with the corporation's requirement for a continuing stream of cash flow-generating innovations, and the rationale for cluster development becomes clearer.

For example, our hypothetical Corporation U temporarily outflanks a competitor with its single well-designed and -positioned discovery. Chest-beating management proclaim their advantage. But any edge proves short-lived. With only a single point of contention to overcome, the rival quickly adjusts.

Cluster Development Illustrated

3M Volition™ represents one of the U.S. manufacturer's 25 Pacing Plus projects identified for early emphasis and development. Volition represents a simple, inexpensive total system for installing fiber optical cable. Advertising claims that the new cable is so durable and easy to install that even the least experienced of field technicians come out looking like pros.

Also at 3M, microreplication comprises a family of products based on a single platform. Master duplicates of polymer structures are developed at low cost. The masters are then used as polymer molds to form thousands of alternative designs. Different materials are used to take full advantage of different physical properties for new applications.

Microreplication scientists discovered that certain combinations of structures and materials resulted in reflective qualities far greater than existing materials. Used in polishing semiconductor silicon wafers, microreplication eliminates the need for polishing liquids. Miniscule facets in a design can create an adhesive effect between different surfaces.[20]

It is interesting to note that most new microreplication products occur after 1990, around the same time that chief executive L.D. De-Simone set a goal of achieving at least 30 percent of company sales from products that are less than four years old.

Pursuing Cluster Innovation I: The Robust Technology Category

For the cluster approach to be optimally effective, research must be organized around a single focal point. The two such focus approaches addressed in the pages that follow are: (1) the robust *technology* with multiple commercial development aspects; and (2) the enduring *function* for which alternative solutions exist.

Global satellite geographical positioning systems (GPS) were originally developed for ship positioning and military surveillance. Applying triangulation techniques from space, a series of satellites precisely identifies the location of an oil tanker or spots a suspected terrorist training base.

GPS has, of course, found myriad uses. GPS has given a blind man "eyes" by granting him the precious freedom to travel, without assistance, wherever he wishes in his home city. Strider™ is the creation of a California not-for-profit company, Arkenstone. Strider uses GPS to guide the user to his destination through voice instructions.

Mike May is a sightless Arkenstone employee. His "map" is provided by the Strider laptop and receiver backpack, which continually track's Mike's position on the ground. Map instructions are provided in the form of a computer-generated voice. Today, Mike can travel wherever he wishes in his home city of Palo Alto with no other assistance but the backpack.[21]

But guiding the blind is just one GPS application. Safeway Stores use the signaling technology to track the position and progress of its truck fleet. Tracker (U.K.) and Lojack (U.S.) use GPS to track a car thief back to the chop shop without the criminal suspecting anything. Boston's Pinpoint Technology uses the satellite to continually monitor the distance between mother and newborn child, to help prevent kidnappings from hospital maternity wards. That application transforms GPS from an outdoors-only technology, as special sensors are set up within wards to permit tracking within buildings.[22]

Pursuing Cluster Innovation II: Ongoing Function, Multiple Improving Solutions

The alternative cluster approach focuses on application, rather than technology group. Whether in hard disk, backup system, or online resource, storage is a key factor behind enduring personal computer usage. The importance of being able to retain, protect, and easily retrieve developed materials has been underscored by the failure of the network computer, in part because of fatal underestimation of the importance of this factor.

Data protection force McAfee purchased Dr. Solomon's, its one-time competitor, strengthening the corporation's commitment to data protection and recovery. Thus, McAfee's online backup, WebStor, represents a different technology but for the same function: protection and (if necessary) recovery. And as storage lends itself to deliberate overlap (covering all alternatives, to prevent data loss), the function-directed approach for developing lends itself to alternative future innovations.

6.6 Process Acceleration: Emphasis on Throughput

Process acceleration means shortening the path of new innovations to market, improving *both* components of throughput: speed and output. Even with no change in the basic demand for the resulting product or service, value is enhanced, as more market-ready innovation is generated, sooner, and at lower cost.

Multiplicity

Combinational chemistry refers to the creation of multiple compounds by drug manufacturers. The strategy uses synthesis and replication techniques to generate up to 1,000 promising candidates over the same time period once allocated for a single prospect.

New techniques for dramatically increasing the number of possible candidate compounds at the beginning of the funnel (see Figure 6-2), qualifying for further screening and investigation. More possible candidates at the top end of the funnel mean a higher chance of discovering a drug that contributes significantly to company profits.

Using traditional manual laboratory techniques, the single researcher might generate 50 unique compounds a year, at an average cost per compound of approximately $5,000 each. These are candidate compounds: initially attractive based on the observed performance or effect, but still far from commercial stage.

Exceedingly few of the prospects make it all the way to the commercial stage. Some of the compounds are found to be unstable and/or inconsistent in performance. Others cause side effects that turn out to be worse than the ailments they were intended to cure. Still other compounds turn out to be orphans—viable cures but directed at market slivers too small to justify further development, at least by the discovering company.

The probability that the separate, promising prospect makes it all the way from the top of the funnel to the bottom—to status as a commercially viable, profitable proprietary drug—remains unchanged. Up to 5 percent in the case of improvement drugs based on prior successful formulas, less than 1 percent for long-odds breakthroughs in new ailment categories.

Thus, under traditional methods, the only means for increasing new output of drugs—for increasing innovation lifeblood—is by increasing the number of research staff. Besides financial constraints, scarcity becomes a factor. Especially in emerging fields of interest, there simply aren't that many scientists available.

It is then necessary that the drug manufacturer seeks out multiplicity techniques. Increasing the number of Stage 1 candidates at the top of the R&D funnel doesn't change the probabilities of success for any one formula. Instead, innovation output increases because of the far larger beginning base.

Combination techniques are based on compound synthesis. High yields shatter output and cost precedents: *Millions* of compounds can be developed for test purposes each year by a single researcher, at a thousandth of the cost per compound. For those formulas that appear to justify further development, fast-track testing opens the promise of halving time-to-market standards from laboratory to the test market.

Synthesis means actual creation of the candidate substance. But even that incurs costs of separate evaluation, storage, sampling, and retention. Costs per candidate compound can be further slashed as *simulation* allows characteristics to be evaluated first in abstract. As the performance characteristics and molecular composition of building block compounds become better known, so does the ability to use non-chemical simulation to hypothesize about possible consequences as different combinations are tried. A further multiplicity step higher.

Process Acceleration Tools

The innovation-dependent corporation can also steal precious months, sometimes years, through improvements to its internal process efficiencies.

Speed Reading at Glaxo Wellcome

Researchers at Glaxo Wellcome's advanced R&D unit personally read and interpret approximately 60 separate research paper pages each day, in line with counterparts elsewhere. But at Glaxo, the research reach is extended by a combination of Internet access and R&D information facilities available on the drug giant's technology intranet. That extension allows them to scroll through 140 additional pages.[23]

Glaxo Wellcome's effort saves precious time in steering an innovation prospect to the appropriate individual, who then acts as a potent development facilitator. Everyone else knows that it is the informal structure of people, capabilities, and relationships that makes the critical difference between the investigation that progresses faster than expected and the prospective breakthrough innovation that becomes stuck in committee.

The informal network knows who says he has expertise in a certain area versus who actually has the critical expertise. The informal grapevine tells who is an administrative traffic cop and who gets things done. These networks note speed, time, and even personal limitations that lead to changes in the development plan for the prospective innovation.

Within Glaxo Wellcome's R&D intranet, one key aim is to fertilize this inevitable grapevine. Descriptions of areas of expertise provide fast answers to the development director's plea, "Give me the name of everyone who knows anything about . . ." Eighteen of the company's twenty-one R&D subunits maintain their own descriptive Web pages for internal consumption. Shared reader comments about new publications help reduce duplicative effort somewhat while broadening the number of publications and other sources that can be efficiently monitored.

Continuous Code at IBM

The innovation created at IBM's Industry Solutions Laboratory is software. Precisely, eight suites of components called "Javabeans" being combined for use in Internet networks. The sun never sets on this development effort. IBM director of software for emerging markets Mark Bilger explains how software in progress is developed by teams in Latvia, Belarus, India, and China, coordinated by a staff of twenty-five in Seattle. Each of the global sites has thirty-one developers.

Part of the appeal of this acceleration approach extends beyond the ability to overcome the mental and physical limitations of development professionals limited to a single location and clock. The individual "going flat out" without sleep eventually slows down, and the mistakes cost far more than the benefits created by his extended hours.

Through groupware "handoffs" from location to location, this development effort is no longer dependent on overwork by one individual or a small team. Equally important, as effort is continuous, there is a constant flow. Without the time waste inherent in familiarization ramp-up time to try to figure out what the previous team did. Ending times for Team 1 overlap with beginning times for Team 2, facilitating communication and understanding.[24]

Scaling Back the Innovation Paperwork Burden

Although process efficiencies in the laboratory tend to be the most dramatic, the site of the throughput improvement is far less important than the degree of time savings. A couple of minutes gained in the lab because of automated testing equipment pales against the man-months of time required to document a process with sufficient precision to create prototypes. An additional drain on resources are the months required to compile, organize, and submit clinical data for central supervisory bodies such as the U.S. Food and Drug Administration (FDA).

Preparatory testing and paperwork involved in a single major drug submission to the FDA may amount to more than $700,000 per submission, and require more than three months. As outside groups are involved, customary wisdom is to treat such costs and time as uncontrollable.

Such wisdom now appears to be under attack, however. Early

document management companies promised one-size-fits-all solutions that were disappointing. For one thing, such systems relied on doctors who rarely used computers to input trial results. Unless physicians' legendary scribbles can be converted into data, chances for simplifying and shortening the approval process are limited.

Boston's PhaseForward is among the second wave of paperwork process specialists who are approaching the FDA issue instead from their own hands-on knowledge of document submission requirements. The three founders include a former clinical technician and an ex–chief technology officer at a database company.[25]

The innovation dilemma remains, prompting an unprecedented wave of R&D consolidation–driven mergers in research-intensive industries. On a traditional accounting basis (i.e., managing by earnings per share [EPS]), consolidation looks like the easy value answer. But EPS-backward thinking inevitably propels the company toward successive series of R&D budget cuts. Penny-wise, pound-foolish, as the corporation achieving The Value Mandate to maximize shareholder worth disregards EPS, and, instead, views innovation as critical value investment in the future.

7

Outperformer Marketing, Sales

Value Creation in the New Marketplace Disorder

Millennium marketplace disorder means continuous, ruthless combat on a features, performance, and cost (price) basis. Nothing new about that. But what is new is that the combination of imploding life cycles plus changes in both the sources and patterns of demand now threaten to obsolete orderly migration planning: the foundation of corporate value from marketing and sales for decades (see Figure 7-1).

It isn't just that the cash cow product relied upon for years is suddenly unprofitable, although that's one symptom. Nor is it that the number of viable competitors per industry is cut in half as the investment required to compete more than doubles on a period basis.[1]

Figure 7-1. Speed as competitive weapon: product/service deployment and pricing.

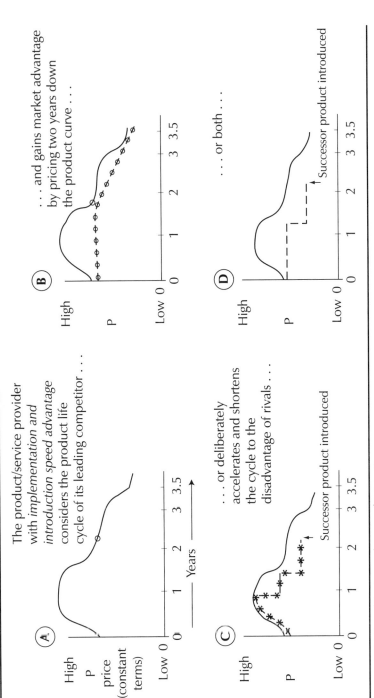

Source: VBM Consulting (www.vbm-consulting.com).

One cannot even contend that market introduction success now depends on achieving most of the profits during the first third of the product-service life.

The scarcely controlled chaos that confronts businesses in the new millennium signals to many that the old rules of engagement no longer apply. And there are potentially devastating consequences for those who continue down the old path. The competitor who missed the market window, yet smugly proclaims that his company will learn from the mistakes of others, is brought to earth quickly. Such deliberate delays provide no added intelligence but do increase the chances of forced exit from the market as at least two truncated cycles are missed.

The Value Mandate corporation and management must scramble to win today, then scramble to re-win all over again tomorrow merely to secure a top global leader spot. Without such day-in, day-out effort, there is a risk of slipping into a twilight existence as an uncertain, middle-tier participant. Uncertain because, in industry after industry, there isn't a viable middle tier anymore. Instead, there exists a churning shuffle zone of has-been leaders being passed by new entrants on the rise.

The company that fails to rebound and contend again starts down a very slippery slope. Forced consolidation or shotgun acquisition looms, as capital flows first and most to the few at the top. In the end, the company applying yesterday's defunct value tactics survives only as a brand name in its acquirer's stable, if that.

In such an environment, there is no acceptable alternative to developing new, effective value approaches to take the place of those rapidly disappearing. Merely stroking a value trend line and affixing some modest incentives is no more than a child's scribble. Incentives alone are not value leadership, but rather a part in an overall series of implementing tools in pursuit of maximum shareholder value.[2]

First things first: The right-thinking CEO knows that value leadership means developing the new value tools and ensuring that they work.

Within industries, the issue is not whether the product or service offerings will be replaced, but rather how soon and by whom. Displacement used to be limited to fully mature products. No longer. In the new market disorder, viable products and services with years of profits remaining are junked by rivals unless the originator destroys them first. Market responses adapt haltingly to each further step reduction in the economic life cycle, caused both by competitors and the company's own reactions. In Figure 7-2(A), a machining center's

Figure 7-2. Dealing with the ever-shrinking product life cycle: reactions.

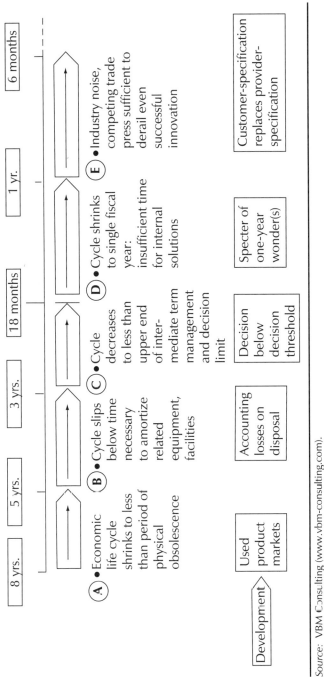

Source: VBM Consulting (www.vbm-consulting.com).

product slips from eight years down to five in terms of economic obsolescence, which is less than the equipment's physical life, properly maintained. That gap prompts an adjustment: support of secondary (used) equipment as the manufacturer finds that his old machines are competing for some orders with all-new production.

Shrinkage from five years down to three—Figure 7-2(B)—means that the equipment may incur a loss in accounting terms if sold at its ideal economic point of replacement, forcing management into an early decision about management by value versus management by accounting numbers. Further shrinkage to shorter periods—Figures 7-2(C), (D), and (E)—causes economic life to slip successively below planning thresholds, development, and planning time. Without dramatic changes in development speed, management finds itself facing forced market exit.

This chapter explores issues that include the splintering of postmigration cycle markets and necessary actions to generate value nonetheless. Established migration patterns splinter into temporary successor roles—interim positions that sustain the corporation over the intermediate term. Legacy corporations that are slow to change get buffeted by the waves. Those companies that price and position themselves based on the lead of another company are driven from the market. Markets transform too fast for reactive companies and their management.

Alternative distribution approaches emerge that are so much cheaper/faster/better than predecessors that the base markets are changed, not merely accelerated. Products are reengineered to exploit the rare financial advantages in an era when increases in real prices are as rare as an Internet company that makes money.

Disintermediation—the push to eliminate middlemen—enters the commercial mainstream on an accelerated basis, thanks to the Internet juggernaut. At issue is *not* whether customers prefer terrestrial stores and their friendly, face-to-face full service over online: extra service is always preferred if all other things are equal. But things aren't equal. The real question becomes whether full-service customers want to pay a premium and yet end up with the same goods.[3]

7.1 Eclipse of Migration Management

Migration management refers to the corporation's systematic approach for coordinating product introductions and withdrawals to patterns of demand in an orderly, recurring manner. This means having a plan that spans that product/service's full economic life, from launch till removal from the market. Specifics may change, but key actions comprising the cycle remain.

The Way It Was

The foundation of migration management is the momentum product—the leading (as perceived by competitors), compelling (as perceived by customers) market offering that establishes a new threshold for performance and pursuit.

Generation-to-generation migration management happens because of capital necessity. The enterprise with nothing more than a one-time product is little more than a project with some sustaining cash flow, which is not the same thing as a going concern. In order to attract the capital that separates the garage invention from ongoing business, a structure must be in place to generate a series of product introductions, not a single flash.

During evolutionary periods, changes occur to the components within the migration plan, and yet the base structure remains intact. Competitors who seek advantage over the market leader on the basis of price, features, and/or performance hope that their edge will be as enduring as their market propaganda proclaims. Customers become used to setting their expectations based on what the market leader offers. The leader rules the roost until dislodged by a radically different and clearly better/faster/cheaper alternative.

Product/service life cycles shrink during such evolutionary times, but only incrementally. The migration paths that persist are fortified by additional obstacles. In the mainframe computer markets of the 1960s and 1970s, IBM exploited customers' risk aversion with the not-at-all-subtle suggestion that no one was ever fired for selecting IBM. Backed by extensive, excellent repair and parts groups, the buyer ignored rivals' claims, even when the rivals had superior performance.

In such periods of persistent but predictable change, industry leaders may rotate from time to time, but the top suppliers' migration formula endures. Consolidation and competition at the margins is inevitable. Followers in rank positions three and four merge after it becomes evident that returns for each company alone are not enough to ensure future capital availability.

Once they are reinvented—with a new strategic plan and the

elimination of costly overlaps—the combined businesses take on the leader. But outright breakdowns in the established market migration are the exception rather than the rule. All legacy leaders need do is drop a few hints of compelling new performance to deflate all but the most tenacious rivals.

Legacy Leaders Face New Threats

Eclipse of migration management doesn't mean that contention just happens at a faster pace; it means that the entire migration structure is shattered. Unwinding the old order results in fragmented, almost random, markets, especially in industries and segments at the cusp of change.

Browsers. Orderly transition? Doesn't sound much like the Internet browser market after the roller coaster that started with Netscape's celebrated IPO in 1996. The browser market reduced to a give-away program aimed at setting up sales of other products. Without an insistence that each product make an acceptable minimum profit, the market becomes a series of dominos; the *next* domino will generate all the profits and cash flow after the string of product introductions.

Orphaned Services of Internet Service Providers (ISPs)

California's Xaact Corporation develops software packages that allow ISPs to differentiate their billing practices based on different groups of subscribers. The software facilitates highly individualized pricing and billing based on each group's timing and usage levels. But new low- and no-charge ISPs draw down *all* fees toward giveaway levels, thus removing motivation and funds for customer segmentation.[4]

The disorder progresses. Customers are no longer responsive to legacy corporations' sales stories about yesterday's leadership, products, or services. Instead, such commercial nostalgia threatens to become *negative* advertising, as customers—who are highly aware of fast changes in their own industry—tag the legacy corporation as being on the innovation *trailing* edge. Customers' blunt challenge question is: "What have you done for us lately?"

Aggressive competitors are motivated to confront the leader in the marketplace. Their key messages include: (1) Canned solutions have no place in fast-changing conditions; and (2) The bloated, legacy company committed to past answers is interested in pushing its past areas of investment, which are not necessarily what the customer needs.

The legacy corporation's managers come to realize that, in order to defend their rank and role in the industry, their company must meet and exceed every thrust. Reacting to the initiatives of multiple challengers with a smug "we'll wait and get it right" no longer works. To customers dependent on a flow of effective innovation for their success, such flip responses identify the company that has abandoned its innovation leadership role.

Unraveling the Old Order

Slippage from migration management to market disorder doesn't happen all at once, but rather in stages. Figure 7-3 shows the challenges an industry leader faces as the company progresses through four successive product generations over 15 years. The first product covers the first half the period. The next three are crammed into the last half.

Period of Competitive Advantage

Management's key challenge is to adapt to the abrupt shrinkage in each successive product introduction. Because shrinkage in the life cycle also means shrinkage of the period of competitive advantage within each life cycle period. The phrase refers to those quarters when most of that product's (or service's) cash flow and value are achieved. Or rather should be achieved, assuming that management has a clear understanding of how and when maximum profitability arises.[5]

The period of competitive advantage comes after the initial launch period—when negative cash flow is expected to gain share and to establish momentum—and before the struggling terminal months, when the cash cow becomes just a plain old money loser.

Fail to adequately exploit this sweet spot of product life, and management faces the threat of falling below the promised minimum return on which the development authorization was based. The occasional product might miss the internal rate of return (IRR) target without necessarily causing undue concern, but a pattern of deteriorating profitability and cash flow raises concerns that there is no value plan for product/service launches.

Figure 7-3. Deterioration of migration strategy: the old order under attack.

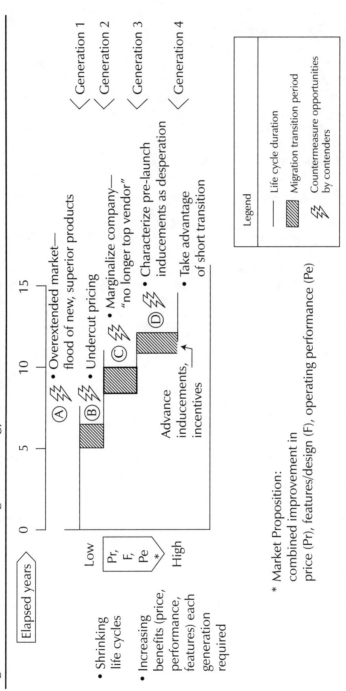

Source: VBM Consulting (www.vbm-consulting.com).

Pitfalls of Market Share Myopia

When workable product-value plans are displaced by reliance on market share alone, it demonstrates that management has no understanding of how positive cash flow will be achieved and sustained.

Share gain is important. But myopic focus on share alone—unless part of a greater value plan—often results in nothing but serial profitless markets. We call this the "Field of Dreams" approach to product development: If you build share (alone), the positive cash flow and value will eventually come. This approach is not necessarily true, Metcalfe's Law notwithstanding.[6]

In Figure 7-3, the three key elements of product/service differentiation (price, functional performance, features/design) are split between the two axes.

Undermining the Leader's Migration Strategies

Shaded areas in Figure 7-3 denote the market migration period, when the manufacturer tries to shift demand from one generation to the next without the competition stealing too many accounts. The lightning bolts signify competitors' actions (separately or together) to try to undermine the leader's orderly migration. The process follows four generations:

1. *Generation 1: Competitors take advantage of the product left too long in market.* Management of the industry's leading company decides to let their cash cow to graze out in the marketplace until results indicate it should be brought in. "Act before you have to" sounds fine in theory, but as long as the product is still profitable (or even merely cash flow positive) the argument arises: "Why leave money on the table?" And yet, there is a risk with leaving an aging product exposed in the marketplace too long.

As shown in Figure 7-3, the risk is that competitors take advantage by launching their newest, most impressive Price (Pr)/Features (F), Performance (Po) counter-products exactly when the comparison is worst for the established company. A few favorable technical reviews later, and some customers who are especially dependent on the market leader for their own technology advantage begin to harbor doubts.

With the established product (and its supplier) temporarily off-stride, the instinct of some competitors is to further encourage customer mutiny with a deliberate product proliferation strategy. They introduce a sufficient number of performance plus price advantages, and customers begin to look at the market differently, questioning the market leader.[7]

2. *Migration from Generation 1 to 2: Competitors respond to inadequate new advantage in second generation.* Slow to react to the new reality of the cash cow product's decline, management's migration approach is limited. The successor product is perceived by customers as an extension of the old. Management encourages that perception, giving the successor product a similar name, features, and appearance. Pricing adjustments are minimal.

If the industry leader's management make the mistake of implying that the next generation product is little more than an extension, then rivals pounce and proclaim the message even more, but with a decidedly negative spin. The rivals' goal is simple: inspire the greatest possible breach in customers' minds between the established provider's product and the new market offering.

If price cuts from Generation 1 to 2 have been inadequate, a deeper temporary cut can help reinforce customers' instinct to avoid the old, known product.

3. *Migration from Generation 2 to 3: Competitors act to change customers' shortlist selections.* The leader has now been off the pace for several years, so competitors' logical emphasis shifts to changing customers' perceptions where they count the most, in the shortlist of designated providers. "How-to" trade articles and studies deliberately ignore the one-time market leader, causing some customers to wonder if they are even still in the field.

4. *Migration from Generation 3 to 4: Rivals take advantage of short transition, other changes.* The industry leader has now awakened and introduced considerable pre-launch inducements to smooth the transition from Generation 3 this time: advance trials, promotion, publicity. Nimble competitors try to turn the leader's (soon to be ex-leader) change in tactics against it, by describing the change as desperation. If the tactics are new, and the transition period is brief (as depicted here), chances are high that something has been missed: performance problems, shipment delays, other confusion. Rivals know well where the most likely stumbles will occur, and offer their own products as alternatives.

But Sitting Out Is Not an Option

Faced with wolfpacks of rivals seeking to take advantage of any slip-up in migration strategy, little wonder that the desired response of many established leaders is to just avoid trying to create value in such vicious short-cycle environments.

After all, life was a lot simpler—and possibly a lot more profitable—when economic cycles were longer. When obstacles to new entrants were more formidable and a competitor with past reputation could almost always count that reputation alone as an advantage, not a deterrent to be overcome.

Desirable for some, implausible for all. Given the choice of competing on a long-cycle or short-cycle basis, almost everyone except some new entrants prefer the former. New entrants choose the shorter life cycles only because that means more decision points, which open up more opportunities to win the business away.

Unfortunately, the direction is instead toward shorter and shorter life cycles, with internal development time acting as the only absolute limit to cycle length. Those new entrants are here to stay, along with their short-cycle practices. Others are forced to mimic some of the entrants' aggressive tactics lest they lose control of too much market share and presence.[8]

Post-Migration: Getting the Future Value Path Right

Predictable, profitable market cycles are threatened. Outperformer management's imperative is to devise a replacement business model. Without new, workable post-migration value approaches, investing in innovation instead threatens to become investing in losses.

Beyond the Proclamations and Value Charts: Addressing Value Creation at Its Source

To increase value, a company's CEO proclaims that there will be significantly more spent on innovation in the future, with at least some of the funds coming from value-diminishing overhead. To lend credence to the statement, analysts note the corporation's historical returns on innovation in excess of weighted average cost of capital.

On the surface, the CEO seems to have a reasonable enough proposition. Indeed, the next chapter of this book concentrates on possible reductions in corporate general and administrative expenses in order to fund new value investment. Arguments in favor of funding shifts from zero return to 15+ percent IRR return are compelling, and value immediately increases.

But the value increases exist on paper. The indicated spread may no longer exist in a market undergoing monumental changes in all areas that affect possible innovation IRR. Factors include life cycle length, period of competitive advantage, number of competitors, and basis of competition.[9] Yesteryear's indicated innovation returns are not necessarily indicative of future returns.

Budgeteers smile at the CEO's proclamation. Shifting funds away from zero return applications (expenses) to projects with much higher yields is a no-brainer, and the corporation's generic value projection model cranks out far greater "value" with the new plug-ins inserted.

Some operations types can't help but be a bit more cautious. Statistical models can be instantly changed to reflect new anticipated value in the future. But without fundamental actions to reconstruct the corporation's value and business model, that's all the statistics are—hope. Don't confuse value modeling with value creation.

A company's legacy innovation prospect for statistical purposes presumes a six-year economic life, with most of the IRR-sustaining cash flow occurring in the second half of that life. The profile generates expected returns of 30+ percent, well above the WACC.

Today's climate demands a more realistic view of that profile, however. Halve the economic life and increase competitive intensity and you get both less revenue and increased required launch support. Then, the required period of competitive advantage shifts to years 2–3 instead of years 4–6. Suddenly, the old innovation numbers are obsolete. More importantly, six-year innovation prospects suffer when introduced into the far different three-year market environment, and returns are easily canceled.

The key issue is not how to devise a better number. Do not fall into the trap of allowing the budgeteer—obsessed with a statistical calculation program but oblivious to value dynamics in the business itself—emphasize a better number as a plug-in.[10]

Statistical manipulations can become a dangerous distraction, especially if management confuses all the number crunching with value creation. In the revolutionary marketplace of the millennium, value starts not with better number crunching, but with a better value and business model. A value approach capable of sustaining the corporation's future growth.

Alternative Paths

Faced with fundamental disruptions to the legacy value and business model (Figure 7-4), outperformer management faces an imperative.

Figure 7-4. Post-migration: getting the future value path right.

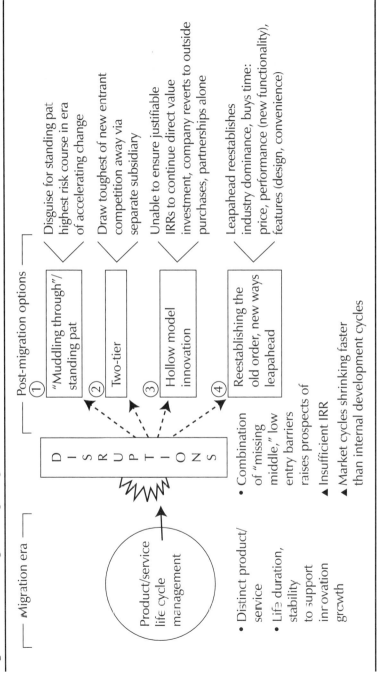

Source: VBM Consulting (www.vbm-consulting.com).

Either devise a new, effective value direction for the corporation or risk slipping back in the pack. Or lower. Or out.

There is no single one-variant-fits-all new value and business model. Competitive circumstances, growth aspirations, and the strength of the existing value-generating engine differ from company to company. And what worked today will not necessarily continue to succeed tomorrow, when the pace quickens even further.

Merely standing pat and responding to crises as they arise is to take no new value direction at all. The corporation's cash flow plunges, as expenditures once proclaimed to be vital investment in the future fail to bring the required business.[11] As shown in Figure 7-4 and discussed below, companies have four strategies:

1. *Muddling Through.* Also known as standing pat or extended inertia, muddling through is the antithesis of initiating of a new value and business blueprint. Nonetheless, just reacting to the challenges as they arise is sometimes confused with a coherent strategy, thus inclusion here.

The past is known, the future is not, which justifies inaction in the minds of many within the corporation when it is experiencing jarring disruptions (depicted in Figures 7-1, 7-2, and 7-3). But while standing pat may be the lowest risk course of (in)action during slow periods of predictable evolution, revolutionary change is another matter.

Management at the car maker that requires four years to develop an all-new model platform from scratch figures that it can afford to coast a bit since models change once every six years. There's still a positive time spread of two years.

But then new entrants—sporting lean overhead structures and faster development speed—actively encourage customers to be impatient with near-custom products that seem to be adapted to instant whims. The new model introduction cycle shrinks to three years, sometimes even shorter.[12] Suddenly, standing pat means missing a couple of market cycles entirely, along with all the value during those periods.

Standing pat is the highest risk position under conditions of accelerating, increasingly non-systemic change. "Don't fix what isn't broken" has already been displaced by "assume it's broken, before it is." But the lagging company's management are the last to know.

2. *Two-Tier.* Two-tier response calls for engaging the new, disruptive competition. This engagement is often through a separate

subsidiary or division, since traditional businesses operate with a far different pace, style, cost structure, and decision approach compared to their upstart competitors.

A global investment bank and a couple of U.S.-based drug store chains both resist their first instinct to add all-new Internet business as product lines within their existing terrestrial organization. This despite furious campaigning within the venerable business for exactly that type of arrangement.

Prestige and budget considerations are both strong incentives for incumbent terrestrial management to try to attach themselves to the new growth area. Corporate gamesmen see the handwriting on the wall. All want to ensure that they are at the center of what will become the corporation's major business by 2005.[13]

3. *Hollow Model Innovation.* One day, management wakes to discover that their development cycle time is longer than new product economic life cycles. Unless something changes, the corporation cannot help but slip farther and farther off the pace each year. Profitability, cash flow, and industry standing are all affected.

Faced with this value catastrophe, management concludes that they have no choice except to exit the internal development part of their business. Their reasoning: limited to their own internal development, the company will perpetually chase others in terms of both the number and pace of innovations. Loss of effective speed in the marketplace is at the center of management's value dilemma. Even if the response is a bull's-eye, delay means that the corporation is left with at most half a market cycle period to earn a full return. The best customers have already been captured by faster rivals and are unavailable to followers.

But opting out of direct internal development does not mean a retreat from innovation. Prospects are developed on a cooperative basis with invention-only companies. The innovation-bankrupt corporation rapidly becomes just plain bankrupt before long. Even now, corporations find themselves looking outside the corporation to ensure sufficient flow in their R&D funnel (refer to Figure 6-2). The funds that would otherwise be directed to speculative research are directed instead to more predictable process improvements.

4. *Reestablishing the Old Order in New Ways: the Leapahead.* Management redoubles its efforts to introduce a combined price, performance, and features proposition that reestablishes familiar generation-to-generation customer control. Emphasis is on performance alone, as both price and design are more easily matched by rivals.

But implementing such a Leapahead approach, consistently, is far easier said than done. A single major breakthrough sufficient to draw away customers from the competition is the never-ending dream of every CEO. But even the most prolific developers at best manage only one breakthrough per five years or so.

The time between breakthroughs is even longer at many corporations. Lotus developers spent the 1980s trying to match the early commercial success of 1-2-3™, without a comparable hit. Even if 1990s Lotus Notes™ is put in the major category, that means only one Leapahead-caliber breakthrough per decade. That is hardly enough for a stand-alone value approach and, of course, Lotus is now part of IBM.

Even when the breakthrough arrives, a lukewarm market reaction cancels all advantage. Digital Equipment Corporation ended its drought in leading-edge technology with the 64-bit Alpha chip in 1992. But sales disappointed, leading in turn to an ill-fated gamble in PC sales, never Digital's strength. The company has since been absorbed by Compaq.[14]

Apple's combination of design (features) plus functionality (performance) with its iMac™ related series appears to broaden the basis for Leapahead effectiveness. iMac's design catches the eye and creates press passion. But it is that series' operating speed that closes many sales. With a winning streak of three distinct models in a row in this series, Apple emerges as that most unique of market competitors: the corporation that can actually reverse its share trend lines in established markets.

But until others can effectively replicate Apple's features and functionality approach, this particular post-migration value path remains one that is unreachable for most. No CEO likes to hear of an opportunity "but not for your" company; presently, however, that's what this more difficult Leapahead approach means.

Moving On Early to Increase Corporate Value

Much of the discussion in preceding pages focuses on companies facing a threat to their business and value from nimble new entrants. The venerable old competitor hangs until forced to act, as all value from the old order dissolves.

It doesn't have to be that way. One of management's best methods for preserving and extending corporate value during tumultuous market times is to command the pace of industry change instead of embracing the no-win proposition of continually trying to catch up to opponents.

Time is money, literally. Value is determined by interpretations of management's projected cash flows, net of investment. If the exact cash flow pattern is moved forward by a year, management discovers that the return increases by 10–25 percent, sometimes more.[15] And that doesn't include some of the secondary value effects, such as: (1) superior access to early, price-insensitive customers; (2) reduced launch costs; and (3) future unsolicited early sales prompted by identification as industry leader.

Figure 7-5 shows the journey of the established corporation from reaction to instigation. "Don't fix what isn't broken" (DFWIB) thinking is solidly entrenched at the onset (1). Each company old hand has his favorite story about Armageddon avoided, only because management had "considered all the options" (read: did nothing). With wholly successful innovations still one chance in ten, inertia is elevated to the level of an attribute.

This reactive corporation begins to plan for migration to the next product generation when unit sales begin to decline. Move too soon, and inert management reasons that money is left on the table. Better to let customers tell you when to exit the market than risk reducing value by embarking on unnecessary actions.

Wary of new competition (2), management comes to the conclusion that the best way to disrupt the competition is to adopt their anticipated actions first, before they can act. With no market reputation and few early advantages except market speed, the new entrants are neutralized even before they begin.

Management's mind-set shifts from DFWIB to ABBII; that is, "assume it's broken, because it is." Inertia is no longer perceived as positive, but rather as a source of value destruction. Now, preparations for the next generation begin far sooner, when the rate of unit sales *increases* begins to decrease. The consequence is a steeper, shorter original product cycle, as management still seeks to achieve all available sales from the generation—but over a visibly shorter lifecycle period.

Combine the earlier transition to the next generation with shorter development cycle (3), and management has the opportunity to fundamentally reshape the marketplace to its own advantage. Caught off-balance, rivals now trail the pace set by another, and must exist on the value crumbs of the market.

Figure 7-5. Moving on early: the outperformer's case for progressing to the next market before it is required.

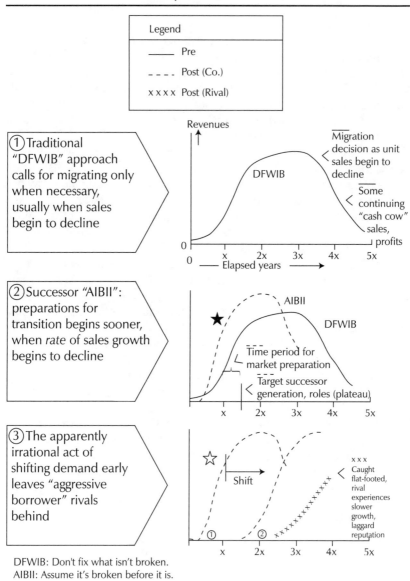

DFWIB: Don't fix what isn't broken.
AIBII: Assume it's broken before it is.

Source: VBM Consulting (www.vbm-consulting.com).

7.2 Changing Adoption Patterns: Threat/Opportunity to Value

Customers are the ultimate font of value creation. No corporate cash flow projection, no present investment-to-future value algorithm is credible unless substantiated by evidence of a supportive market foundation. Answers to two questions help determine whether an underpinning exists for new value development, or not:

1. Who and where are the critical customer groups counted upon by management to provide the sustaining cash flow during key products' periods of comparative advantage?
2. What specific actions have been taken by management to establish proprietary influence over key buyers and recommenders, and what indicates that the corporation's strategies will be more effective than competitors'?

One of management's key value imperatives is to influence future customer innovation adoption patterns to that corporation's advantage. Over near and intermediate terms, control of the industry's most valuable customers is a zero sum proposition, as identified by projected cash flow/revenue measures (CF/R). But customer innovation adoption patterns are changing rapidly, influencing account profitability and changing the pace and pattern of purchase. The once-familiar customer adoption curve (Figure 7-6[A]) is replaced by a successor which is barely recognizable: shorter, steeper, with pivotal purchase influence shifted from the last half of the cycle to the first (Figure 7-6[B]).

The retreat of established products' profitability undermines prior corporate value assumptions. It is not enough just to generate more products, sooner, in response to shorter economic life cycles. That additional investment is wasted without new marketing and sales strategies that ensure the new purchase influencers are captured, first.

Departure of the Cash Cow: Value Implications

At least for valuation formula purposes, Investment today used to translate into immediate value today. Historical IRR statistics suggest that a CF dollar invested today generates, say, six in Year 5. Discount that stream of future cash flows back to the present, and the *indicated* result is an increase in today's value for that corporation.

Figure 7-6. Changing innovation adoption patterns.

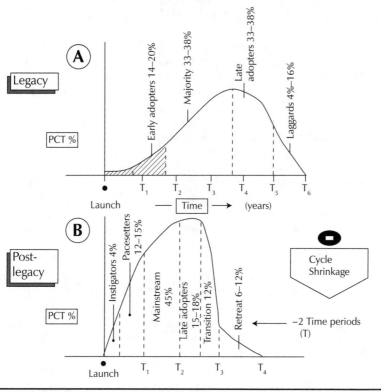

A. Legacy developed from Figure 1A, Hellmat Schütte, "Asian Culture and the Global Consumer," *The Financial Times,* Mastering Marketing, September 21, 1998. Reprinted with permission from *The Financial Times.*
B. *Source:* VBM Consulting (www.vbm-consulting.com).

But when the fundamental customer adoption model changes, the lockstep investment-to-value relationship also comes into question. Shortened life cycles mean less time to generate required returns. And demand peaks sooner in the life cycle: The corporation accustomed to marketing established and mature products finds itself without a viable strategy.

Migration Era: Value in Later Periods, Assuming Effective Advance Investment

In the migration era, the long-enduring cash cow product generates value for the corporation as a direct result of expenditures made years before. Expensive launch support, introductory discounts to encourage trial, saturation advertising, and special trade promotions all aim at securing as much share as possible, as quickly as possible.

Management's presumption is that a commanding market share means future high value. Once the product is established, the migration era math calls for deleting support costs faster than prices to customers are lowered. The result is a positive margin of cash flows to revenues, creating value. Demand is reflected by the familiar skewed bell curve pattern of adoption, such as shown in Figure 7-6 (top).

That goal is often achievable in markets of moderate competitiveness. Learning curve efficiencies (manufacturing and assembly) partially offset the downward pricing to customers. If we factor in reductions in advertising, promotion, and distribution budgets, management has reason to be optimistic about their positive cash flow projections. The cash cow's primary customers are Late Adopters (Figure 7-6[A]). Before committing to purchase, these deliberate foot-draggers justified their slowness as learning from the mistakes of others. They later discover that they are the ones committing the mistake, and that they cannot afford to take chances. Assuming that the selling company's product is established as a leader, the customer is relatively price-insensitive at this point.

Post-Migration Era: Value Contribution Plunges, from First to Worst

But the established manufacturer—with established product—faces guerrilla tactics such as those depicted in Figure 7-1(D). Timing *and* pricing *and* features *and* superior performance are brought to bear by earnest rivals who treat Late Adopter accounts as their market sustenance.

The once-lucrative cash cow product slumps to a cash-draining shadow of its former self, and can only be sold at deep discount. The rumors start, first within the corporation, then leaking outside: The company loses money on every unit.

A Catch-22 dilemma arises here. Management comes to the conclusion that support costs must be scaled back drastically to offset disappointing revenue, a strategy that's even more value-destructive. Material reductions in early cycle support elevates the possibility of value-crushing losses to certainty. Funding for trials, continuous ads, and special trade arrangements disappear, causing target account

awareness to plunge. The company risks becoming invisible to its target customers. Everyday trade noise, new product hype, and all the
information overload that comes with faster-paced times increases.
Increased promotion is required just to be heard over the din.

Critical Value Role of Earliest Adopters

Management's mistake above is trying to hold on to the old order too
long. "Assume it's broken, because it is" applies. Ineffective patches
just rob time and resources necessary to confront the new post-legacy
adoption pattern.

Post-Legacy Cycle

The adoption curve now is shorter and steeper. The Post-Legacy life
cycle (Figure 7-6, bottom) as shown is about two-thirds the legacy life
cycle and shrinking. The launch period is briefer, so both market
share and profitability must be achieved earlier. Mainstream demand
starts after about a year, representing almost half of the total. The
foundation of the legacy cycle, late adopters, are almost invisible.

But the most conspicuous change occurs at the beginning of the
cycle. Early adopters, once treated as a homogeneous group, are sub-
jected to segmentation analysis as companies seek to capture those
early purchasers and those who influence them.

Approaching the New Influencers of Corporate Value

The earliest adopter sub-segments rarely, if ever, identify themselves
voluntarily. Unless discovered and developed, the only outcome is unrealized potential. If customers are the ultimate point of origination
for the company's wealth, then instigators and pacesetters are the
gatekeepers.

Instigators (4 Percent of Total Demand, Estimated)

These are the post-Legacy *earliest* adopters. The category corresponds approximately to *innovators* in Figure 7-6(A) with one critical
difference: Targets are actively pursued just on the basis of their expected influence on subsequent buyers.

Thus, the high-impact approach of deliberately placing clothes (Versace) and cars (Jensen Interceptor) with celebrity users, which generates wanna-be responses.

There is also the techno-snob appeal. Grid laptops in the 1980s and Nokia's 9000/ 9000i Communicator in the 1990s were both featured at trade shows. Only. This helped convey exclusivity for executive and imitating middle managers alike. But early pricing eliminated the temptation for the latter to try to somehow slip one into his expense report.

Pace-Setters (12–15 Percent of Total Demand, Estimated)

A second earliest adopter category, pacesetters, hope that they are confused with desirable instigators. In order to gain maximum benefit from this proclivity, the seller times this category to be just a few months after the first. Rate of growth for pacesetter demand depends on the seller's methods for: (1) identifying and securing the right instigators—those exerting the greatest influence on subsequent buyers; and (2) seller's access to the media for extending the message.

Mass advertising is rarely effective in generating full demand from this category, as it erases the exclusivity sought by the pacesetter. Alternative means can be as subtle as personal evaluation by an industry leader or as deliberate as managed spot shortages to create word-of-mouth about waiting lists.

7.3 Exploiting the New Disintermediation

The motivation underlying the instinct to *disintermediate*—to cut out the middleman—is to increase corporate value. The original producer/developer (and sometimes the customer) covets the intermediary's 8-to-12-point margin as value that they forgo.[16]

Value from disintermediation increases in importance in the millennium because of automatic price increases. Warranted or not, perceptions in the marketplace are that arbitrary, unexplained price increases in excess of the rate of inflation are a thing of the past. Any sellers violating the unwritten rule risk being branded as gougers, with ongoing value destruction as penalty.

Even if there is evidence of new inflation after 2000, it will take several years for the old price-tolerant attitudes of the 1970s and

1980s to become reestablished. After all, long-standing inflationary expectations were only broken after more than 15 years of somber price news.

Until (and unless) that happens, companies must look inside for value. They must look to their internal cost structures rather than pricing as the primary mechanism for increasing corporate value. Which means special attention is paid to the role of intermediaries, given continuing perception that some services are overpriced and others unnecessary at any price.

Conflicting Value Contribution Perspectives

The age-old contention from producers and some end-user customers is that many intermediaries are paid for doing nothing, or their actions are worth far less than the amount being paid.

Such contentions are rarely admitted openly. Easy pricing opportunities are over, which means that effectiveness in squeezing dependent middlemen may make the difference between whether or not the corporation's cash flow projections are met. And that, in turn, determines value.

The initial reaction of resellers, wholesalers, agents, and distributors to being bypassed is a combination of shock, denial, and indignation. After all, they insist, each are essential cogs in the commercial chain from order to customer. But essential is another of those accolades that is only credibly provided by the customer. And with new alternatives for middlemen emerging daily—including various forms of end-user self-access on the Internet—fewer and fewer services are seen as irreplaceable.

Intermediaries who deal with physical wholesaling and transfer services that require massive infrastructure investment argue convincingly that true savings from trying to do it yourself are usually far less than many realize. The small Northern California producer may dream of selling directly to Ralph's Supermarket in Southern California—thus keeping the margin for himself—but try that, and the producer probably wipes itself out of business with all the extra, unanticipated costs.[17]

The momentum for value bypass is accelerated when ultimate user and producer team up against the intermediary. For example, both airlines and their business travelers agree that adding 8–10 percent to a travel ticket for routine flight arrangements, which can easily be executed online, is absurd.

End Users Face Disintermediation: Are You Willing to Pay for Inefficiency?

At the end-user level, momentum toward value-based distintermediation focuses on a simple question to customers: "Are you willing to pay more for a familiar but less efficient process?" Raising that question encourages end-user customers to make decisions based on the value impact of middlemen to them, personally.

Downes and Mui set the cost-per-transaction of a routine banking transaction at ten cents, compared to $1.07 for a comparable face-to-face transaction via bank teller. *The Economist* suggests that "processing (an airline) ticket on the Internet costs $1, compared with $8 through a travel agent."[18]

At a corporate level, as described in the next chapter, those bypassing their own procurement department can expect to save 70–80 + percent on transaction charges for recurring purchases such as office supplies (assuming pass-through).

The "are you willing to pay more?" question above is one that beleaguered intermediaries hope is never asked. Which is precisely the reason why it does emerge. Advertisers for retail online brokers are particularly artful in suggesting that traders may not be operating with a full deck if they are paying a "full-service" transaction fee for an ordinary buy order when do they own research.

Defending the less efficient, more expensive service is the spin doctors' nightmare. For every story about a folksy country bank where customers gladly pay more for a friendly smile and greeting from the teller, there are ten hardboiled New Yorkers who respond, "Great, so long as I'm not charged any more than your most efficient service."

Deflation stories, Priceline.com-style name-your-price bidding, and free-everything on the Net emboldens customers to hold out for special treatment. Companies have to pay attention to this attitude because stickiness (customer near-term loyalty) is critical whether the store is terrestrial or cyber. Even if the seller cannot sustain a highest service/lowest cost combination for long, the hit-hungry merchant's temptation is often to do whatever is necessary to first lock in the customer. Then one can deal with the profit problem at another time.

The New Disintermediation: "Bit," "Box," and "Crossover" Products/Services

In the emerging disintermediation era, the starting point is separation of businesses into the two broad categories popularized by MIT's

Nicholas Negroponte: *bit* (data) businesses versus *box* (physical) businesses.[19]

Crossover

A category in between bit and box is referred to here as *crossover*. These are physical products capable of being transformed into online alternatives, either now or in the future. Examples start with the most familiar: books, music, videos, photos, software, data storage, investment research, and online newspapers.

Normally, adapting products and service to the channel would be considered backwards, even suggesting regression to product-push arrogance of times past. But with possible online cost advantages of a times-ten magnitude, management is challenged to see how far they can reach in converting pure box products into crossover hybrids. Hybrids might be new forms of services or new service-product combinations never before introduced to the marketplace.[20]

The U.K. version of the *Encyclopedia Britannica* costs between £845 and £3,000, but a CD-ROM version costs a mere £125. The CD version has far fewer illustrations than the hard-copy, and some users prefer flipping through the pages to clicking the return button on their PC's keyboard. But compact size, speed of information access, and certainly weight all favor the alternative channel. In 1999, Britannica went a step farther, and solved the pricing problem comparisons to Microsoft Encarta and other online encyclopedias. Britannica made the transition to an online encyclopedia service, with no price at all.[21]

The imploding insurance market also encounters an urgent need to shift from face-to-face service to online, revolutionizing industry cost, business, and value structures. Conning & Co., estimates that industry consolidations plus retirements mean a drop of 20 percent in the numbers of career life insurance agents and their counterparts selling property and casualty coverage.[22]

Combine these manpower shifts with radically lower cost channels, and the question becomes not whether agents in the insurance business will go the way of high payout commission salesmen for encyclopedias, travel, stocks, and cars, but rather how quickly.

The old insurance industry value model was based on a first-year payout structure unthinkable in almost any other industry. Whether the coverage was sold by direct mail, through brokers, agents, or a branch office, first-year payouts regularly exceed premium inflows in the legacy value model (Figure 7-7). With channel costs about the

Figure 7-7. First-year life insurance premiums, by channels.

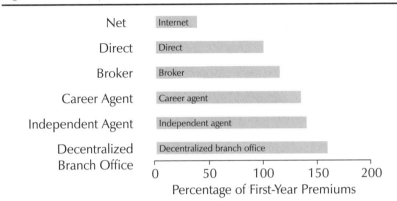

Source: First Boston, in Thomas Easton, "$800 Billion at Risk (Bits Not Brokers")", *Forbes Global,* November 29, 1999, page 96. Reprinted by permission of *Forbes Magazine* © 2000 Forbes 1999.

same, insurance company viability and value for shareholders largely hinges on future lapse rates; that is, how long the insurance remains active, with full premiums paid.

Betting the business on lapse rates is treacherous, because the insurance company is not in control. Customers can terminate for a variety of reasons—budget restraints, alternative coverage, or belief by the insured that the coverage is not needed anymore—and the insurer cannot prevent it. Spend the time and money necessary to actively reduce lapse rates, and the extra costs easily cancel out any benefit.

But add radically lower cost channels to the prospect of an agent shortage, and the industry value model shifts tremendously. With Internet sales costing less than 25 percent of first-year premiums on a comparable basis (Figure 7-7), companies face an opportunity to liberate themselves from dependency on lapse rates to determine value creation effectiveness. CS First Boston estimates that use of toll-free telemarketing or Internet saves around 20 margin points compared to independent sales agents, and 10–15 points compared to captive agents.

The tough truth? As with *Britannica,* above, an army of high-commissioned agents switches from a resource to a liability, except for customers eager to pay a much higher premium that reflects the cost differential. For those companies slow to shift to the new value model, acquisition by those willing to make the change looms. Suggests *Forbes'* Thomas Easton: "For those (insurance) companies that can move to electronic selling, a hugely profitable business awaits. As for the rest of the insurers? There're the ones that are truly at risk."[23]

The ultimate limitation to the speed of crossover transformation is customers' pace. The engineering outsourcing brokerage company, Sub-contract UK, is owned by Wigart, the Swedish information company. Wigart's U.K. operations parallel its similar businesses in Sweden, Finland, U.S., and Australia in which the company capitalizes on demand for outsourced components. Historically, specifications for outsourced components are made available to subscribers by mail, with engineers receiving the detailed drawings in paper form.

The switchover to online is progressing rapidly, but old habits are sometimes difficult to break. Engineers' preference for working with physical blueprints, rather than electronic media, slows growth, Wigart management admits.

Online Sales Alternatives: Six to Seven Points to Propel Value

Net-direct sales have emerged as a distinctive channel that by their nature tend to attract adaptive customers with a built-in appreciation for the benefits of channel speed and simplicity. But adaptive does not mean insensitive to price. To the contrary, the Net buyer knows all about prospective cost advantages up to 10:1, and is not about to be shortchanged.

Back in the Net pre-history era of 1996, antiviral software producer McAfee combined early sales momentum with pricing that passed many of the cost advantages of online onto its customers. The combination made the competition look like gougers, as McAfee prices fell as much as 50 percent below the competition.

The result: McAfee effectively redefined the entire antiviral software business to its own advantage.[24] It then dominated that new segment that it created. Now known as Network Associates, McAfee acquired key rival Dr. Solomon's. Invariably, the less-expensive channel almost always prevails. It prevails more often when that lower cost channel is the Net.

Heard the phrase win-win? Now familiarize yourself with *lose-lose*. Companies in fields from PCs to toys, travel to insurance, destroy value by permitting internal politics to prevail over channel common sense. No one wants to be excluded, with the result that disastrous dog-cat multichannel compromises are devised, destroying value while alienating everyone:

Online Buyers

If online end-user purchasers even *begin* to suspect that prices are pulled upward because of pressure from resellers, the online traffic departs in droves. A few clicks of the mouse, or reference to one of the comparative sites, is all it takes for traffic to be lost to the online competition, perhaps permanently. And the online grapevine is even faster than the one within your corporation.

Resellers

As long as the resellers still control least half the industry's profitable volume, they remain a force with which to contend. Furious at dual channel suppliers undercutting them with better deals online, the reseller can swing volume on the floor from one nameplate to another in a matter of days.[25] But even that reseller is bypassed if the market judges its extra services as not worth the extra cost.

Or worse, the terrestrial store is treated as nothing more than a display case for online purchases by buyers. The avid book buyer samples the cappuccino at the opulent Main Street book emporium, but then jots down the book title and orders from amazon.com later that evening. The target objective for sales cost reductions through conversion to online is half the total selling costs, expressed as a percentage of revenue. Assuming that sales (including sales administration and overhead) comprises 12–14% percent of revenue, that amounts to six to eight margin points savings on an ongoing basis. Or about a $250 million increase in value per billion dollars in annual revenue. A narrowing of that company's Value Opportunity Gap by a quarter of a *billion* dollars.

That's a target. The exact amount depends on factors including the current channel mix and value-channel strategy, and the exiting of present dominant structures such as preferred supplier arrangements. Complex systems sales and relationship management arrangements are not conducive to online success.

But much of what is sometimes embellished by the salesperson as "relationship selling" turns out to be little more than order taking. A test: offer to pass the salesman's former sales commission to the customer as a temporary gesture of goodwill, and see how many "relationship management" accounts are eager to lock into online alternatives, such as automatic reordering arrangements.[26]

7.4 Extending Value Advantages of Confirmed Order Scheduling to Marketing and Sales

Chapter 5 introduces confirmed order scheduling as an essential requirement in demand pull/ flexible assembly. But flexible production works only if the specific build schedule for that day is known and all arrangements are made at least several days in advance.

The daily production plan, flow configuration, cell assignments, and inventory arrangements can all work as intended assuming that everything is planned in advance for that specific build date. There must be sufficient assurance that all arrangements regarding delivery of JIT parts and component subassemblies will be completed. There must also be no order cancellation without stinging penalty to the salesperson.

Foot-Dragging: Holdover Legacy Employees Slow to Adapt

Despite the advantages to the corporation and its shareholders from deployment of *full and complete* demand pull/flexible production, some stand in the way, for their own suboptimal reasons.[27]

The predecessor stack-and-wait manufacturing manager was kicked upstairs to a ceremonial management role long ago. He doesn't understand demand pull/ flexible, which seems backward to him. His reasoning: "The work in process should go to the machine, which is supreme, not the other way around." He has good reason to fear that his group will be among the first to go when cuts are made to adapt to the new sourcing order.

Inflexible suppliers and their purchasing office counterparts built their longevity on the basis of the more parts, the more suppliers, the better. The prospect of a stock-out stopping production ceased being a serious concern years ago, yet the structure remains. The structure is still in place because there are jobs tied up in the bureaucratic maze of contacts and parts.

Legacy sales and marketing employees also have a considerable stake in the old order. With the customer declared as king, a salesman with even a moderate order book commands enough clout to bully the manufacturing process to his will. Never mind that his frequent cancellations and last-minute orders destroy more value than they're worth. And never mind that there's suspicion that the corporation is paying top commission rates for mediocre goals. Until and unless an individual profitability assessment is developed, executives insist on referring to these as the corporation's value creators.

Selling from Excess Finished Goods Inventories: Value Destruction Consequences

The foot-dragging sales rep complains that any departure from the tried-and-true practice of manufacturing to finished goods inventory threatens his sales performance, and ultimately results company-wide. There are enough things missed already as it is, and any removal of the excess-inventory grease that makes everything work could cause havoc, he reasons.

The ubiquitous new car salesman blanches at the prospect of having anything less than multiple models of every type and color on his lot. Other salesmen want to know that multiple warehouses are filled with product, so they can quote confirmed delivery dates with confidence.

This is sales suboptimalization at its worst. Appeasing these salesmen means robbing the corporation of value. Investment in standing finished goods inventory is passive, absorbing high-cost funds that could be alternatively put to use on high-yield internal projects or other value projects.[28]

Costs involved in storing, handling, and transporting finished goods inventory are invisible to the customer, who is the ultimate determiner of value. The end user doesn't care whether the product has been in storage ten minutes or ten weeks, handled by two workers or 200. Such costs are not part of the performance, features, and price equation on which the customer bases his or her decision to buy. With no apparent positive value role, the logical assumption is that these invisible expenses instead destroy corporate value.

Radical, High-Value Product Sales: No Inventory, Confirmed Orders, in Advance

In the old order, the productive salesman rules supreme. After all, without revenues, there can be no value. But new methods emerge for limiting finished goods inventories, such as sharing data about goods in stock. But partially fixing a defective approach so that it destroys less value doesn't make such sense. Especially if the alternative is a system designed from the onset to enhance new value.[29]

The selling approach that corresponds to demand pull/flexible production is advance confirmed orders. Before assuming that this is a disguised product-push mentality, consider this: Sales demand is facilitated by the substantially lower costs and prices made possible through the radical production breakthrough.

Porsche Boxsters were subject to huge backlogs in the late 1990s, with style, price, and features combining to set demand ablaze. Sales of Stevenson Furnaces (American Standard) are helped by a dramatic increase in model range, as are Clark shoes in the U.K. Levi Strauss sells custom fit jeans through advance, confirmed orders. Virtually every major U.S. personal computer maker also sells through advance, confirmed orders.

In the U.K., Daewoo of Korea institutionalizes the approach by using salaried salesmen rather than high-pressure, commissioned closers; with low prices doing most of the work of the close. In Japan, confirmed order selling is long established in the auto industry and has expanded into other sectors. Salaried salesmen travel to the customer's home with catalogue and specification form, driving their own car to the house as the test drive model. In addition to the sales attributes in the performance-features-price assessment, additional corporate value is created, as there's no need for an expensive main street showroom, with all the related costs that such an operation involves.

Extending Demand Pull/Flexible's Advantages: Perceived Custom

As the millennium gets under way, radical systems, approaches, and technologies that create new corporate value extend beyond their original industries into other sectors.

Jc-I-T's Costanza, Lean Enterprise Research Center's Jones, and others are propelling the potent three-in-one combination of radical demand pull/flexible production, component assembly on flexible platforms, and preferred supplier program–based procurement from car making to almost every industry struggling to resolve two apparent contradictory forces: (1) lower unit cost and increased production throughput with (2) greater model diversity and speed-to-market.

As the advantages of demand pull/flexible and related developments (described in Chapter 5) become better known and more widely adopted, companies that are slow to react will have to scramble to avoid being left behind. The stack-and-wait producer melts away in the face of demand pull/flexible and related watersheds. Initially, inertia rules. Gradually, whole industries radically transform themselves. Whatever the spark, the direction is set. When one or two competitors in the industry convert to demand pull/flexible, the market advantages in terms of lower cost, greater diversity, and speed exert tremendous pressure for others to change as well. Three levels of players face the new challenge.

Level 1: Backs against the Wall

The first to act are those who must embrace the radical performance improvement approach because they have no other choice. These adopters have no other choice but to ensure success of the new performance order or fade away.

Level 2: Advantage Seekers Who Don't Need to Change (But Do So Anyway)

Once the radical approach is proven, next come the opportunistic managers of corporations that don't have to change (at least not yet), but proceed anyway, in order to stay ahead and increase pressure on laggards who either cannot or will not make the value transition.

Level 3: Laggards: From Top to Bottom in Three Years

Last to convert are the laggards, who in some instances have fallen from low-cost producer to high-cost producer in just three years. Rendered numb by their collapse and the failure of the "don't-fix-what-isn't-broken" mind-set, some are no longer viable, going concerns, although residual cash flow and communications from management will try to keep hold of some past supporters for a while longer until collapse is finally undeniable.

In the car industry, today's reality is that a manufacturer probably cannot obtain financing unless the plant and plan calls for flexible production with platform assembly. The new approaches aren't magic bullet solutions, but rather minimum requirements for continued operation, enforced by capital providers.

In other industries, New Order (demand pull/flexible production incorporating platform component assembly) has been embraced by

Level 1 companies (discussed above), with some inroads into Level 2. But the New Order will not become dominant until sometime in the next decade. Jet engines, shoes, furnaces, PCs, and bathroom fixtures are all ripe for the New Order.

Micro-marketing to specific needs of preferred customers is combining with the ongoing need to be an industry low-cost producer. The new imperative: Optimize the maximum number of unique models from the minimum number of components and distinct product platforms.

The goal: to provide customers with desired range and diversity, but without fragmenting the provider company into unfocused model proliferation or uneconomic one-off custom manufacturing. This goes hand-in-hand with achieving significant increases in the range and diversity of products offered to market, but without canceling the ongoing economic advantages of demand pull/flexible caused by too many parts and related costs.

Levi Strauss now produces customized jeans to fit specific contours for additional cost. Toyota only assembles a car when a customer makes a firm order, and suppliers only provide parts when the Japanese auto giant needs them.

But that increased flexibility for customers is not without some limitations. Custom Levis require a wait of several days, contrasting starkly with the norm of instant fulfillment when it comes to ready-made clothes for Gen Xers. The Toyota customer is limited to choosing from a list of options and alternatives that are updated from time to time.

Compaq management acknowledges that competition from direct sellers such as Dell (direct online sales) and Gateway (print ads combined with inbound telemarketing) has forced them to become increasingly vigilant about inventories, effective speed-to-market, and sourcing flexibility.

Compaq has followed in the steps of Dell, IBM, and others to build on a modified made-to-order basis, which some refer to as "near custom." Balances are achieved between number of separate components and numbers of distinct models. Model diversity is emphasized: The customer is encouraged to believe that he has almost limitless flexibility to configure his equipment the way he wants. But the options are limited, and the customer must wait a couple of days for the configuration to be completed. No "take it home right now" impulse close.

Variations in the type and level of processor power and memory emerge as a key ordering difference among ultimate customers. Compaq trades some market control to achieve additional speed-to-market, implementing what is now the PC industry norm (except for Dell) of shipping units to distributors-resellers without processors or memory. The resellers adapt the Compaq unit for the customer's specific needs.

In terms of value consequences, some results of the changes are already apparent. An increase in the annual number of inventory turns (sales divided by inventory)—from 7.1x to 10.4x—frees up more than $5 billion by mid-1997. Those funds are now available for critical new development efforts.[30]

Tsunami Marketing: Overwhelming the Competition with Deliberate Proliferation

"Tsunami" means tidal wave in Japanese. As used here, the word describes product model/service version proliferation aimed at:

- Overturning the existing market order, displacing the leader all at once, instead of through gradual incremental tactics.
- Dominating the segment so that customers almost completely forget competitors. Buyers look to the new dominant to find out "what's new," reasoning that most of the innovation momentum is controlled by that source.

Tsunami reflects the challenger company's rejection of incrementalism. Merely contest the industry leader on a launch-versus-launch basis, and the lead will always remain just out of grasp. The challenger carves out a small niche, but little more. Customers are inclined by inertia to continue past behavior until and unless there's a reason to do otherwise.

Incrementalism by the challenger works to the incumbent leader's advantage. Using the challenger's pattern of one major introduction every six months, management at the legacy company organizes accordingly. New features are absorbed, or their characteristics incorporated in the legacy company's responding launch, three months later. Three months later is still near enough to the incremental challenger's timing for the incumbent to still appear to be in command of innovation in the segment. Some legacy companies actually succeed in transforming their slowness to market into an asset. Deleting one or more of the drawbacks of the challenger's product, the incumbent argues that "we took the extra time to get it right" in trade advertisements.

If such an image persists, the challenger's image is scarred by a perception of unreliability compared to the market leader. Customers have yet another reason to stick with their traditional source. But the legacy company's defenses can be overwhelmed by the tsunami wave. The challenger starts producing too many new models, too quickly, for the leader's plodding reverse engineer-or-deflect strategy. The challenging corporation makes full use of its two greatest weapons: (1) development superiority when it comes to high-demand innovation and (2) speed, in all parts of the organization. But such advantage depends on two key factors. First, that all activities and functions in the development sequence are of equal fast pace. Any advantage from lightning-swift innovation is canceled if market testing or supplier arrangements lag, as the pace of the innovation introduction to market overall can be no faster than the slowest component activity.

Second, the corporation's sourcing capabilities and in-place resources and processes fully support highest volume/highest diversity/lowest unit cost production as described for demand pull/flexible production in Chapter 5. The challenger who can introduce no more than two new models per year because of limitations in his batch-and-queue production commits corporate suicide by trying to implement a tsunami-type approach in the marketplace.

Effective, deliberate proliferation means distinctive, high-demand products and services. Each product must command stand-alone appeal for the proliferation approach to work. Cosmetic alterations (such as changing trim or nameplate) or mere line extensions are accurately perceived by knowledgeable customers as imposter innovations, leaving the erring company worse off than before.

The key test is whether each separate new introduction commands strong stand-alone appeal. Otherwise, product distinctions blur. Customers cannot tell one model from another, and eventually don't care. Competitors take advantage, contrasting their own crisp product family boundaries with the errant challenger's approach.[31]

Tsunami works best when purchasing motivations can be narrowed down to just a handful of critical decision factors. The greater the number of points of differentiation attempted in the introduction, the greater the risk of proliferation without an edge.

With its 1998–1999 new models, Nokia established the design momentum for the top-end segment of the cellular phoneset market. Not just smaller models, but more distinct models, as well. This one-two punch propelled Nokia to industry leadership roles, as most rivals offer only one or two models in the smallest size bracket.

Lamy established minimalist style as the dominant purchase motivation for its premium range pens. The German company emphasized highly functional, even stark designs with minimalist beauty. Multiple Lamy models relegated the limited range of 1980s bulbous fat pens to a different era and executive mind-set. If a pen could suggest the difference between the ruthless high performance of the 1990s versus meandering excess of the 1980s, Lamy is it. One of the most notable tsunamis occured, appropriately, in Japan. Yamaha Motorcycle Division dominated the domestic market of the early 1980s. Challenger Honda Motorcycle doesn't merely mounted a strong battle against the legacy-incumbent, Honda almost swept Yamaha aside in two years, 1981–1982.

How? First, by isolating design diversity as the most important purchase motivation for Japanese buyers in that market. And then, implementing its model proliferation strategy based on that discovery.

Honda introduced 80 new models over the two years, catching Yamaha in the full force of its tsunami. The fading leader could only manage 34 models over that same period.[32]

Although most of the examples of tsunami involve product segments, that does not mean that services are excluded. Citibank developed new mortgage products and innovations at a pace that put competitors on the defensive. UPS's European unit tried to generate new momentum against FedEx in the market for small, overnight parcels to the U.S. by offering multiple delivery times, including early morning to some locations.

Schwab Online and E*Trade both tried tsunami tactics in the booming online retail stock brokerage marketplace. Each attempted to establish itself as the online brokerage alternative of choice for the short time that traditional terrestrial brokerages remained asleep.

Success keys for services are comparable to those for multiple product introductions. Each separate service must command distinct appeal on its own as a stand-alone service. Otherwise, confusion and cannibalization result. An effective services proliferation strategy requires more advertising and promotional support than products, in order to compensate for the absence of physical presence.

7.5 Field Sales: When "Added Value" Means Value Destruction

The sales force needs to join other major potential sources of new value from operations. To do this, the force's direction and resources must be recast away from the account manager (AM) as caretaker of previously discovered accounts and toward major revenue source development.

The account rep has no match from other paths to market in some regards, despite cost disadvantages.[33] The effective field salesperson can actively position the product or service while most alternatives rely on the buyer to initiate. The catalogue cannot gently influence the client's purchase specification at an initial meeting, establishing advantage in responding to the Request for Proposal issued weeks later. The account manager can.

Ads and trade promotions are at best indirect inducements. And Net data overload threatens to reduce ad effectiveness still further, as customers take active measures to separate critical intelligence from cyber-fluff. Many ads are disregarded, others actively blocked as the enabling technology to do so comes to market.[34]

New Emphasis: Major Revenue Sources

And yet, as new, far lower cost paths to market emerge, management is forced to rethink the field salesperson's value role. The order-taking caretaker posing as self-proclaimed "relationship manager" is no longer affordable. But the developer of major new revenue sources pivotal to starting the all-new revenue stream is close to indispensable.

The AM who maintains the account created years ago by someone else while picking up the odd, on-site order is no longer tenable. Combinations involving pricing breaks, spot contacts, automatic reorder from stock, preferred supplier arrangements, third-party agents, and online order placement now emerge as viable substitutes for servicing the stable maintenance account.[35]

As this maintenance account has already been cultivated, no new major outlays are anticipated. Thus, the sales issue is less a matter of creating all-new demand than to harvest embedded demand already in place. At $350–$500 + per successful close (EN 7.33), the field salesperson appears to be a highly inefficient means for such mere order-taking.

By contrast, the AM as major new revenue source developer has no substitute. The rare Corporate Key Contributor (Chapter 3) salesperson who makes the target account his own while rivals are left to dropping off business cards at reception is a corporate source of value. He or she establishes the base for future worth that didn't even exist before. Either from an all-new target company or from a new opportunity within an existing contact.

This emphasis on new value creation forces tough decisions about the composition of the salesforce. Some forces are dominated by a rotating caretaker AM, but few or no true CKC business developers. In such a case, management's challenge is to reconstruct its sales staff for the new goals. The alternative is to rely on other channels entirely if no suitable top talent can be attracted and retained.

Three specific opportunities emerge for the CKC addition to establish a new value sales base, described in the pages that follow: (1) circumventing the customer's Request for Proposal Stage; (2) master contract placement; and (3) relationship sale with diverse decision makers.

Overcoming the Customer's Request for Proposal (RFP)

Speed-to-market doesn't apply just to product development and launch plans. The salesperson with superior speed attempts to insert his corporation's proposition at the beginning of the client's decision process—before competitors even submit a bid; before the specification is even finalized. Ideally, the salesperson is involved as the buyer's original requirement is first being formed.

There is evidence to support the contention that sales closed prior to reaching the formal Request for Proposal stage usually mean higher prices and greater profits for the winning company. Pre-RFP issuance, the effective CKC salesperson can act to help make the bid a one-supplier proposition. But after the RFP is issued, almost any seller can win the bid.

Once specification is set, qualifying bidders are invited to submit their best prices. Automated bid systems, such as General Electric Information System's Tradenet, further expand the potential universe of pursuers by automating spec information, making bids easier for smaller suppliers. The goal is to eliminate the RFP step altogether. That requires a salesperson capable of influencing the buyer's specification early enough in the process to eliminate the need for other bids. Such influence needs to be conducted in a manner that is readily defended as best meeting the customer's requirements.

For the salesperson, this means maintaining sufficient knowledge of the buyer's coming purchase plans to anticipate those items best suited for Selling Corp.'s products. It also means establishing sufficient contacts with principal decision makers to make favorable modifications in the spec stick.

These two capabilities help distinguish the caretaker account manager from the true value creator. The first is unaffordable. The second creates worth for the corporation and its shareholders that didn't exist before.

Master Contract Placement

With face-to-face sales costing ten times as much as some other transaction alternatives, piecemeal unit sales by reps is unthinkable. As the corporation's most expensive channel, the field salesman now is affordable only when matched with the highest-dollar-level, highest-profit-margin products and services.

Better still, the salesperson should be armed with contracts. As the millennium nears, experimentation with online sales of consumer big-ticket items such as cars proceeds. But no one suggests that the Internet can help Selling Corporation secure a slot as one of only three sources in the client's new preferred supplier program (Chapter 5). Nor is a Web page and electronic catalogue of much help in negotiating the new, complex master contract covering multiple products and years.

The emphasis here is on new contracts. Merely presiding over the existing arrangements doesn't create additional worth. Rather, such actions only serve to slightly reduce the possibility of loss. Staff the corporation at any level with employees who merely maintain the present level of performance, and status quo is about the best one can expect. More likely, though, the salesperson and corporation satisfied with coasting invite rapid decline.

Over the near to intermediate term, the battle for any account tends to be zero sum in nature. Rapid expansion of preferred supplier programs and similar initiatives reduce the number of winning sellers. If Selling Corporation doesn't succeed in securing one of the target customer's preferred supplier roles, that probably indicates that a fierce rival has succeeded. For the provider that loses out, the likely consequence is exclusion from that buyer's business for five years or longer.

Relationship Sales with Diverse Decision Makers

The master contract, the preferred supplier arrangement, and influence on product/service specifications all help avoid low-profit RFPs.

All three initiatives by the stellar field salesman, however, presume existence of a special relationship with the preferred customer. A relationship that extends far beyond conventional seller-buyer roles.

Relationship management is another of those phrases that has been reduced over time to the level of mere corporate mantra. Such a relationship once implied a connection between salesman and customer so strong that the external salesman exerted as much clout within his customer's company as many internal senior managers. This relationship endured, and could hardly ever be unwound by competitors.

Now, management may use the word relationship, but it means much less. Today's salesman slaps the mantra on any company where he is on a first-name basis with at least one decision maker or key influencer.

This weakened version of relationship management is value-destructive. The reassuring phrase provides the false impression that everything possible is being done to develop the value from that account. But unless there's solid evidence of new value creation in the form of RFP avoidance, preferred supplier roles, and/or master contracts, chances are great that the relationship is far less powerful than the salesman conveys.

The difficulty of securing a true relationship management role increases as the number and dispersion of decision makers grows. Bigger sales mean involvement of more decision makers, with the salesman's traditional contacts far removed from decision influence.

Often those original contacts are no longer employees of the target customer at all. The salesmen accustomed to contacting their individual liaison in the old-style staff-intensive corporate purchasing department are shocked to discover that the department shrank to improve profitability months ago. The old contact is gone, along with the glad-hands style of business development that once sufficed.

Major sales that potentially cross departmental boundaries require a sales rep who can command credibility with different disciplines, even if the initial proposed placement is to one department only. The telephone operating company—already perceived by its account primarily as a default supplier of voice and data equipment and services—is put on the defensive when attempting to place advanced Internet Protocol services with target customers.

But that gap becomes an insurmountable chasm when the salesman hopes that his customary contact with the IT manager/telecom manager is sufficient to position his proposed sale on Internet and intranet services. Not only is the traditional contact only one of several key decision contacts, but the IT/telecom manager's goals are likely to be diametrically opposed to major systems that encourage greater user access, such as corporate-wide intranets.

Value Destroyed by Bottom-Trawling Quotas

Trawlbottom Corp. is the name used here for a multi-billion-dollar worldwide technology services unit. Trawlbottom is competitive worldwide in most product/service categories of its industry, but not the services category representing the highest source of ongoing profits for the company's largest competitors.

Senior management at Trawlbottom Corp. figures that up to $100 million in profits are abandoned each year by an approach that lags far behind rivals.

Top management is interested in closing its own Value Opportunity Gap in this key product area.[36] The start point is to recognize why value is being destroyed at Trawlbottom Corp.

Extrapolating Underperformance: Future Projections Based on Yesterday's Value-Destroying Performance

Nowhere is the value-destructive impact of "steering the corporation by staring in the rearview mirror" clearer than when annual sales projections are based primarily on the prior year's base number. At Trawlbottom's services unit, the manager repeatedly tries to scale back new sales targets, based on the fact that the increase is more than 75 percent above prior year levels.

But the 75+ percent statistic is both meaningless and misleading, as it merely reflects the cumulative effects of setting bottom-trawler goals several years in a row. Better to base expectation on comparative performance of those doing it right than sustain under-performance by extending past underperformance into the future.[37]

Trawlbottom Quotas: Missed Markets, Abandoned Value

The value destruction represented by minimalist projections is pushed down into equally modest individual sales quotas. The department manager wants to get along with his field salesforce, and thus goes along with pursuing less than half of the available and accessible market.

The result is that Trawlbottom's sales and resulting value from this product sector are deliberately "dummied down" until those levels match the trend line of past performance and the talents of the incumbent field salesforce.

Extraordinary Rewards for Mediocre Results

Corrections to the pattern of value destruction are delayed further, since salesmen are rewarded for underperformance in industry terms. The goals are based on legacy sales levels, extending underperformance still further.

Department and individual sales quotas emerge as potential value destroyers when goals are based on past underperformance trends. Management insists that the quotas represent "maximum shareholder value." But if the quotas are developed first with the goal of assuring bonuses, rather than maximizing corporate worth, the inevitable result is value destroyed, as certain as if a trade secret was stolen by a competitor.

As long as the quota structure based on past trend data persists, the threat of slipping backward to suboptimal, value-destroying performance remains. The alternative approach of setting corporate targets based on percentage of available demand usually helps counteract the result of years of persistent low target setting. Until and unless the alternative view is pursued, management probably believe that the division's salesforce is creating value.

New attention focuses on the adequacy of the quota method to keep pace with corporate efforts to accelerate growth. The salesman scrambles to reach his quota number for the present fiscal year, distorting performance in the fourth quarter as excess sales are pushed forward to the next year if possible, adding a personal cushion for the next quota negotiation.

Although positive for the individual salesperson, these efforts to make quotas are value-destructive for the corporation. The salesperson's energies that might otherwise be directed at the next client are instead involved in a nonsense activity of shifting numbers on paper.

7.6 Pursuing the Unconventional, Fast-Developing Markets

Maximizing shareholder value calls for early pursuit of high-growth, high-value market prospects. Whole categories of opportunities exist that focus on market development. These coincide with R&D's cluster development course, as described in Chapter 6 (see "The Case for Cluster Development").

In our environment of accelerating change, the strategy of reacting to others' market initiatives is only slightly less precarious than standing pat.

Where to look? At the millennium, some of the so-called "can't miss" market areas have a disturbing sense of shakeouts waiting to happen, particularly in Internet retail. How many more book/electronic trading/auction portals are needed? Probably less than there are now, and that's not even taking into account the one-a-day IPO additions.

Does that mean that there are no broad areas for proprietary new business development? No. Two are summarized here: (1) marketing to the customer's cost side and (2) selling to high-intensity markets.

Marketing to the Customer's Cost Side

The indications are that there is a boom market for products aimed at cutting internal costs. With pricing flexibility limited by deflationary mind-sets, sometimes the corporation's key value growth opportunity is within. Systematic cost reductions combined with efficiency and productivity improvements create value opportunities within the selling company.

Revenue-side products and services help customers grow their own profit stream. Products for resale help the customer earn merchandising margin. Marketing studies, such as new product or customer investigations, are growth-oriented. Search fees for top salesmen are justified on the basis of expanding revenues.

From the selling corporation's perspective, the key problem with revenue-side emphasis alone is that orders stop when the customer's customers stop buying. Management argues that the environment isn't right to stress selling, as recent campaigns have disappointed, so why not come back later, after the customer's customers start buying again?

The customer's revenue-side purchase mentality turns conservative in flat to down periods, despite the fact that for two decades down periods have been typically sharp, deep, and brief. Short slumps, combined with accelerating change, typically lead to fast recovery and argue for continued expansion through such flat periods. But rare indeed is the Buyer Company CEO with the vision to look beyond short-term dips affecting the industry or the economy overall as an opportunity to expand while others become mired in short-termism.

Selling Corporation management gnashes its teeth over their predicament. Consistent earnings and net cash flow growth are perceived as essential to supporting the corporation's stock price and value. Short-term thinking can lead to corporate value destruction, especially if preserving EPS growth is ranked higher by management than sustained cash flow generation. Potential divergence between near-term EPS levels and ongoing value becomes especially acute as revenues flatten. Profits from sales are off at Selling Corporation, made more acute by price cuts to preserve share. The only way that management can make "the number" (target historical EPS) is to cut costs.

Assuming that easy cuts have already been taken, that leaves substantial invest-spend programs aimed at creating significant new value in key parts of the corporation. Management argues that stretching out the corporation's transition from stock-out-based procurement to preferred supplier programs can be deferred with minimal effect on the corporation. Competitors smile to themselves. When management diminishes their corporation's value on their own, no assistance is needed from them.

What does work are specific products and services aimed expressly at helping customers cope with their new cost-reduction obsession. But legitimate cost-side innovations cannot be improvised over the short term; they require as much or more development time and attention as revenue-side counterparts.

The potent expense-side product—which is not a hurry-up expedient but rather a mainstream innovation of Selling Corporation—can be as marketable in expansion periods as in economic downturns. Management of the purchasing company committed to maximizing shareholder value in *their* company views every dollar of savings as funds to be transformed from low (or negative) value use to positive value creation, when directed at the company's major new value initiatives.

Some examples include sensors that diagnose cracks in underground pipes before disastrous leaks occur, reducing repair expenses dramatically. Corporate videoconferencing can cut intracompany travel costs, freeing funds to flow directly into high-yield internal projects.

From the buyer's perspective, financial benefits from cost-side product/service purchases probably seem far more secure than purchases based on seller's expansive claims about revenues that can be achieved. Vendor's forecasts of revenue benefits for buyers reflect the seller's goals first. Even if those optimistic scenarios prove to be realistic, profits from such revenue-side purchases are only achieved when costs are also on schedule.

Selling to High-Intensity Markets

High-intensity here refers to the passion of the end-user customer. Delight when the product or service truly exceeds high-end expectations. This is not to be confused with late-1990s standard-issue baffleprose, the syrupy "delight the customer." High intensity means unbridled fury if the customer's experience is negative.

Positive or negative, the high-polarity situation can represent an extraordinary sales opportunity and a legitimate market edge. On the positive side, the unsolicited word-of-mouth recommendation is far more effective than advertising; which, after all, is just the company putting itself in the best possible light. Customers of Seattle-headquartered Nordstrom have built a franchise business out of that retailer's uncompromising pursuit of positive recommendations.

But the poisonously negative customer perception may be even more promising for developing proprietary market advantage. That is, assuming that the replacement is able to radically improve perceptions, decisively and consistently. Circuit City runs one of the largest home electronic chains on the East Coast. Management was already well-acquainted with the age-old complaints about used car dealers' treatment of customers—the old maximum-pressure, humiliate-'em-but-sell-'em-at-any-cost tactics. Circuit City management figured that they could flip extreme negative perceptions by treating the customer as royalty, not as a mark. The results have been remarkable.

Kingston Technologies competes in one of the world's most ruthless markets: add-on memory chips for PCs. Margins are paper-thin for most industry participants, with the result that most companies figure that they can't afford exceptional service and support.

Kingston figures that it can't afford *not* to provide Nordstrom-level attention to its key customers. For a moment, forget the margins. Kingston's extremely motivated employees go far beyond the requirements to ensure that customers act as positive referrals in the future. The contrast with the conventional in that industry makes Kingston's stance all the more visible.

8

Unwinding the Crony Bureaucracy

Toward the High-Value Support Administration

Managers want to build empires; shareholders, numerous and unorganized, have often been powerless to stop them.
— "All Fall Down," *The Economist*,
February 28, 1998, page 81

8.1 The Value-Destroying Crony Bureaucracy
8.2 Toward a Systematic, Value-Directed Approach
     to Administrative Functions
8.3 From Full-Service to Self-Service: Intranet Revolutionizes
     G&A Costs, Performance
8.4 Downsizing: One Last Time, from the Top Down
8.5 Value-Critical Implementation Issues

The crony bureaucracy and its imperial headquarters are no longer affordable. Management of the Value Mandate corporation faces an imperative to fund significant increases in value-driving investments. In order to remain competitive. To narrow the company's Value Opportunity Gap. To maximize shareholder value.

The crony bureaucracy receives the bill. The outperformer CEO first seeks to fund the stepped increases in value investment by unwinding the corporation's crony administration and its underlying functions, processes, departments, and buildings.

The working assumption that a new value investment with an internal ROI of, say, 35 percent, can be pursued only if those funds are first generated from redesign or elimination of expenses creates deliberate dilemmas in the corporation. These tough choices in resource allocation are often disregarded as administrative budgets are extended because of inertia rather than need.

The corporation that consumes 40–60 percent of its own internal cash flow for continuity is like the farmer's family that eats the seed corn instead of planting it. Opportunities for value growth are self-limited because the support administration is too rich. First in line for funds, the champions of innovation projects must cope with whatever is left over. Management at established "Venerable Corp." wouldn't think of jeopardizing consistent maintenance of headquarters' impressive front lawn for a couple more projects in one of the firm's key development areas.

As a result, Venerable finds itself outflanked by hair-on-fire entrepreneurs who invest 200 + percent of their internal cash flow each year, every year, in frantic search for the next marketplace miracle.

The first time Venerable loses a market battle to these upstarts, the longer-established company's spin doctors are practically convincing as they characterize the event as a fluke. But by the *third* such rout, the upstart owns the global market, and Venerable is left reeling in disarray.

Another excellent company bites the dust as it believes its own market and cannot or will not adapt fast or significantly enough.

In the past, Venerable's crony bureaucracy always seemed to sail above the frequent reorganizations and most urgent expense reduction initiatives. Armed with the most skilled office-politics minds in the company, the cronies expertly defused or at least deflected to lower ranks the most strident call for efficiencies.

But at least at the Value Mandate corporation, the CEO recognizes all the palace intrigue and its eager players as value-destroyers, spinners' illusions notwithstanding. Endgame.

Double-digit general and administrative expenses, expressed as a percentage of revenues, face mandatory shrinkage to single-digit levels. In some cases this means *halving* the corporation's G&A/R ratio, such as happened at Xerox Corp., during the brief regime of CEO Rick Thoman.

Once *one* major copier manufacturer reduces its G&A/R percentage from 12 to just 6 percent, competitors face a mandate to follow.[1]

A competitor who wants to stay that way wouldn't dream of permitting a rival to establish an uncontested six-point margin advantage on the factory floor. An unassailable cost and performance advantage at HQ is no less devastating to continuing competitiveness.

For continuing support operations, the tired bureaucratic stratagem of linking threatened reductions in services with reductions in budgets (whether or not such a connection exists) is recognized at the top as a ruse and prohibited. Only those functions with confirmed track records in terms of both performance and costs will survive as part of tomorrow's streamlined, high-value support administration.

For noncontinuing support functions or portions, prospects are abrupt. The owners of the corporation now recognize that any support that is *not* the most effective and efficient destroys value. Shareholders ask, "Why should we continue to subsidize value-destroying operations and reduce our own returns as a result?"[2]

But even for those activities that do survive, continuity of the *function* does not ensure continuation of the present processes or their providers. The lowest cost alternative is probably *not* addressed unless holdover approaches are rigorously challenged. Unless management selects the best performing support solution regardless of source and process, value will be destroyed relative to potential. The Value Opportunity Gap widens, and shareholders are, in effect, asked to subsidize the inefficiencies.[3]

The basic math of value progress is straightforward. Link the requirements to create value and close the corporation's VOG to general and administrative expenses, and the case for material reforms to the administration's embedded cost structure becomes a mandate.

The starting point in that endeavor is significant expansion of the number of value investments with the size and yields to significantly impact the VOG. Value investment isn't limited to external markets, but it also includes key internal "expense-side" investments capable of generating continuing hard dollar savings, such as intranet infrastructure, which we address later in the chapter.

In order to encourage tough but necessary decisions about spending for show versus spending for growth, outperformer management's working assumption is that all value investment is met through internal cash flow.

Practically no corporation in a growth industry can finance its full value investment requirement out of internal cash flow, so the practical consequence is to require reductions in some ongoing expenses. For analysis purposes, say external financing is available only to the extent that new value investment requirements cannot be covered internally.[4]

Suddenly, all the "essential" expenses associated with the crony bureaucracy take on a whole new light. The Northwest U.S. corporation's grand campus with corporate logos on all the doorknobs? Even if the value impact of that misdirected investment is just one prototype forgone, who's to say that the missed window wouldn't have been the unassailable blockbuster that disrupts the old order in the industry? Separate dining rooms to keep the suits from having to eat with the lowly workers? The prices at this restaurant are expensive: three medium-sized value investment initiatives forgone, two VOG points missed. That make-work "strategic planning" assignment devised for the friend whose last solid contribution was five years ago? These exemplify two more value opportunities left for the competition to discover.

The second aspect of administration's stretch-performance goal is more difficult to quantify than the first (cost reduction, efficiency improvement), but equally important: improving the administration's support.

Anyone can slash expenses viciously if consequences are removed from consideration. But unless structural reforms accompany those cuts, the expenses quickly return. Required: a systematic way to continually raise those issues that the professional empire builder hopes will never be asked, such as:

- What will *really* happen to the corporation if the incumbent activity (or component) is discontinued, consolidated, or significantly redesigned and simplified in terms of content, service, and means of delivery?
- What is the fastest/most effective/most efficient means for fulfilling those service and provision roles that continue, anticipating both best-of-industry and best-of-function alternatives?
- Finally, assuming that any "best solution" today is only temporary, how long will it be before today's approach is displaced by something better? And how can that successor "best" solution be anticipated while the existing one is still in place, so that management can act before forced to do so by competitive pressure?

The last question is especially jarring to the department empire-builder who treats the department as his personal fiefdom. Those days are over. The owners of the business refuse to pay for the crony bureaucracy any longer.[5]

8.1 The Value-Destroying Crony Bureaucracy

The crony bureaucracy obliterates corporate value, in absolute terms, with dollars squirreled away in the crannies and deadwood positions of budgets. This occurs in relative terms, as better processes or cheaper/faster/better employees are mysteriously passed over while holdovers with no advantage except inertia are retained.

When inertia rules, shareholders pay the price in terms of a discounted corporate value and a gaping VOG, which leaves the corporation increasingly vulnerable to the takeover wolfpack.

Fat Returns

The occasional shock downsizing action aside, evidence suggests that administrative fat in many companies is far from eliminated. Even after conspicuous delaying, outsourcing, and outright elimination of positions, people, and departments irrelevant to corporate value, the administrative ranks continue to grow.

A 1998 study sets U.S. white-collar workers at around 51 million, with the percentage of white-collars in the workforce increasing ten points over a decade, from 30 to 40 percent. That increase is only partially explained by the long-term swings from manufacturing to services.

Extravagant regrowth during extended boom periods is a factor. The underused data clerk *never* survives the acknowledged recession, but as soon as times are good again, management's mind-set reverts back to the old thinking: What's the harm of a single extra hire?[6]

Expansive economic times mean that the shakeouts that periodically wring out marginal functions and excess budgets are deferred indefinitely. With no immediate threat of an internal crash crunch, spin doctors seek to repaint the padding in planning, corporate communications, and general administration as necessary to protect the growth. "Growing, but lean" rivals "maximizing shareholder value" as the spinners' best verbiage.

Fortune's Thomas Stewart suggests that selling, general, and administrative (SG&A) expenses increased a full point as a percentage of revenues from 1986 to 1997, translating into $13 *billion*. Or, as Stewart notes, "more than the annual revenues of all but ninety U.S. corporations."[7] That amounts to $13 billion in value destroyed. Far more if you take into account the lost value from returns forgone as internal capital was steered into period expenses rather than value investment.

Explanations for the apparent continuation of the fat are surprising but not inexplicable. Surprising—as 1986–1997 spans the peak and crash of the 1980s leverage buyout boom; one of the favorite themes of the LBO raiders was increased efficiency, made necessary by the need to service debt piled on by those same raiders. Surprising—as the 1986–1997 period includes the 1992–1994 period of highly conspicuous downsizing announcements.

But trying to use downsizing to calibrate available staff for manpower requirements is like using a shovel to stir a can of paint. Crude at best, possibly worse than nothing at all, especially as the consequence is an inevitable bounce between over- and understaffing.

During lean periods, flat to declining sales mean that G&A expenses appear to be exploding out of control when expressed as a percentage of revenues. Pressure mounts to cut G&A immediately, in any way possible. Arbitrary staff downsizing actions have the advantage of speed if not effectiveness.

The return of expansive expectations is the signal to career bureaucrats that the pressure is off. In the best traditions of the never-ending corporate budget shell game, it is time again to plump staff while inventorying the various forms of phantom staff and funding authorizations that can help deflect future cutdown attempts.

Expense Multipliers

To scale down the crony bureaucracy while generating additional funds for value investments, we need to understand the principal *expense multipliers* within high headcount/high budget departments.

As used here, the phrase refers to characteristics that result in an apparent staffing requirement, such as (1) range and number of responsibility items; (2) clients and contacts, both within and outside the group; or (3) documentation requirements. Increase just one of these factors, and the amount of additional work is minimal, perhaps not even requiring additional staff. But increase all three multipliers at once, and the number of positions requested soars.

Understanding the multipliers is also critical to unwinding the bureaucracy's costs and how they are getting met. Eliminate or significantly reduce one key multiplier, and staff growth (and its costs) can probably be capped. Eliminate two categories, and the fundamental nature of the service is changed. Eliminate more than two, and material changes in how the service is provided emerge, along with significant reductions in ongoing costs and thus increases in corporate value.[8]

Precedent, Procurement

Procurement/purchasing is one of the two sourcing functions, as we described in Chapter 5. Also it is one of the corporation's largest bureaucracies.

Head count coverage starts high where the core philosophy of the department is to prevent stock-outs, almost regardless of cost. That mind-set in turn leads to proliferation of the number of suppliers, number and range of separate components (stock-keeping units [SKUs]), and the number and complexity of monitoring processes and forms. Each element is padded: If five is enough, ten is good, and twenty great.

The more SKUs and suppliers involved, the more frenetic the pace of activity in the department becomes. Each additional part means extra storage, documentation, handling, and tracking costs. Each added supplier means credit and payment tracking, price negotiation, delivery status verification, and quality assessment.

The product of SKUs times vendors times documentation times storage of it all causes staff numbers to soar. To the leader of the department, it seems as if a 10 percent increase in SKUs plus a 10 percent increase in suppliers and staff means almost a doubling of administrative expenses.

Alternative approaches to individual parts stocking (SKU reduction campaigns, component supply), processes (online ordering), and supplier relationships (preferred supplier programs) emerge to scale down both scope and cost of procurement administration while increasing effectiveness and speed. Suddenly there are fewer staff needed and less to record, store, and handle—less expense required to perform the department's essential functions.[9]

Other Expense Multiplier Situations, Elements

Somewhat parallel multiplier situations arise with the corporation's various expense centers. Key expense drivers include the number of staff and the number of separate expense centers.

The greater the number of administrative employees, the greater the costs, and not just because of staff salary and overhead, but also because of the costs that result from interaction with others. Factor in a marked increase in the number of separate organizational units, and the CEO *swears* that there's a 50 percent increase in costs because of all the endless meetings.

But the meetings are symptoms. CEOs such as Robert Ayling at British Airways deliberately try to discourage unnecessary conferences and the "meetings culture" in general, as posturing discussions are sometimes confused with work.

Other actions strike directly at the cost drivers themselves. Incumbent internal functions that destroy value, or that are eclipsed by a superior alternative, become subject to discontinuation. Third-party outsourcing, internal outsourcing (captive contract group or remote office), and end-user direct access can change the entire nature of the services provided.

8.2 Toward a Systematic, Value-Directed Approach to Administrative Functions

A systematic approach to examining G&A functions involves examining the "customer" and "supplier" environments within the corporation, which emerge as corporations seek to set up internal trade arrangements that mimic outside markets.

Assessing the Support Group's Value Contribution: *Different* Customers

Value is ultimately judged by the customer— the intended beneficiary—or at least the one who receives the bill. Identifying the support group's customer and relevant service scenario is critical to accurately assessing the relative value of the G&A service provided and either to increase the incumbent service's value or seek an alternative.

Welch on Job Security

Shortly after succeeding Reginald Jones as chief executive of General Electric in 1980, John F. Welch, Jr., faced pressure from employees to provide answers to their key concern: job security. Maximizing Shareholder Value is fine in theory, but self-preservation comes first.

GE administrators sought clarification from the new CEO about their future roles in the corporation. Bureaucracies such as strategic planning and internal audit had grown rapidly at GE during the 1970s as part of Jones's command and control superstructure. By the early 1980s, the internally proclaimed "renown" groups were massive.

But there was now concern. Early statements from the new CEO emphasized market impact and resiliency more than measurement and control. Then there were the stories about Welch's impatience with vapid questions from clerks seeking to fill in blanks in their budget questionnaires.

Staff didn't like what they heard from Welch: "Companies can't give you job security, only customers can."[10]

Sales stars yawned. The pacesetters had learned the reality long before: Their only security is their sales numbers and their accounts' ongoing profitability. They are only valued as much as the expected profits from the next major sales campaign.

But the administrators were sweating bullets. *What customers?* Lacking any external revenue, the implication was that there were no "customers" to vouch for the support bureaucracy. Instead, stature at headquarters was assessed in other ways. In *Control Your Own Destiny or Someone Else Will*, Tichy and Sherman describe how a new GE hire in the 1980s was at first perplexed as staff wandered into his office, staring at the ceiling and saying nothing. His visitors, he learned, were counting the number of ceiling tiles, comparing the sum with the number in their own offices. One quick calculation, and the visitor knows whether to kick ass or kiss ass. And that B-School finance course is finally put to use!

Interpretation, Payback

The impact of Welch's "only customers can" comment was devastating, even more outside GE than within. CEOs who had anguished for years about their own introspective, value-draining bureaucracies welcomed the long overdue expression of common sense.

An early consequence of "only customers can (give you job security)" was abrupt pruning of overview staff at GE and at other companies as well. Anyone with "planning" or "analysis" in their job title became a possible headcount reduction target.

Some interpreted Welch's comment as justification for a general staff-bashing. "Customer" was narrowly defined by the bashers as applying only to buyers from other companies. Extend such thinking to its extreme, and anyone who generated any revenue from outside the firm could be perceived as a value contributor, while those without an external revenue connection might languish as second-class corporate citizens.

This was an exaggeration, but at some firms, not by much. Payback was sweet for some division leaders who had been forced to squirm over a fraction of a percentage point variance just a couple months earlier.

Some staff-bashing was revealed to be diversionary. This field sales laggard might have a connection to the external marketplace, but that alone didn't mean that he was a corporate resource. To the contrary, in relative terms the laggard destroys corporate value if a counterpart at a rival company sells more, at a higher margin. Perhaps the struggler thought that by diverting the spotlight, the ax could be diverted too.[11]

Then there were those employees who generated no external revenue and yet who clearly increased the corporation's worth through their actions. They might have included the insurance buyer pro who could slash ongoing premiums by 10 percent with no sacrifice in coverage; the CFO whose impeccable timing in equity and debt issues could be worth two points off the WACC, compared to rivals with lesser financial talent; or the procurement-function senior administrator who would spearhead preferred supplier, component purchasing, and online order initiatives simultaneously to adds tens of millions to the corporation's value.

Addressing the "Customer" Issues

If *only customers can provide job security*, it is necessary to understand the different placement or "selling" environments that the G&A support groups face.

Despite the splash caused by Welch's comment, follow-through has been incomplete. Certainly in terms of two questions that emerge if "only customers can" is applied to corporate G&A overhead staff: (1) who are the G&A staffs' customers? and (2) what are those customers' purposes in requiring support?

The second question is central to a thorough assessment of the support service and its value to the company. The new corporate staff function emerges because a competitor has one and arguments to not be left behind strike a resonant chord, or someone read an article proclaiming the imperative for a chief (fill in the blank) officer.[12] Far less, if anything, is heard about whether the function serves an essential role for prospective clients within the firm or is irrelevant.

Assume that the internal client for the G&A service is one of the company's top product managers. The success of this client's launch plan to the outside market hinges on the availability of extranet applications that permit external customers to dynamically configure their own proprietary version of the company's products. This flexibility provides a huge edge over rivals limited to one-size-fits-all sameness.[13]

If the selling corporation's internal Information Technology group opposes intranet and extranet development (because of concerns about losing control, for example), the product manager is sunk even before starting, unable to bid. Even if IT is a reluctant developer, an unremarkable extranet application produces the same result, as the company can no longer assume that rivals will miss using the Net to establish a major account development edge.

Practically speaking, the standing G&A staff group is limited to "selling" its services within its own corporation.[14] Table 8-1 depicts four such internal customer groups and scenarios for G&A services. Each group is characterized by its primary purpose, which shapes the nature of its highest value support.

Market Support: (1) New Development

New Development internal clients require several forms of G&A support in order to launch all-new products and services. The novel revenue and future cash flow sources it generates are critical to corporate value growth.

Such sources include market research requested by the project manager to hone the product's design and to effectively segment diverse buyer groups in a way that accelerates market share gain, or professional pricing of the product to optimize market penetration rate and business case cash flow.

For the staff "provider" group understandably concerned first with its own survival and secondarily with benefits to the corporation, various tactics help ensure that there is no competition.

The suboptimalizer's dream arrangement is involuntary allocation. Product groups elsewhere in the organization find that they are "charged" for a pre-set percentage of the G&A unit's budget,

(text continues on page 220)

Table 8-1. Toward an assessment of G&A relative value.

	Market Support			Staff Support
	1	2	3	4
Profile	New Development	Incremental/Extension	Terminal	Staff-to-Staff
"Marketplace" Scenario	New innovation. Cash flow and profit negative, 6–12 + mo. Early share grab	Life cycle extension revenue. Marginal revenue vs. marginal cost considerations	Cash flows to end of life cycle Requirements: (a) spot support to slow pace of CF deterioration, (b) consistent, aggressive cost decreases	Expense centers recast as service centers. Rough marketplace simulation, as clients have no true cash flow
Support Assessment	Overall Internal Rate of Return versus next best alternative	(2) $ Cost, Plus Margin (Cost/Increm. Rev.)	(2) $ Cost, Plus Margin (Cost/Increm. Rev.)	$ Cost
Support Issues	Projected support for specified development, launch plans	Marginal support of add-on or extension to point of forecast unprofitability	Period-by-period support based on very short term cash flow projections. Quick exit.	Lowest Cost Sustainable Service Based on Spec (not just spoiler bid)

How Suboptimizers "Beat the System"	Unrequested allocation Inertia lock in: No reconsideration, deletion once established Underestimation Overestimations: time period (t), overall return Underestimations: support speed, cost	Unrequested allocation Inertia lock in: No reconsideration, deletion once established Underestimation Absence of ongoing profitability assessment: no internal funding for support	Unrequested allocation Inertia lock in: No reconsideration, deletion once established Lack of replacements: non-viable products cannot cover support costs	Unrequested allocation Lock in: No deletion once established Overly complex spec by internal provider as protection against competition
Beating the Suboptimalizers	Simplifying support requirement to broaden external competition START with standardized support available from multiple sources: How can requirement be adapted?	Simplifying support requirement to broaden external competition START with standardized support available from multiple sources: How can requirement be adapted?	Simplifying support requirement to broaden external competition Standard external alternatives prescribed, internal on exception basis only	Simplifying support requirement to broaden external competition START with standardized support available from multiple sources: How can requirement be adapted?

Source: VBM Consulting (www.vbm-consulting.com).

whether they use the services or not. The white-collar featherbedding is automatic, regardless of whether the internal service provided is perceived as spectacular or disastrous. If disastrous, substitutions or corrections might be made in the future, but that matters little to the product/project over the near term, because the business has been lost.

Budget tricks entrench the internal supplier regardless of performance. With budget dollars "already paid" in terms of overhead, the internal supplier can make a persuasive argument: You're already paying for us anyhow, might as well use us.

If charges for internal services are automatic, any action by the internal client to look outside appears wasteful to headquarters. The internal client who finds homespun capabilities lacking must pay double: first by the allocation, a second time for the external service from market.

Then there's the form of "payment" to internal service providers, as contrasted with the external. Payments to the internal suppliers are made in the form of pretend budget dollars, whereas the external alternative requires actual currency. The latter means more forms, barriers, and signatures, with the same question asked repeatedly: We already have some people who do that. Why not use them?[15]

Imposing a *requirement* to look at external sources first helps prevent some of the value destruction that can result from the opposite posture of getting by with internal support only, regardless of relative performance compared to all available alternatives. A requirement to look outside first forces the internal client to answer this question: How can the requirements be slightly adapted for inexpensive off-the-shelf services and approaches, rather than relying on overly complex homespun internal custom services?

Market Support: (2) Incremental/Extension

The product/project manager client's base requirements change, which in turn change the characteristics of support needed. This revision occurs around the middle of the product's market life. The manager's objective is to sustain and extend profitability—buy additional time, generate more cash flow—to support the corporation's other innovation initiatives.

Both cost and margin considerations apply. Revenues become increasingly unpredictable as the product begins to show its age in the market, with abrupt reductions in revenue possible at any time. Management's challenge is to ensure that components of G&A can be quickly reduced as necessary to protect margins.

Meeting this challenge invariably means some changes in the form of support and sometimes *who* is providing that support. For example, an advertising department headed by a manager who can think only in terms of grand media events is, instead, forced to think small.[16]

Much of what is described as "new" product development revenue in this category is instead incremental/extension product. A potential mismatch emerges if the internal support group is accustomed only to high-spending launch campaigns. The product manager needs short-term services capable of ensuring more profitable years, producing a few points' higher margin than would otherwise be achieved. The grand launch period is long past.

Market Support: (3) Terminal

Yesterday's cash-generating star product tries to hang on for a couple quarters more before negative cash flow finally dictates pulling the product to prevent further damage to market reputation and corporate value. Most internal support groups are hard-pressed just to respond within the time period, much less deliver fast enough to make a difference.

Support takes the form of spot services because there is no longer sufficient cash flow/revenue margin for full support, even if desired. Price cuts late in the aging product's life cycle are necessary if the product is to remain in the market at all. In some instances, the product manager must retreat from a superior but no longer affordable product.

One necessary cutback as the product reaches full maturity is customer service. The real-time call-center coverage provided by an internal group is no longer affordable. It is also no longer necessary because the product has been in the marketplace for some time, and the most frequent questions about its use and application rarely arise. The far lower cost alternative is a Web-based help desk with a limit to the number of free inquiries, but the internal group does not support this, which it considers to be a "second class" service approach.[17]

Similar issues of cost and flexibility serve to exclude internal services in other areas including market research, promotions management, and facilities support. Looking outside the corporation first for standardized, multiple provider packages is no longer a suggestion but, rather, an imperative.

Staff Support: (4) Staff-to-Staff

Regardless of any pseudoprofit-center terminology used for the purpose of a company's internal transfer pricing system, staff organizations are almost always expense centers: groups that absorb the corporation's cash flow. The expense center does not generate any actual revenue to offset costs.[18]

"Staff-to-staff" exchanges between expense centers are a prime source of potential corporate value destruction. The elements are all in place. Pretend budget dollars "buying" paid-for services that sometimes have little to do with comparable services outside or even what the internal client requires. When the "payment" is in the form of an automatic allocation, the internal supplier doesn't even have to provide a minimally acceptable service in order to receive sustaining budget.

But as of the Millennium, internal services groups are scrambling just to survive to the next budget. A continual march of alternative providers offers an ever-widening range of substitute services, some of which are invariably equal to or better than the homespun approaches. Due to technology, scale efficiencies, and use of standardized formats, the outside alternatives are sometimes offered at far lower cost than the incumbent services.[19]

To the head of the internal services provider group, the handwriting is on the wall. The question is less *whether* the long-enduring internal group will be displaced, but rather, *when.* One by one, functional departments once considered part of the corporation's core support are redesignated as peripheral to the corporation's base business and farmed out to the best performing, cheapest specialist group.

And away they go: first payroll processing, then overnight funds investment, management of temporary employees, and benefits administration. Next, telecom system management, facilities management, fleet management, accounting services, and security. Before long, full departments are feeling the ax, starting with IT, but extending to other staff-intensive groups: HR, accounting, risk management.

The manager of the internal expense center seizes upon outside providers' standardization to try at least to slow the pace. Goldplating (creating artificial complexity) emerges as a survival tactic—

devising services so idiosyncratic, so complex, so narrowly defined that no one else will bid for the business or contest the budget. Finally, persuade the internal end user to specify the fluff extras as critical, and the ruse is complete: The outside providers couldn't or wouldn't match our exacting specification, so we went with our familiar internal source.

But this "full-service" waste endures only when extra costs are tolerated within the corporation. This occurs occasionally because the extra costs and value destruction are unknown. The corporation's 12–16 percent ratio of G&A to revenues is treated as untouchable, with dire warnings from self-interested staff that any significant reductions in G&A/R will jeopardize the corporation as a going concern.

8.3 From Full-Service to Self-Service: Intranet Revolutionizes G&A Costs and Performance

Any serious assault on the value-creation stretch goal of cutting G&A/R in half depends on two fundamental new developments.

The first is to replace expensive, real-time face-to-face standing staff organizations with online alternatives where feasible. This means applying the 10:1 cost advantage cited in Downes and Mui and other sources in the form of online transaction costs, which are one-tenth that of face-to-face transactions.

The related second challenge calls for ensuring that the infrastructure exists to place control of such online services in the hands of the end user. And that priorities and deployment strategies are in place to justify the corporation's full investment in its commercial intranet.[20]

User Self-Access Poised to Displace Market Make-Believe Internal Service Centers

> Applied Materials Inc. of Santa Clara estimates that it has saved $6 million since it first introduced self-service three years ago.
>
> —*The Wall Street Journal*, October 8, 1999[21]

Some degree of end-user influence over centralized internal services is nothing new. But shifting control of the services from provider to the end-user "client" *is* novel.

As of the Millennium, user online self-access (sometimes referred to as self-service) is gradually displacing face-to-face service from standing expense-center bureaucracies.

Online Self-Access: Fast Track

Economic and speed advantages dictate that this alternative to internal service will dominate by 2005, and even a couple years sooner as corporations pursue maximum shareholder value.

The pace of corporate adoption will accelerate dramatically after the Millennium as third-party providers in two categories fight for share. Enterprise Resource Planning (ERP) systems providers (e.g., Germany's SAP, U.S.'s PeopleSoft) contend with third-party providers of specific intranet-based applications from companies such as American Express and CFOweb.com (www.cfoweb.com).

The target is the sweet spot of the Business-to-Business market: internal staff-to-staff services already in the corporation's budget and funded. Demand is *not* the issue. Hundreds of billions are *already* spent for services ranging from internal directories to car fleet management, from travel purchases to videoconferencing arrangements, from risk management to market research.

But savings and performance *are* salient issues. When a manager discovers that he or she is being charged $150 for office supplies that cost $15 in the stationery store just down the street, it will be clear that the corporation's internal transfer pricing mechanism has failed, regardless of its grand design.

Why? Because the cause of the problem remains. Permit a high-cost service bureaucracy to continue, and that organization will figure out some way to divert the corporation's internal cash flow stream in order to survive. Innovation may be the corporation's value lifeblood (see Chapter 6), but the individual unit depends on continuing internal subsidy.

Data entry, storage, rekeying, and multiple transfers from one station to another cause the documentation accompanying a transaction to soar. Dr. Peter Farley is a partner of Iameter, a San Francisco area company that measures the quality and cost of health care. He suggests that "submitting a paper claim costs about $20 each time it's done. On the Internet, I've seen numbers as low as 57 cents."[22]

Overcoming Limitations of Make-Believe Internal Market Transfers

Permanent organizations must meet client needs that are sporadic. This fundamental mismatch bloats corporate costs while encouraging a "we own the service" poisonous mind-set among entrenched providers.

The expenses associated with administration of the transfer/service system itself destroy value. The corporate fantasy world of profit centers, expense centers, and responsibility centers generates its own avalanche of reports, memos, meetings, and measures. The fact that none of these have any use or visibility outside the walls of the corporation itself suggests their true worth.

The pretend market mechanism limits the internal customer to an unacceptable reactive role. Overselling of the service and/or under-delivery by the internal provider devastates the internal client's operations.

An inside "client" that, in 1997, was considering entry into the network computer market relied on the company internal research group's analysts. It received little more than a compilation of the glowing market projections and near-vertical projections of demand from major and minor research houses. All wrong, as it turns out less than two years later. *Support* cannot mean just any response at all, regardless of worth. In the case of the internal research group that will not or cannot see beyond the lemming projections, the payment should arguably go the other way.

Yet for the internal client steered wrong, there is effectively no recourse except to buy elsewhere when the current "contract" period is over. Nor is there any assurance that the next provider won't be even worse than its predecessor.

Control Is the Issue

The first time an internal user group asked for an exception from a 1970s IT department's batch-processing dictum, *control* has been an end users' obsession. Internal providers facing possible loss of funding view the control issue as a matter of defending turf. But to the responsible "client," it is all just a matter of effectiveness.

Scientists at GE's research unit in upstate New York tire of foot-dragging by their data processing bureaucracy about creating a department-wide intranet designed to pay for itself quickly. The intelligence-sharing tool would enable the researchers to avoid unnecessary overlaps and paperwork while improving coordination.

But the IT managers are concerned about the very aspect of the intranet that holds the greatest appeal to the scientists: control. The researchers delight at the prospect of controlling their own exchange of data, with data processing reduced to the role of bandwidth provider and maintainer and wasting no more steps, either by duplicating analysis already conducted or by completing make-work forms and service requests. The researchers *insist* that this core productivity tool be implemented.

In the past, such "unreasonable" demands of internal users have been suppressed with a single word: *costs*. Starting with that first group requesting an alternative to batch processing, the users are told that whether the service originates from inside or outside the corporation doesn't matter: The same rules of scale apply. Special or different means unaffordable costs or unavailable time.

Consequences of "Internal Bypass"

Availability of online services shatters the old scale rules, including services pricing.[23] For example, if all the corporation's internal research group does is compile and overview canned research, the salaries and overhead of that unit become value destruction if managers can instead access reports of comparable quality themselves, directly from online sources. Who needs some corporate bureaucrats to put a different cover on some Gartner or Morningstar research when the recipient can simply order it himself?

Where actual expertise is required, the user-buyer group is liberated from the travesty of a choice that isn't really a choice. The office manager has just had extra functions added as risk manager, and that new budget will be defended to the death. But the internal client insists on expertise, and couldn't care less about which amateur has recently been assigned the role. The client's decision is too important to rely on a service that is merely adequate or worse.

Rumblings from entrenched internal service provider organizations, now facing the *real* impact of full market competitive conditions? Not from those services with the reputations, performance, and demand that verifies the wisdom of management's decision to set up this separate internal capability in the first place.

The payback is most conspicuous in terms of end users' perspectives, on a comparative basis for like transactions. Instead of paying $150 for $15 of office supplies from the internal procurement organization, Barclays Bank employees order online, at market or submarket cost per transaction. On a comparable basis, German automotive components supplier Robert Bosch GmbH opens up its ERP system to enable employees to buy supplies directly as needed.[24]

The Corporate Intranet: Commercial Priorities First

Ensuring that commercial priorities are first is essential to justifying full funding and future development of a corporation's intranet infrastructure. This means understanding key uses and establishing an order of which applications receive priority.

Office Technology Disappointments: The Underutilization Problem

In the case of technologies of the past, one of the key causes of disappointments has been mis- and under-utilization. Initially, some personal computers were used as expensive typing machines but little more. Complex systems emerge in pursuit of the impossible: an Executive Information System with one-button control of the entire enterprise.

The corporation's internally accessed intranet makes user self-access possible, but not if bandwidth is diverted to high visibility/low value bulletin board uses. No self-protective internal bureaucracy is without its own storefront on the corporate intranet, and some have several, if propaganda about them is accessible from outside the company.

Bandwidth is limited. The imperative for preserving the intranet's capacity and the skills of support developers for the most important applications is lost if company officials confuse the number or percentage of *users* company-wide with the *value* of those uses.[25]

Intranet Value Application Categories

What *is* relevant to the company are the range, type, and number of support applications. Converted from "full-service'" via entrenched internal bureaucracy to online access, provided by whoever happens to be the most effective and efficient at that particular time.

What *is* important are applications capable of reducing internal traffic to practically nothing, helping management deal with the travesty of bound internal manuals, which although updated periodically are never current.

What *is* important are the extranet applications that enable and encourage the target account to close a compelling sales proposition, helping the top field salesperson make one more major sales call per day without extra exertion.

What *is* important are those applications that help the corporation create three days out of one overtime: for bid preparation, for sequential stage work, for off-hours maintenance.

And, what is important are the applications that help the corporation with the expensive headquarters office slash facilities and personnel costs.

The applications described above are important because they create corporate value. In some cases, massive new value is manifested in a few points deleted from the corporation's central G&A/R ratio.

How best to ensure that the most important applications are not crowded out by trivial uses? Table 8-2 shows one priority list for possible applications based roughly on the combination of implementation feasibility and the size of the expected value improvement in relative terms. The priority list for any company depends in large part on which areas of value development are its most critical.

A. Transformation of Active Archive Data

The corporation is filled with hard copy manuals, most for internal use, that must be current and yet never are because of continuing changes. These include company directories, parts lists, standard catalogues, price lists, field installation instructions, and formulation and process details for new products and new machines. Materials costs and confidentiality concerns add to the problems of these documents, which are obsolete as soon as they are produced.

Mazda–North America used to generate thousands of printed pages on service records, repair manuals, and technical service data by model and part. All required periodic update but were nonetheless obsolete as the update schedule could never keep up with the changes. Increasing the number of updates per year was the opposite of the direction that management wanted to go. Costs would soar, and some of the data would still be DOA.

Printed reports are now replaced with online ccess. The mountains of paper are eliminated, unless the user requires a hardcopy download.[26]

Table 8-2. Justifying the intranet infrastructure: categories of value application.

Secure internal e-mail and access to the external Internet continue as the largest intranet uses. But as the intranet evolves, issues of application value priority emerge

Type	Description
(A.) Transformation of Active Archive Data (RT)	Conversion of regularly updated hard copy data to online, in priority of value impact, alternatives. Corporate directory, parts lists, service updates
(B.) Full Serve to Self-Serve I Conversion of Standing Support to End User Access, Non-Expert (Var)	Simplified online internal service offering, based on existing priority services, combined—e.g. T&E submission/review/reimbursement Vacation, flexible benefits changes
(C.) Online Sales Tools & Support (RT)	Externally accessible sales/promo/order sites Field sales support: scheduling, demonstrations, pricing, contracting
(D.) Full-Serve to Self-Serve II Conversion of Standing Support to End User Access, Expert (NRT)	Specified analyses—e.g., fleet management, payroll processing, computer maintenance Tiered response schedule
(E.) Intracompany Travel Reduction (RT)	Internal travel replacement communications 24/7 RFP/development support
(F.) Online Analytical Tools (Var)	Combination of external, internal tools from CAD/CAM to standard planning data, CAPEX worksheets, budget submissions and reports
(G.) Alternative Format Internal group display info, other archival info. already retained in alternative form (Var)	Internal "bulletin board" applications Non–real time archival data, internal news company internal shopping

RT	Real time availability
NRT	Non–real time
Var	Mixed

Source: VBM Consulting (www.vbm-consulting.com).

B. Full-Serve (FS) to Self-Serve (SS), I

Many existing services that in the past have been provided by stand-ing departments lend themselves to ready conversion to online appli-cation with only limited revisions in processes and formats. This FS-to-SS category involves a relatively low level of required "supplier" expertise.

Some simplification is usually necessary before conversion to on-line, including removing goldplating added by the internal unit to discourage competitors.

As an example, the group administering flexible benefits deliber-ately maintains thousands of different combinations, providing a scope of operations that appears to require a standing staff. But when it becomes apparent that over 90 percent of demands can be met with five configurations, the make-work illusion disappears.

C. Online Sales Tools and Support

Dynamic support for the field salesforce is now limited to elephant accounts as online sales progressively take over contact for clients ordering in smaller volumes. Sales are changed to higher-margin, faster-moving. In 1999, Nike permitted customers to add a few colors and features to a special line of online shoes sold at high premium. Tomorrow, a recurring network client submits a basic idea for a net-work configuration on a client workpage on the intranet (beats using a napkin), and receives a detailed proposal and completed draft net-work diagram from a relationship manager within 12 hours.

A far less exotic but possibly far more profitable intranet-based application is Web-based automatic reordering. Similar to negative checkoff communications (see "Value-Critical Implementation Is-sues" later in this chapter), the customer agrees to reorder at certain stock levels unless there is an explicit indication to the contrary.

If the intranet/extranet's monitors extend into the customer's actual stock levels, the account is locked into the seller's system, with little opportunity for competitors to strip the account away. Elec-tronic Data Interchange without EDI's costs and scope limitations.

D. Full-Serve (FS) to Self-Serve (SS), II

For functions such as fleet management and requests for new tele-phone systems, the major efficiency is in the form of front-end data gathering, as a single-entry replaces paper forms. As most of these online services involve delayed responses, the company has the opportunity to improve value by access to international labor market differences (e.g., computer maintenance and systems design).

Tiered services—certain expert-based support such as risk management—lend themselves to different levels of service and timing urgency and thus differential charges.

With the limitations of printing and distributing pricing lists removed, the company is able to change regular prices more frequently, while responding to customers' pricing initiatives almost immediately. The corporation able to change prices weekly or daily "encourages" customers to become locked-in to that seller's extranet, in order to keep up with the most recent changes.[27]

E. IntraCompany Travel Reduction

Explicit linkage of the new online service with an existing expense category provides credibility at executive and Board levels that the intranet is achieving real hard-dollar value improvement, not just theoretical advantage. The ban on most intracompany travel is coupled with purchases of desktop-to-desktop videoconferencing and officing systems.[28]

Officing tools and online CAD/CAM also assist in the 24/7 Request for Proposal and work schedules described in preceding chapters. The corporation increases its chances to make the shortlist by responding faster to the RFP as development work is handed off between three different teams approximately six to eight time zones apart.

Based on the nature of the company's operations and the pace at which rivals adopt similar "time charting methods," team organization shifts to a series of different handoff groups worldwide. A, B, and C engineering teams for RFPs and premium value, short schedule work, D and E teams for payroll administration worldwide and computer software maintenance, also on a 24/7 handoff basis.

F. Online Analytical Tools

The corporation's master file closet of proprietary and general tools ensures projections and analysis on the same basis throughout the firm. Examples include standard planning data (prevailing assumptions for interest rates, capital cost elements, stick price range, and other data), analytical tools (e.g., for value assessment and creation purposes, APV [Appendix A]), and the corporation's own ongoing VOG analyses, comparable to Figure 2-2.

G. Alternative Format

This category refers to the remaining applications of modest (and sometimes no) value contribution to the corporation. Examples include department general information Web pages and online versions of company newspapers, announcements, and speeches. A key risk is that expensive Web development talent is diverted to these low-value applications, potentially diminishing corporate worth in two ways: (1) adding unnecessary costs to company expense centers and (2) missing priority intranet opportunities with tight timing windows, especially those in Category C above.[29]

Company-approved employee shopping via its own intranet represents a special situation. As of the Millennium, most such early experiments are limited in scope and number of sponsors involved. But the essence of such arrangements is not much different from ads and special offers in the corporation's newspaper. Deftly developed and managed, such sponsorship can help significantly reduce ongoing intranet running costs. In other words, diminish value destruction that otherwise goes with daily operation of the corporation's intranet.[30]

Internal audit is an often overlooked item in this category even though it is essential to preserving corporate progress. Typically understaffed, the auditors are sometimes easily dominated by more powerful groups in the corporation, negating any effective review function. The intranet provides an opportunity for a far more rigorous capability.

Justifying the Intranet Infrastructure Purchase

The intranet infrastructure competes for scarce corporate funds against alternative value investments from both revenue and expense sides. Bromides such as this as a strategic imperative are more likely to harm than help. Only by ensuring that highest value applications are deployed as early as possible do proponents of the intranet purchase face a realistic prospect for approval. The deployment schedule is the intranet justification.

Office Technology: Past Disappointments

"Overhyped, overpriced, underperforming": Disappointed with office technology that solves no one's problems except the box-pushers' sales quotas, corporate buyers reject the argument that new technology must be purchased just because it is shiny and trendy.

In the mid-eighties, Office Automation (OA) promised a dream of paperless offices and electronic precision to replace the clutter. But purchasing companies were not yet ready for "paperless" and the high-tech toys merely shuffled old documents faster. About a decade later, the Network Computer (NC) entered the marketplace—and exited almost as fast. Despite formidable support from powerful Microsoft rivals, proponents overlooked one minor detail: Customers didn't want the product.

These and other disappointments now mean that office technology faces the same return requirements for approval as other prospective value investments. At a minimum, a return exceeding the corporation's Weighted Average Cost of Capital (or a higher hurdle, if multiple projects are competing for scarce capital) is required.

Highest Value Applications: First in Line

But if management ensures that highest-value applications are deployed first, the intranet infrastructure at least has a fighting chance of competing for limited investment capital against revenue-side innovation prospects and against other expense-side technology, which is also justified primarily on the basis of reduced costs and improved efficiency.

The CAPEX discounted cash flow justification model resembles the corporation's basic value model in many ways (see APV in Appendix A). Ensure that the intranet applications, which generate the greatest cash flow, are pursued first, and Internal Rate of Return numbers soar. But implement low-value propaganda applications first, and IRR plunges. Sometimes by enough to kill approval.

Figure 8-1 anticipates the challenges associated with authorizing purchase of expensive network-based technology. The figure and the legend show the seven value application categories described in the preceding pages and listed in Table 8-2.

The axis on the left side of the graph in Figure 8-1 indicates the level of implementation difficulty. First, we might as well secure the easiest value applications, such as converting recurring in-house catalogues from hard copy to online. The early, tangible savings generate cash flow to help finance later implementation phases. More important, a break is established from the visionary but profitless high-tech OA of years past.

The axis on the right side of the figure shows hard dollar value

Figure 8-1. Justifying the intranet infrastructure: focus on highest value applications.

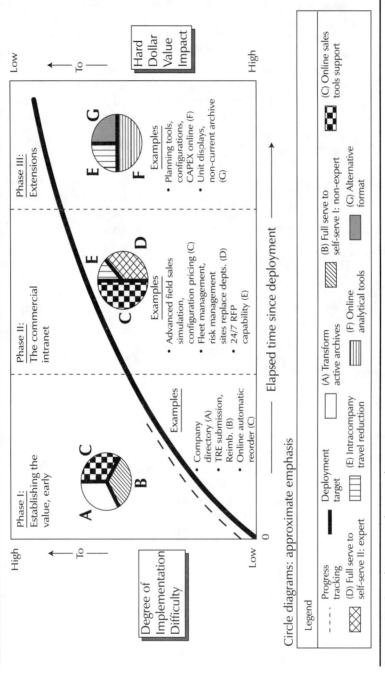

Source: VBM Consulting (www.vbm-consulting.com).

impact, in reverse scale. The emphasis here is on *hard*. In a rush to generate the highest numbers possible, some intranet vendors damage their case by commingling actual savings with a variety of "soft" dollar numbers, for example, future expenditures that might be avoided if the intranet is purchased today. Far from increasing the case for purchase, these exaggerated estimations actually undermine the case for purchase, as reviewers recall the funny numbers of office technology propositions past and get indigestion again.

During Phase I, the deployment plan calls for the optimal balance between large applications in terms of hard dollar cash flow and ease of implementation. Some example applications from Categories A, B, and C are shown.

There are now a sufficient number of manual conversions from hard copy to online (Category A) that this form of intranet application is widely accepted as a key value source. Close behind are travel and entertainment report submission, review, and reimbursement online, combined with company credit card use (B). Some automatic reorder sales opportunities (C), which were too expensive under EDI, suddenly become possible with the far lower transaction costs of the Net, represent an early opportunity to lock in major accounts.

By Phase II, deployment moves into the mainstream of commercial applications. All archive transformations and non-expert full-service to self-service conversions are complete. Category C, D, and E priority applications are next in order, such as the three examples shown: field sales closing support and instant pricing (C), fleet management (D), and development of 24-hour RFP response capability.

By Phase III, the major deployment actions have been taken as management attempts to add the lower priority, more difficult to implement prospects. Standard planning data and tools (F) and business unit storefront display sites are next in order.

The deployment plan is the financial justification. But waiting three to five years to assess the performance of the intranet is too long. The dashed line depicts management's actual deployment progress on an interim basis. If this corresponds to the planned implementation schedule in terms of the types of intranet applications and results, then the assumption is made that the program is on schedule.

8.4 Downsizing: One Last Time, from the Top Down

Serial downsizing is an admission of management failure. Corporate officers who will not or cannot systematically match personnel with their firm's highest value work requirements try to compensate for years of value destruction with a lightning stroke. But rather than a fast fix for a chronic problem, the arbitrary cutdown usually causes more new problems than old ones are solved.

Yet there is one aspect of the corporation where crude head-count or dollar targets may be the only way to stop long-enduring value destruction: deadwood. This is the manager who has been "kicked upstairs" beyond his or her level of value contribution.

In the corporation that pursues maximum shareholder value for real, there is no provision for such white-collar featherbedding. The informed "supervisor" presides a level or two above those who are actually doing the work. The faster moving the markets, the more complex the technology, and the more likely it is that the supervisor is totally dependent on those being "managed," making a joke of control.[31]

General Downsizing as a Last Resort

Hope springs eternal among analysts and others who together influence "Prolific Corp.'s" market value and price/cash flow multiples. Prolific's management deliberately suppressed value for years by choosing to maintain too many on staff, and in the wrong places.[32] And yet, the corporation still lacks the key skills necessary to ensure survival beyond the current business cycle.

Finally, Management Is Going to Do Something

Announcement of Prolific's initial corporate-wide downsizing action raises hopes for change. Value-influencers know that downsizing is about as effective at addressing the root causes of staffing ills as attacking anthills with a sledgehammer, but they figure the announcement at least signals that management now acknowledges that changes are necessary. Perhaps the old order of value destruction is at an end.

And long overdue because indirect labor is easily Prolific's largest discretionary expense category, as at most companies. Some observers have pointed to the apparent correlation of high price/cash flow multiples to high levels of operating efficiency, as suggested by high cash flow/employee ratios for that industry on a global basis.[33]

Until recently, Prolific's spin has been that little can be done about employee costs, which are effectively fixed or at least unmanageable. Then a change occurs in the mind-sets of both Prolific's senior management and some of its larger investors, prompted by the realization that the financial community *is already* penalizing Prolific for its excessive and mismatched staffing.

Forget posturing statements about "creating value." Unless this problem is solved, the corporation's value will continue to be unnecessarily suppressed. Prolific's major activist investors are increasingly inclined to hold management personally responsible for *their* wealth forgone. The way they see it, each dollar of continuing wasted expenditure translates into at least four dollars in value extracted from their pockets.

The corporation that cannot effectively manage its staff levels and costs relative to today's and tomorrow's world competitors finds its claims of global competitiveness undermined. In the late 1990s, prior to the Olivetti acquisition, Telecom Italia's massively oversized financial public relations department proclaimed that company to be a world player in the global telecommunications industry.

In the capital markets at least, the actual image was quite different up to the Millennium, with continually changing management and an embedded high cost structure. As of early 1999, Telecom Italia's ratio of employees per installed telephone line was several times the level of the regional Bell operating companies of the United States.

Such images translate directly into value destruction. The "institutional favorite" in an industry typically enjoys a price-to-cash flow (PCF) multiple more than 25 percent over the multiple of industry also-rans. Apply that higher multiplier to increased cash flow from other corporate value-enhancing actions, and the result is a visible boost in corporate worth.

Once established, a downward spiral in value proves difficult to halt. Reduced value investment means less cash flow, followed in turn by reduced projections of *future* cash flow, and the latter is the primary basis on which value is determined.[34]

General Downsizing: Fast and Flawed

Back at Prolific Corp., management sees the light and is eager to shrink this portion of their company's persistent VOG.

It might just be *too* eager. Instead of making fundamental reforms aimed at maximizing value from the corporation's overall personnel while minimizing costs, one-dimensional downsizing is pursued. Management cites the need for speed. Arbitrary, across-the-board 15 percent reductions in head count are pursued as the fastest action. But such "cures" may be worse than the "disease" they confront. While all eyes are on management's percentage goal, the true personnel issues central to corporate value are missed:

1. *CKC Critical Mass.* The issue is whether the corporation possesses a sufficient number and type of true CKCs to propel future value. Without a sustaining critical mass of value talent, the firm is arguably better off being sold before the market gets wise.

The corporation is in a downward spiral but management is oblivious to its plight. If Prolific Corp. has not managed to secure its industry's key CKCs, that means that its competitors have.[35]

Prolific misses out even if CKCs bang on its door. A hiring freeze is on, all incoming applications are discouraged—even those from candidates who are critical to the corporation's future.

2. *Activity-Lead Staffing.* At issue is whether to fit the work to the employee or the other way around. The ever-accelerating pace of change argues for the latter, as capabilities critical to maximizing corporate value today change in concert with the shrinking pattern of product and service life cycles. Try to force-fit a skill base to the changing pattern of required expertise, and organizational layers grow to compensate. One executive gets the title, another the responsibility for actually doing the job, and a third to prepare for the future of that role.

Despite the fact that the first manager's skills and experience are now grossly out of step with the corporation's updated requirements, he or she is retained. Additional hires help to cover this shortfall (doubling costs), with the original manager "kicked upstairs" to an ineffective supervisory role.[36]

Other Value Destruction through Downsizing

Multiple downsizing events, hiring freezes, and administration of the downsizing by department heads concerned with their function first amplify value destruction.

Multiple Downsizing Actions

If the first downsizing announcement generates a positive signal to the markets that something is being done, subsequent announcements have the opposite effect. Within the company and outside, confidence in management's skill at managing the corporation for value dissolves, with lingering consequences. *Why didn't they get it all—get it right—the first time?*

The second downsizing event confirms that the first wasn't effective. Because dramatic downsizing is at best a last-resort tactic, repeated use suggests that management is still far from commanding a more consistent, effective approach to personnel costs. Generous, even excessive departure payments are used to entice some headcount reductions. However the action might be explained, value destruction is unavoidable when marginal employees with little demand in the outside marketplace somehow pulls down a fee well in excess of their value.

This is not to begrudge any individual any negotiated fee. But rather, to note that the value benefits from reducing headcount can quickly be canceled by huge departure payouts. In some instances, it is better to keep the head count.[37]

Hiring Freezes: Side Effects

An unintended consequence of the arbitrary hiring freeze is that some value-destroying holdovers become even more difficult to remove. This is so, not because of any increased capability, but rather, because they are "protected" by the freeze on the inside while possibly superior candidates are excluded from contesting for that position from the outside.

Without a freeze in effect, incumbents face the prospect of a continual challenge that a better/cheaper/faster competitor will walk in the door and take away his or her job. For everyone, today's reality that *you're only as good as your next game* (Chapter 3) is unavoidable. Corporations are no longer willing to trash their value to carry noncontributors, as that action endangers the entire enterprise and every job in the corporation.

Continuous competition for roles in nonfreeze times provides the subtle but essential message that *no one owns any job*. One occupies that position until it is eliminated by change or a superior candidate comes along.[38] This sounds obvious, but it is easily forgotten when the suits contend that they *are* the company. Look back at an annual report from five years earlier, and a different set of suits was saying the same thing.

No one knows exactly how it is that the striving organization pursuing value as an obsession becomes a coaster corporation, on its way out of the industry entirely. One cause is that a block of managers in key positions treat their jobs as personal possessions rather than as goals to be continually renewed.

Insider Job: Downsizing Administered by the Departments Themselves

When a certain percentage of across-the-board cuts are allocated to each department for decisions at that level, it is based on the reasonable-enough argument that this is where the best knowledge about all the employees in that department resides. But portioning headcount cuts to department heads has the practical effect of authorizing the foxes to guard the chicken coop.

Instead of decisions being made on the basis of corporate benefit, any parochial concern may be applied in its place. The top-performing but irritating new employee—perhaps tomorrow's possible CKC—is often the first to go. The myopic department head now has a device to take action, and decisions are rarely challenged from above.

Other head-count reductions are pushed down to lower-paid, lower-level positions, dramatically reducing the dollar savings of the downsizing campaign overall. But it's still "Jobs for the Boys"—the cronies who nod on cue, who are rewarded for their pliability.

Once More, but This Time from the Top Down

With all the pitfalls of downsizing, why should any corporation proceed with another, only this time from the top of the organization downwards? Because if the corporation has limited itself to conventional downsizing to date, there's good reason to suspect that value-diminishing fat is collecting in the top ranks: deadwood managers, still employed although no one can imagine why. As long as those walking, talking sources of value destruction continue to be employed, maximizing shareholder value is a bad joke.

Minor value impact? Every bit helps when it comes to closing the VOG, and ten deadwood managers, each at half a million dollars total support cost per year, translates into a minimum $20 million in value improvement.

That's only the immediate value impact. Factor in other considerations such as (1) overlapping communications, (2) missed value investment opportunities because of a decision pace, and (3) loss of top talent who want nothing to do with an underperforming crony bureaucracy, and the value destruction soars.

Deadwood has nothing to do with age, per se. The individual value destroyer can be 26 or 66. What is relevant is expected value to the corporation tomorrow and over the intermediate term. The past is relevant only to the extent that it points toward expected future performance. The faster the pace of market change, the less reliable past history is as an indicator of future performance.

A specific "top down" downsizing approach becomes necessary because adjustments in the executive ranks are rare, at least compared to the every-other-year reorganization, interspersed by purges, that confront the rest of the corporation.

An announcement that scores of division executives are being dismissed usually coincides with the announcement of bankruptcy. Apparently, all those EVPs and division heads were affordable up to the point of the Chapter 11 announcement, but not afterward. Only a few stop to wonder whether that kind of purge a few years earlier might have prevented the announcement.

Occasionally, headquarters executive ranks are cleaned out as a last-gasp measure for the corporation now "in play," and with very few moves left to it in trying to fend off acquisition bids.[39] Management has opened the door to unwelcome acquisition bids by failing to create enough value in the firm earlier. Standard acquisition defenses have already been enacted. Management hopes that the elimination of even more overhead might boost the company's market value, closing the firm's VOG somewhat and placing its stock price out of reach.

If such tactics were enacted years before as part of a systematic, overall value review, the tactic might actually work. But steep cuts made under duress raise concerns that takeover defense is the key concern, not value preservation. Some question whether muscle is being cut out along with the fat. (Probably not, as competitors generally have already poached the top talent early in the crisis.)

Top management purges of profitable companies experiencing a slump were once unthinkable. Now, the value math is unavoidable, and management faces pressure to take action. Aging products and problems with recent innovation development cause a corporation's cash flow PCF multiple to slump by as much as 20 percent from its historical levels. Combine that impact with a similar slump in cash flow (both current and projected), and the value destruction is apparent to all.

Venerable Marks and Spencer's stumbles in the late 1990s, as the U.K. company's unique structure and marketplace approach began to show wear, particularly in the face of voracious new forms of online and Main Street competition. Changes were made at the top in January of 1999, followed by some massive restructuring of senior management ranks shortly thereafter.[40]

Post-millennium? Outperformer chief executives face a challenge to act before they are forced to do so, to clean out deadwood management early enough that such action benefits *present* shareholders, rather than a new set of owners.

Avoid the deterioration that comes with a G&A level five to seven points greater than it has to be in the first place, and the corporation's PCF multiple is defended or may even increase. Factor in the improvement in projected cash flow that comes from a leaner, faster-moving administration, and the consequence is value creation, not value destruction.

8.5 Value-Critical Implementation Issues

Empire defenders interested in crippling the pace of value reform in the administration can count on chaotic implementation as an ally. It starts with instant management principles that leave the corporation worse off than before and goes on to missing the safeguards that ensure that newly created value is preserved.

Avoiding the Distractions: False Principles

Detours slow administrative value-reform progress. Diversionary fads that promise improvement without pain seem too good to be true because they are.

These instant principles emerge about once a quarter and take the forms of instant business books, PR slightly disguised as objective articles, and high-hype, low-content consultant seminars. When the fad unwinds under ordinary scrutiny, the practitioners have already moved on to providing the *next* cure-all.

The fads are allowed to arise in the first place because someone has spotted symptoms of a legitimate problem. Advocates of the paperless office in the mid-1980s noted massive waste and memo-shuffling, choking management responsiveness. Fifteen years later, "shared services" instant seminars highlighted the legitimate symptom of too many overlapping internal services, by too many different alternative providers within the company.

But simply describing a symptom is almost valueless on its own. Today, the meetings-attendee who does nothing more than raise issues is a deserving target of business cartoon parody. This empty suit is soon "invited" to explore other opportunities. Anyone can articulate a symptom. The skill is in being able to resolve the root problem.

Canceling the "Loss of Business" Rationale by Administration Expense Centers

A common budget tactic of the crony bureaucracy must be retired for good to forestall value destruction. That tactic is to oppose significant change in administrative priorities with the argument that the corporation will lose X amount of revenues and related profits.

The argument is hollow, even misleading, in the case of support removed several steps from the marketplace. The field engineer directly involved in installation may be essential to customer satisfaction, and the same may be said of that post-sales customer services agent who resolves problems before they become account-threatening crises.

But back in divisional headquarters, administrators are deluding themselves and others if they pretend that their departure would mean a comparable, immediate effect. Chances are great that the project manager isn't even aware of any admin service of value being provided and views the allocation as an internal tax. *I'm paying for that?* Give me the budget instead.

Following through with FTE: Ensuring that *Possible* Head Count and Cost Changes Become Actual

FTE stands for Full Time Equivalent employees: the number of whole positions that result when fractions of activities of numerous employees are summed for analysis purposes. But unless indicated FTE reductions are translated into *actual, current* staff cuts, the FTE analysis is a waste of time and money.

Assessing employees on the basis of individual activities helps spot any disparities between budgeted, authorized priorities and how those individuals actually spend their time. Such an analysis also is fundamental in making commonsense adjustments in funding various G&A activity categories.

If it turns out that each of ten employees spend one-tenth of their time on an activity that management designates as valueless, the clearest and most direct reform action is to eliminate one full position—not some paper adjustment involving an "authorized but unstaffed" phantom position, but an actual reduction of an existing position and an employee.[41]

Sometimes there is no budget at all for an activity being pursued by staff anyway. Vague position descriptions plus expansive department mandates set the stage for rampant off-budget "borrowing." The conventional response is to waste funds by spending time on overly precise wordsmithed descriptions of both. But a strong case can be made that it is better to concentrate on what the individual *does*: how he or she uses time and the value of those activities.

Actions shape the corporation's performance, not position and department descriptions, which are rarely accurate and, having been written, almost never emerge from the file cabinet. A minimum of position documentation is necessary for broad guidance and legal reasons. But excessive time on such documentation is value destructive.

If value is created one internal initiative at a time, it is supported and sustained one individual at a time. The employee who skips from one meeting to another as a futile issues raiser is rarely revealed by position description alone. Yet this value-destroying games player is immediately revealed by occasional, objective, spot independent analysis of what he or she *actually does*. [42]

Sunset Provisions for Functions and Individuals: Alternative to Management by Inertia

Sunset provisions provide for automatic funding expiration for key administrative costs at particular (usually one or two years) points in time. The timing is set in accordance with the corporation's key development and decision cycles, which synchronize roughly with life cycles of the corporation's products and services.

Management is often reluctant to go out of its way to spotlight a value-losing operation or the value-destroying individual. Confrontation is awkward, as are the questions that arise from such actions: "Why did you wait so long to before acting to stop the value losses?"

Sunset removes the requirement to act by assuming that the pace of change is such that all activities and staff become non-contributing in a year or two. Those activities and individuals that are provably contributing are permitted to continue. The bias is switched from inertia to action out of necessity, as the risks to the business from standing pat increase with each escalation of the pace of change.

If allowed to convert FTEs to actual head count without being told exactly who is to be cut, department heads may well choose to protect their familiar crew, sometimes to the detriment of value creators and the corporation overall. There is no sure means for preventing such cronyism.

But sunset provisions for individuals and departments help reduce such incidents. Applied to individual employees, sunset means that value contribution is reassessed periodically, whether or not the individual is under contract. The value assessment cannot be some meandering performance review, but rather need to answer two specific questions as precisely as possible. First, what is the individual's *actual value* contribution on an objectively considered basis? Second, does that *actual value* exceed total dollar cost by at least five times?[43]

Applied on a functional basis, sunset contradicts the department head's presumption to "own" a particular internal service activity until that rare event when it is wrenched away. Instead, it evaluates the activity and who does it competitively, with no particular advantage to the incumbent except familiarity.

Negative Checkoffs: Ensuring that Internal Decision Speed Keeps Pace with the Marketplace

A "negative checkoff" means that the decision is already made unless a better alternative is presented. You are probably familiar with book and record clubs, which automatically send the next pre-selected choice to you unless you respond otherwise.

What is an annoyance when it comes to buying books at home, though, can help to prevent chronic inertia when it comes to corporate decisions that impact value. The bottleneck employee reduces corporate value by causing the corporation to miss some time-sensitive opportunities in the guise of being conservative and prudent.

There's nothing wrong at all with being careful—if that's the reason for the delay. But a negative checkoff means that the probable best decision proceeds *with full approval of everyone* unless something else better comes up. No office political games of "It wasn't my decision." Permit the negative checkoff decision to proceed, and that is the equivalent to suggesting that solution yourself.

Obviously, the preferred response by the corporation is to eradicate the bottleneck at its source. But effective process redesign is often not fast enough, and some redesign efforts merely substitute new obstructions for old ones. In the meantime, the chief executive cannot afford to stand idle as the corporation's opportunities for value growth are turned down, not as a consequence of a negative decision, but rather because the organization cannot respond rapidly or effectively enough.

Negative checkoff provides a reasonable period of time for response. But with no response, the proposition proceeds as stated, with the nonrespondent's active agreement assumed.

In the old linear structure, decisions crawl from one point to the next. The next decision influencer down the line faces few if any time constraints. Delays are blamed on the project manager or whoever is trying to speed the decision process in order to meet an urgent market window.

But the bottleneck and his or her tactics are immediately revealed by the negative checkoff. Miss a couple of input deadlines, and the CEO begins to believe that the process can get along quite well without that obstacle.

In its place comes the requirement for decisions that facilitate positive action. Limited to the CEO's initiated directives or to others as carefully controlled by the CEO, with the proposal automatically considered when transmitted by secure internal email. The internal shell game of "never received that" is over, along with the bottleneck's subterfuge of long-delayed deliberation.

Epilogue

Readers of *The Value Mandate* are cordially invited to visit VBM Consulting's shareholder value intelligence freesite, The VBM Resource Ctr. (www.vbmresources.com). The site contains key articles, columns, and news updates of interest to the manager seeking to maximize shareholder value across the corporation.

VBM Consulting's corporate Web site is www.vbm-consulting. com. To contact the authors, send your email to peter.clark@vbm-consulting.com and/or stephen.neill@vbm-consulting.com.

VBM Consulting's Value Opportunity Audit (VOA) is an intensive initial investigation of substantial value opportunities for client firms. Key principles from *The Value Mandate* are applied in this two-to-three month highly focused investigation. The Value Opportunity Gap (VOG) structure described in this book's first two chapters provides a continuous framework for pursuing maximum shareholder value today and tomorrow. We probe all five of the key value sectors within the firm, and help devise specific actions in each designed to narrow the value opportunity gap. Additional description is provided at www.vbmresources.com.

APPENDIX A

Using APV: A Better Tool for Valuing Operations

by Timothy A. Luehrman

A PV (Adjusted Present Value) is a key methodology for measurement of company current worth, and is referenced at key points in this book.

If you learned valuation techniques more than a few years ago, chances are you are due for a refresher course. You were certainly taught that the best practice for valuing operating assets—that is, an existing business, factory, product line, or market position—was to use a discounted-cash-flow (DCF) methodology. That is still true. But the particular version of DCF that has been accepted as the standard over the past years—using the weighted-average cost of capital (WACC) as the discount rate—is now obsolete.

True, business schools and textbooks continue to teach the WACC approach. But that's because it's out there as the standard, not because it performs best. Today those same schools and texts also present alternative methodologies. One alterative, called *adjusted*

At the time of this article, Timothy A. Luehrman was a visiting associate professor of finance at the Massachusetts Institute of Technology's Sloan School of Management in Cambridge. Translated and reprinted by permission of *Harvard Business Review*. This article was originally published under the English title "Using APV: A Better Tool for Valuing Operations "by Timothy A. Luehrman, *Harvard Business Review,* May–June 1997, pages 145–154. Copyright © 1997 by the President and Fellows of Harvard College, all rights reserved. This translation copyright © 1997 by the President and Fellows of Harvard College.

present value (APV), is especially versatile and reliable, and will replace WACC as the DCF methodology of choice among generalists.
(See "What's It Worth? A General Manager's Guide to Valuation," in
the May–June 1997 issue of *HBR*.)

For managers with businesses to run, the question of which valuation method to use has always come down to a pragmatic comparison of alternatives. What might you use instead of WACC? Just like
WACC, APV is designed to value operations, or assets-in-place; that
is, any existing asset that will generate future cash flows. This is the
most basic and common type of valuation problem that managers
face. Why choose APV over WACC? For one reason, APV always
works when WACC does, and sometimes when WACC doesn't, because it requires fewer restrictive assumptions. For another, APV is
less prone to serious errors than WACC. But most important, general
managers will find that APV's power lies in the added managerially
relevant information it can provide. APV can help managers analyze
not only how much an asset is worth but also where the value comes
from.

All discounted-cash-flow methodologies involve forecasting future cash flows and then discounting them to their present value at
a rate that reflects their riskiness. But the methodologies differ in
the details of their execution, most particularly in how they account
for the value created or destroyed by financial maneuvers, as opposed
to operations. APV's approach is to analyze financial maneuvers separately and then add their value to that of the business. (See the
exhibit "APV: The Fundamental Idea.") WACC's approach is to adjust the discount rate (the cost of capital) to reflect financial enhance-
ments. Analysts apply the adjusted discount rate directly to the
business cash flows; WACC is supposed to handle financial side effects
automatically, without requiring any addition after the fact.

In reality, WACC has never been that good at handling financial
side effects. In its most common formulations, it addresses tax effects
only, and not very convincingly, except for simple capital structures.
However, its compelling virtue is that it requires only one discounting operation, a boon in the past to users of calculators and slide
rules. Today that advantage is irrelevant. High-speed spreadsheets
make light work of the extra discounting required by APV. More than
20 years after APV was first proposed, its unbundling of the components of value, always very informative, is now also very inexpensive.

APV is flexible. A skilled analyst can configure a valuation in
whatever way makes most sense for the people involved in managing
its separate parts. The basic framework can be highly refined or cus-

tomized according to tastes and circumstances, but a simple example illustrates the essential idea.

An APV Case Study

Roy Henry, president of IBEX Industries, has his eye on an acquisition target: Acme Filters, a division of SL Corporation. Acme is a mature business that has underperformed in its industry for the past six years. After an internal campaign to boost performance fell short of senior executives' expectations, SL Corporation resolved to sell Acme. Working with division managers from IBEX Industries who know Acme's operations and with some external professionals, Henry has targeted the following specific opportunities for value creation:

- Acme's product line will be rationalized, and some components will be outsourced to improve the company's operating margin by three percentage points.
- The same changes will reduce inventory and boost payables, producing onetime reductions in net working capital.
- Some of Acme's nonproductive assets will be sold.

APV: The Fundamental Idea.

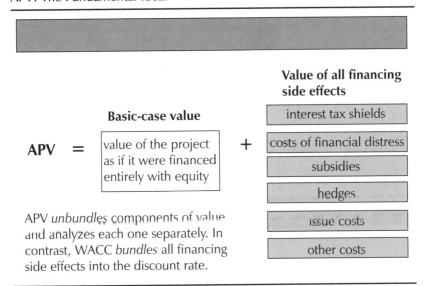

Basic-case value

$$APV = \begin{bmatrix} \text{value of the project} \\ \text{as if it were financed} \\ \text{entirely with equity} \end{bmatrix} + \quad$$

Value of all financing side effects

interest tax shields

costs of financial distress

subsidies

hedges

issue costs

other costs

APV *unbundles* components of value and analyzes each one separately. In contrast, WACC *bundles* all financing side effects into the discount rate.

- Distribution will be streamlined and new sales incentives introduced to raise Acme's sales growth from 2% to 3% annually to the industry average of 5%.
- Some taxes will be saved, mostly through the interest tax shields associated with borrowing.

The seller's representatives have indicated that SL Corporation is reluctant to accept less than book value (currently $307 million) for Acme, despite the division's recent lackluster performance. Henry's financial experts believe that a deal at book value could be financed with about 80% debt, comprising senior bank debt, privately placed subordinated debt, and a revolving credit facility. (See the pro forma balance sheets in the table "Step 1: Prepare Performance Forecasts.") Henry expects to pay down that debt as quickly as possible (and the lenders will insist on it) and to arrive at a debt-to-capital ratio no higher than 50% within five years. He will try to hold fees down to $15 million, but they could well reach as high as $20 million or more.

Acme does not have publicly traded shares, but a few similar companies do, and they provide benchmarks for estimating the cost of equity. One such company, with a historical debt ratio of 45% to 50%, has an estimated cost of equity of 24%. Another, with no debt in its capital structure, has an estimated cost of equity of 13.5%. In general, Henry's equity investors expect significantly higher returns—of 30% to 35%. For comparison, let us suppose that the return on long-term government bonds is 5%.

Executing an APV Analysis

Now let's estimate the APV of this acquisition target. The first task is to evaluate the business as if it were financed entirely with equity. Then, because it will not be financed entirely with equity, we add or subtract value associated with the financing program that we expect to utilize. (See the exhibit "Steps in a Basic APV Analysis.") Presumably, the net effect of the program will be positive; otherwise, we would use only equity financing.

To determine the value of Acme Filters using APV, carry out the following five steps:

Step 1: Lay out the base-case cash flows. The base-case value is built on financial projections that would be prepared for *any*

Step 1: Prepare Performance Forecasts.

(in millions of dollars)

Pro Forma Income Statements

	Year 0	Year 1	Year 2	Year 3	Year 4	Year 5
EBIT		$22.7	29.8	37.1	40.1	42.1
Interest		21.6	19.1	17.8	16.7	15.8
EBT		1.1	10.7	19.3	23.3	26.3
Taxes @ 34%		0.4	3.6	6.6	7.9	8.9
Net income		0.7	7.1	12.7	15.4	17.3

Supplemental data

	Year 0	Year 1	Year 2	Year 3	Year 4	Year 5
Depreciation		$21.5	13.5	11.5	12.1	12.7
Capital expenditures		10.7	10.1	10.4	11.5	13.1
Δ Net working capital		−12.3	1.9	4.2	5.2	6.1
Δ Other assets		9.0	6.9	3.4	0.0	0.0

Pro Forma Balance Sheets

	Year 0	Year 1	Year 2	Year 3	Year 4	Year 5
Assets						
Net working capital	$60.0	47.7	49.6	53.7	59.0	65.1
Net fixed assets	221.0	210.3	206.9	205.7	205.1	205.5
Other assets	26.0	17.0	10.0	6.6	6.7	6.7
Total assets	307.0	275.0	266.5	266.2	270.8	277.3
Liabilities and equity						
Revolver @ 7.5%	$13.0	0.2	4.8	11.7	20.9	20.0
Bank loan @ 8.0%	80.0	60.0	40.0	20.0	0.0	0.0
Subordinated debt @ 9.5%	150.0	150.0	150.0	150.0	150.0	0.0
Long-term debentures at 9.0%	0.0	0.0	0.0	0.0	0.0	140.0
Total debt	243.0	210.2	194.8	181.7	170.9	160.0
Equity	64.0	64.7	71.8	84.5	99.9	117.2
Total liabilities and equity	307.0	275.0	266.5	266.2	270.8	277.3

Supplemental data

	Year 0	Year 1	Year 2	Year 3	Year 4	Year 5
Interest paid	$0.0	21.6	19.1	17.8	16.7	15.8
Principal repaid	0.0	32.8	15.5	13.1	10.8	10.9
Dividends	0.0	0.0	0.0	0.0	0.0	0.0

Base-Case Cash Flows

	Year 0	Year 1	Year 2	Year 3	Year 4	Year 5
EBIT		$22.7	29.8	37.1	40.1	42.1
− Taxes @ 34%		7.7	10.1	12.6	13.6	14.3
= EBIT (1 − t)		15.0	19.6	24.5	26.4	27.8
+ Depreciation		21.5	13.5	11.5	12.1	12.7
= Operating cash flow		36.5	33.1	36.0	38.5	40.4
− Δ Net working capital		12.3	−1.9	−4.2	−5.2	−6.1
− Capital expenditures		−10.7	−10.1	−10.4	−11.5	−13.1
− Δ Other assets		9.0	6.9	3.4	0.0	0.0
= Free cash flow of assets		47.0	28.1	24.8	21.8	21.3

DCF approach to this problem, including the WACC-based valuation most companies already use. The projections consist of expected incremental operating and investment cash flows for the target business. For Acme's figures, see the table "Step 1: Prepare Performance Forecasts." (To save space, we have omitted the above-the-line items that go into the EBIT forecast.) In the first year, for example, Henry expects after-tax operating cash flow to be $36.5 million. The chart shows a reduction (a net inflow) of net working capital in the first year as he liquidates inventory and increases payables, followed by new investment (a net outflow) to support subsequent growth in sales. Capital expenditures represent another cash outflow. Finally, the change in other assets picks up after-tax cash proceeds from liquidating the nonproductive assets mentioned above. The operating cash flow, plus or minus those investment effects, gives "free cash flow of assets."

Step 2: Discount the flows using an appropriate discount rate and terminal value. As with any DCF valuation, we need a discount rate and a terminal value. How these items are treated is where APV begins to diverge from other methods. Start with the discount rate. We want an opportunity cost of capital; that is, the return Henry's investors could expect to earn by investing in some other asset with the same riskiness that the target assets would exhibit if they were financed entirely with equity. Our best benchmark for this opportunity cost is 13.5%—the cost of equity for a comparable company with an all-equity capital structure.

The last ingredient is a terminal value for the assets. This is simply the estimate, at some terminal horizon, of the assets' value, taking into account everything after the terminal horizon. For a

Steps in a Basic APV Analysis.

| Prepare performance forecasts for the target business. | Prepare a valuation spreadsheet for each component of value. | Add the components of value. |

Step 1:
Prepare performance forecasts and base-case incremental cash flows for the business.

Whole business

Income statements

balance sheets

base-case cash flows

Here the components of value are bundled together.

Step 2:
Discount base-case cash flows and terminal value to present value.

Base-case valuation spreadsheet

estimated operating and investment cash flows, including terminal value

Step 3:
Evaluate financing side effects.

Side effect: interest tax shields

present value of estimated interest tax shields from borrowing

Here they are unbundled.

Step 4:
Add the pieces together to get an initial APV.

APV

base-case value
+ value of financing side effects
= **adjusted present value**

Step 5:
Tailor the analysis to fit managers' needs.

Finally, they are rebundled.

Step 2: Discount Base-Case Cash Flows and Terminal Value to Present Value.

(in millions of dollars)

Base-Case Value

	Year 0	Year 1	Year 2	Year 3	Year 4	Year 5
Free cash flow of assets		$47.0	28.1	24.8	21.8	21.3
Terminal value of assets						263.4
Discount factor @ 13.5%	1.0000	0.8811	0.7763	0.6839	0.6026	0.5309
Present value, each year		$41.4	21.8	17.0	13.1	151.1
Base-case value (total)	**$244.5**					

going concern, we usually choose as the terminal horizon the earliest point after which we can regard the assets as a perpetuity or some other simple financial construct. Suppose we expect free cash flow for years six and after to grow at 5% per year in perpetuity. The value (at the end of year five) of such a perpetuity is simply the year-six cash flow divided by the result of the discount rate minus the growth rate (0.135 − 0.05 − 0.085), which equals $263.4 million.

Now we discount the free cash flows and the terminal value at 13.5%, as shown in the chart, to obtain a base-case value of $244.5 million. Note that this figure is lower than the book value sought by the hopeful seller.

Step 3: Evaluate the financing side effects. Of the several possible side effects of Henry's proposed financing program, we will examine only one here: interest tax shield. Interest tax shields arise because of the deductibility of interest payments on the corporate tax

Step 3: Evaluate Financing Side Effects.

(in millions of dollars)

Interest Tax Shields

	Year 0	Year 1	Year 2	Year 3	Year 4	Year 5
Interest tax shield		$7.4	6.5	6.1	5.6	5.4
Terminal value of tax shields						122.4
Discount factor @ 9.5%	1.0000	0.9132	0.8340	0.7617	0.6956	0.6352
Present value, each year		$6.7	5.4	4.6	3.9	81.2
Total present value, tax shields	**$101.8**					

return (versus the nondeductibility of dividends). Why is this a side effect? Because the projected tax payments in the base case are too high—the hypothetical all-equity-financed company pays no interest and receives no tax deduction. With the capital structure Henry is contemplating, the interest deduction will reduce taxable income by the amount of the interest and so will reduce the tax bill by the amount of interest times the tax rate. In the first year, the interest tax shield is $7.4 million ($21.6 million × 0.34). In the second year, it is $6.5 million, and so forth, as shown.

As with the base case, we still need a terminal value and a discount rate. Academics agree that tax shields, like any other future cash flow, should be discounted at an "appropriate" risk-adjusted rate—that is, a rate that reflects riskiness. Unfortunately, they don't agree on how risky tax shields are. A common expedient is to use the cost of debt as a discount rate, on the theory that tax shields are about as uncertain as principal and interest payments. Of course, there may come a time when you can afford to make your interest payments but can't use the tax shields. This suggests that tax shields are a bit more uncertain and so deserve a somewhat higher discount rate. Others argue for an even higher discount rate, observing that managers will adjust leverage up or down according to prevailing business conditions or the fortunes of the company. If so, then future interest payments, along with the tax shields, will fluctuate for the same reasons that operating cash flows fluctuate and therefore deserve the same discount rate. Following the most common approach, we used a rate of 9.5%—a figure a bit higher than the average cost of debt and thus on the high side of the lower end of the range just described.

For a terminal value, suppose first that at the end of year five the company refinances its outstanding debt with a new $140 million issue of long-term debentures at 9%. In subsequent years, indebtedness grows as the company grows—say, at 5%. So, too, will interest tax shields grow. In year five, the value of this perpetually growing stream of tax shields is $122 million. Discounting all the tax shields back to the present gives a value for this side effect of $101.8 million.

Step 4: Add the pieces together to get an initial APV. By adding the base-case value and the value of the interest tax shields, we get an initial estimate of the target's APV:

$$\text{APV} = \$244.5 \text{ million (base-case value)} + \$101.8 \text{ million (value of side effects)} = \$346.3 \text{ million.}$$

Step 4: Add the Pieces Together to Get an Initial APV.

(in millions of dollars)

	Year 0	Year 1	Year 2	Year 3	Year 4	Year 5
Base-case value	$244.5					
Side effect: tax shields	$101.8					
Adjusted present value	**$346.3**					

- We say this is an initial estimate for two reasons. First, we have ignored other financing side effects here to shorten the presentation. And second, even within this simplified example, we can push the APV analysis further and obtain more insight. So far, our analysis suggests that buying this business for $307 million is a good deal: Henry would increase his investors' wealth by the net present value of the acquisition, or about $39 million. (NPV = $346.3 million − $307 million.)

Step 5: Tailor the analysis to fit managers' needs. How much of Acme's value is already there, and how much is Henry creating by assuming ownership and implementing changes? How much value does each of his planned initiatives create? Do the executives responsible for realizing that value know how much it is? Do they know what it depends on? Finally, how much of the value that is to be created will be paid over to the seller at closing? The fifth step of an APV anaylsis can examine these and other managerially pertinent questions.

Start by unbundling the base-case cash-flow projections into separate cash flows associated with Henry's value-creation initiatives. In the table "Step 5: Tailor the Analysis to Fit Managers' Needs," the base-case free cash flows are decomposed. Baseline cash flows are derived from recent operating results and represent the business in its current underperforming configuration. Then these are increments for each of the proposed initiatives; margin improvements; net-working-capital improvements; asset liquidations; and higher steady-state growth. When each of these is taxed and discounted, we see that the baseline business is worth $157 million and that operating improvements would add $87 million. (Both figures exclude interest tax shields.) About a third of the $87 million comes from short-term initiatives: selling unproductive assets and reducing working capital. The rest comes from ongoing initiatives: improving margins and boosting growth. Most likely, those four tasks will be in the hands of different people. It's crucial that they do their jobs well,

Step 5: Tailor the Analysis to Fit Managers' Needs.

(in millions of dollars)

Baseline Performance

	Year 0	Year 1	Year 2	Year 3	Year 4	Year 5
EBIT baseline		$20.4	26.8	33.4	36.1	37.9
− Taxes @ 34%		7.0	9.1	11.4	12.3	12.9
= EBIT (1 − t)		13.5	17.7	22.0	23.8	25.0
+ Depreciation		21.5	13.5	11.5	12.1	12.7
− Operating cash flow		35.0	31.1	33.5	35.9	37.7
− Δ Not Working Capital		−4.0	−4.0	−4.2	−5.2	−6.1
− Capital expenditures		−10.7	−10.1	−10.4	−11.5	−13.1
= Free cash flow, baseline		20.2	17.0	19.0	19.2	18.5
Terminal value, baseline						172.8
Discount factor @ 13.5%	1.0000	0.8811	0.7763	0.6839	0.6026	0.5309
Present value, each year		$17.8	13.2	13.0	11.5	101.6
Baseline business value	**$157.2**					

Increments: Value-Creation Initiatives

	Year 0	Year 1	Year 2	Year 3	Year 4	Year 5
1. Margin improvement						
Incremental EBIT		$2.3	3.0	3.7	4.0	4.2
− Taxes @ 34%		0.8	1.0	1.3	1.4	1.4
= Cash increment		1.5	2.0	2.4	2.6	2.8
Increment to terminal value						25.9
Present value, each year (@ 13.5%)		1.3	1.5	1.7	1.6	15.2
Value of margin improvement	**$21.3**					
2. Net-working-capital improvement						
Incremental cash flow		$16.3	2.1			
Present value, each year (@ 13.5%)		14.4	1.7			
Value of net-working-capital improvement	**$16.0**					
3. Asset sales						
Incremental cash flow		$9.0	6.9	3.4		

Present value, each year
  (@ 13.5)   7.9   5.4   2.3
Value of asset sales   ⎡$15.6⎤

4. Higher steady-state growth
Incremental terminal value $64.7

Value of higher growth   ⎡$34.3⎤

*Sum of baseline and
  increments*   **$244.5**
+ Value of interest tax shields $101.8 (as before)

= Adjusted Present Value $346.3 (as before)

APV Is Rich in Information.

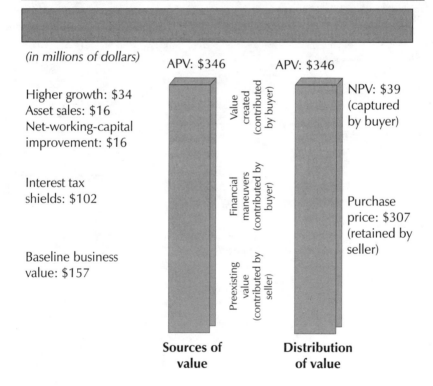

(in millions of dollars)   APV: $346   APV: $346

Higher growth: $34   NPV: $39
Asset sales: $16   (captured
Net-working-capital   by buyer)
improvement: $16

Interest tax
shields: $102   Purchase
                                                                    price: $307
                                                                    (retained by
                                                                    seller)
Baseline business
value: $157

Sources of   **Distribution**
value   **of value**

Although the buyer is creating $87 million—and still more
in tax savings—all but $29 million is paid to the seller.

because even though $87 million of value will be created, only $39 million (the MPV) will be retained by the new owners. The rest will go to the seller as part of the sale price.

We could push the analysis still further in several ways, depending on what would help managers, negotiators, or financiers. We could examine different scenarios for each category. We could reassess tax shields to look at different proposed deal structures or to allocate debt capacity to the different parts of the business or specific initiatives. We could reassess risk, perhaps adjusting the discount rates in the subpart valuations. Suppose, for example, that working capital improvements came primarily from liquidating excess raw-materials inventories; the associated cash flow would likely contain less business risk than normal operating cash flows and so would deserve a discount rate somewhat lower than 13.5%. Alternatively, suppose the margin improvements came from increased automation and, hence, higher fixed costs; this would suggest that those incremental cash flows deserve a somewhat higher discount rate.

Could these extra analytical features be performed with WACC? Maybe, but first we'd have to get the WACC computed correctly. (See Appendix B.) Then if we wanted to consider that different cash flows may have different risk characteristics and so deserve different discount rates, we'd have to compute the WACC for all the different value-creation initiatives. That would force us to think about the capital structure of, say, net-working-capital improvements. And have we expressed the debt ratio for that structure in market-value or book-value terms? Does the ratio change over time? The exercise is even more prone to error than the simple formulation in Appendix B. APV is both less cumbersome and more informative.

APV's signature characteristic is that no discount rate contains anything other than time value (the risk-free rate of interest) and a risk premium (according to the riskiness of the cash flows being discounted). Any value created by financial maneuvers—tax savings, risk management, subsidized debt, credit-enhanced debt—has its own cash-flow consequences. You treat those consequences by laying out the cash flow in a spreadsheet and discounting them at a rate that reflects time value and *their* riskiness, but nothing else. In other words, APV is exceptionally transparent: you get to see all the components of value in the analysis; none are buried in adjustments to the discount rate.

APV has its limitations, of course. Some amount to technicalities, which are much more interesting to academics than to managers. But two in particular are worth knowing about because they introduce consistent biases in the analysis. First, income from stocks—as opposed to bonds—may be taxed differently when the investor files a personal tax return. This usually causes an analyst to overestimate the net advantage associated with corporate borrowing when computing the present value of interest tax shields. And second, most analysts neglect costs of financial distress associated with corporate leverage, and they may ignore other interesting financial side effects as well. More generally, we should bear in mind that for all its versatility, APV remains a DCF methodology and is poorly suited to valuing projects that are essentially options. The most common formulations of WACC suffer from all these limitations and more.

What should you do to learn APV? The good news is, if you've gotten this far, you've already learned it. The basic idea really is that simple. There are indeed fancier formulations that examine, for example, additional side effects, such as financial guarantees or subsidies. And I have glossed over important concepts that help you to select or create sensible discount rates, for example, and to reconcile different benchmarks for the cost of equity. The relevant concepts are well covered in basic corporate-finance texts. For a glimpse of fancier formulations, look at books devoted to fancier problems; the classic example is cross-border valuation, for which APV is enormously helpful. Beyond that, all you need is practice.

APPENDIX B

The Pitfalls of Using WAAC

by Timothy A. Luehrman

We can evaluate Acme Filters without APV, using the same pro forma cash-flow projections and discounting at the weighted-average cost of capital (WACC). Unfortunately, this is not as simple a procedure as textbooks often make it appear. A sketch of the approach many companies take to this analysis highlights some of its pitfalls.

In a WACC-based analysis, we discount only once—the discount rate has to be adjusted to pick up all the costs and benefits of a selected capital structure. Not surprisingly, a lot of analytical energy goes into computing it. WACC is just what it says it is: a weighted average of the after-tax costs of different sources of capital, in which each is weighted by the fraction of the capital structure it represents. In our example, there are three kinds of debt (four if you consider the refinancing in year five) and one kind of equity. See the calculations in the table below to observe how we obtained a WACC of 9.7%.

When we discount the free cash flows from this business at 9.7%, we obtain a value for the business of $417 million, which implies an NPV of about $110 million (NPV = $417 million − $307 million). That is 275% of the figure we got using APV, which itself was probably an overestimate. Obviously, if Henry got into an auction for this

(in millions of dollars)

WACC Calculations

Source of funds	Amount	Percentage of funds	After-tax cost	Weighted cost
Debt				
Revolving credit @ 7.5%	$13	4.2%	0.050	0.2%
Bank debt @ 8.0%	80	26.1%	0.053	1.4%
Subordinated debt @ 9.5%	150	48.9%	0.063	3.1%
Equity	64	20.8%	0.240	5.0%
Total funds	307	100.0%		**9.7% = WACC**

Discounting Free Cash Flows at WACC

	Year 0	Year 1	Year 2	Year 3	Year 4	Year 5
Free cash flow of assets		$47.0	28.1	24.8	21.8	21.3
Terminal value of assets						481.2
Discount factor (WACC)		0.9120	0.8317	0.7585	0.6917	0.6308
Present value, each year		$42.9	23.3	18.8	15.1	319.0
Asset value (total)	**$417.1**					

business and bid the price up to $417 million, he would transfer a lot of value from his investors to the seller's shareholders.

Why the difference in estimated values? There are several reasons, but the most important is that we made some common errors and miscalculated the WACC. Let's start with the cost of equity, which we assumed to be 24%. One of our benchmarks for the cost of equity was another company in the same business, with about 50% debt in its capital structure. That company's cost of equity is 24%. Since we are aiming for the same amount of leverage, 24% seems a reasonable estimate. But we won't arrive at that capital structure until year five, and in the meantime our leverage is substantially higher. In fact, our debt ratio at closing will be about 80%, which suggests a cost of equity of about 40%, not 24%. But even this figure can't be used alone, because the cost of equity changes every time the debt ratio changes—every year. For the same reason, simply plugging in 30% or 35%, the benchmarks associated with Henry's investors, is also misleading. In short, none of the raw benchmarks Henry has are suitable for WACC.

Another problem is that we used book values to generate the weights in the WACC, whereas the procedure is valid only with market values. To illustrate, suppose for a moment that the value of the business at closing really was $417 million. That implies a *market-value* debt ratio at closing of 58%, not 80% or 50%. And this, too, is subject to change every year. Of course, if we knew the true market value of the assets, we wouldn't need to do the analysis in the first place. One expedient is to guess at the market value or use book values and then iterate—fill in the computed market value as the new guess, then recompute another guess, and so forth until the guess and the computed values converge.

There are other difficulties as well. In fact, every element of WACC presents computational challenges in all but the simplest, most sterile of settings. Can those problems be addressed? For the most part, yes, though demonstrating that is not the point of this article. Suffice it to say that making the indicated adjustments to the simpleminded (but very common) calculation shown here is at least as difficult as—and less informative than—using APV.

Endnotes

Preface

1. The tactic of increasing the ratio of debt-to-capital in order to decrease weighted average cost of capital and thereby increase the value of the company (all other things being equal) is well-established as of the millennium.

Shareholder value lecturers have been pressing the point for more than two decades. Leveraged buyout (LBO) raiders seized the point for their own purposes starting about 1982. The research unit of the Financial Executives Institute has focused on this nominal value issue (Davis, Henry A., *Cash Flow and Performance Measurement: Managing for Value* [New York: FERF, 1996]).

Inner workings of the WACC-to-value relationship have been explored in several *Harvard Business Review* articles since the mid-1980s. Appendix A in this book describes Adjusted Present Value (APV), a primary valuation methodology developed by Professor Thomas A. Luehrman: "Using APV: A Better Tool for Valuing Operations," May–June 1997, pages 145–154.

The basic theoretical underpinning of Miller & Modigliani as applied to valuing companies is depicted in Figure 2-4 and described in numerous texts, including the author's *Beyond the Deal: Optimizing Shareholder Value* (New York: HarperBusiness, 1991, pages 78–93) and thus is not repeated here. Reference is made to two books written in the early 1990s that provide considerable coverage of that topic: (1) Stewart, G. Bennett III, *The Quest for Value* (New York: Harper-Business, 1991), and (2) Copeland, Tom; Koller, Tim; and Murrin, Jack, *Valuation: Measuring and Managing the Value of Companies* (Wiley, Penn.: McKinsey & Co. 1990).

Value-Optimal Capital Strategy is to be addressed in the second book in the VBM series, *The Value Challenge* (preliminary title).

2. Miller, Merton, and Modigliani, Franco, "The Cost of Capital, Corporation Finance and the Theory of Investment," *American Economic Review*, June 1958, pages 261–297, "Dividend Policy, Growth and the Valuation of Shares," *Journal of Business*, October 1961, Vol. 34, pages 411–433.

3. "Acquisition Bids as Indicators of Value Performance," see Chapter 1 and Figures 1-3, 1-4.

Chapter 1

1. From VBM Consulting's Value Opportunity Audit (VOA) Program; see the Epilogue of this book or www.vbmresources.com or e-mail at outperform@vbm-consulting.com.

2. "Shareholder" here refers to investors with an active interest in the continuity of the corporation. Davis cites Boeing's SVA plan: "institutional investors with a long-term perspective."

The activist institutional investor who has bought its shares as a hold investment epitomizes the owner for whom maximizing shareholder value, for real, is directed first and foremost. In retrospect, it can be seen that pass-through speculators such as LBO acquirers in the 1980s kidnapped the rhetoric of MSV to gain control, but sometimes not to build stronger corporations.

In its simplest definition, total shareholder return refers to appreciation in stock price plus cash dividends. Total Shareholder Return (TSR) is a relevant measure only in the context of alternative returns for that same capital (*Beyond the Deal*, pages 16–23). But the CEO of the corporation who contrasts his firm's TSR to long-term government bonds is only doing part of the necessary analysis. Unless the firm's current TSR is also compared to both best-of-industry measures and that company's own TSR under optimal performance, the analysis is incomplete:

Best of Industry TSR ([2] in text)—Top TSR performance is indicated, rather than just an industry average. But merely reaching mid-range performance fails to ensure even ongoing survival in the industry, much less leadership.

Company Optimal Performance ([3], in text)—Major subject of this book. When the CEO proclaims different performance levels at different times as all "maximum shareholder value."

3. The high correlation between changes in market value (stock price levels) and changes in discounted cash flow are cited in Cope-

land/Koller/Murrin, page 85 (Exhibit 3-7). Davis, page 11, Grant, pages 4–5, 44–46, and 84–87.

The very *low* correlation between earnings per share and price-to-earnings multiple has also been investigated at length. An extensive McKinsey & Co. analysis, reported in the 8 Feb. 97 *Independent* (Lon.) 27, resulted in an R-squared (correlation) of a very low .024. The study examined average Earnings per Share (EPS) growth for 1983–1987 against PE for the same periods.

The corporation's stock price is a reflection of corporate value, which means that changes in stock price generally parallel changes in analyzed value. The two are not identical, however. Several approaches exist for adapting market value to analyzed value.

The methodology described in Appendix A of this book is Professor Timothy A. Luehrman's Adjusted Present Value methodology, as explained in his 1997 *Harvard Business Review* articles. Unlike some other approaches, Luehrman's APV reflects changes in the corporation's weighted average cost of capital (WACC) throughout the period of value assessment (see Appendixes A and B).

4. Many economic expansion cycles progress through three phases in terms of the level of acquisition intensity. During the last full economic cycle in the 1980s, the third and concluding phase occurred in 1988–1990, as evidenced by peak average acquisition premiums over pre-bid market value (five days before offer announcement) of 41.9 percent with 410 completed transactions (*Beyond the Deal,* pages 11 and 25). Deal volume and acquisition premium patterns suggest that 1999–2003 is emerging as a parallel in this cycle to the 1980s boom period. Other factors:

- *Cheap Stock as Currency.* High stock prices mean reduced weighted average cost of equity (WACE). The pragmatic CEO is always eager to take advantage of a bargain, especially if that bargain is the corporation's own stock. But as with any asset that has inflated in value, the holder sometimes believes that benefit is achieved only if the shares are exchanged for something else, something tangible. Such as another corporation.
- *Emergence of Takeover Syndicates.* Cash flow from the boom's first two periods funds third-party acquisition syndicates: fi nancial acquirers with staff who are evaluated solely on the basis of deals closed. These entrants supercharge the M&A environment during each cycle, since each creates a multiplier effect. As the pure financial buyer cannot exploit any opera-

tional synergies, the syndicate must rely on later resale, or, simply turn back to the public market.

Phrases such as "undervalued" and "overvalued" are more for financial press impact than conventional analysis, as efficient market theory rules out any long-enduring instances of either. But what does occur—and what is often mislabeled as "undervaluation"—is undermanagement in value terms.

The corporation's value is 100 now, and value could be 150, despite management's protests that this is impossible. So existing management does not or cannot achieve the additional value, and the self-confident acquirer seeks to seize the missing value.

5. The simple value-to-cash flow (VCF) multiple of four times represents the low end of the four-to-six times range from *Beyond the Deal* and thus is a deliberately conservative estimate.

But the corporation that manages to narrow its Value Opportunity Gap (potential value minus present value) exhibits a far greater VCF multiple. Which means higher valuation for each extra dollar of cash flow generated, compared to companies with huge value gaps.

6. Chapter 2 is dedicated to the Value Opportunity Gap; this section provides an introduction. Factors influencing each corporation's unique VOG change over time. Thus even if it *is* possible to get the range down to a single-digit percentage number, it is arguable whether such an analysis is worthwhile.

Per the Preface, emphasis throughout this book is on devising the actions necessary to close the value gap: This is what is meant by "Value Gets Down to Business." Priority corrective action takes precedent over passive analysis.

7. Tichy, Noel, and Stratford Sherman, *Control Your Destiny or Someone Else Will* (New York: Currency Doubleday, 1993), pages 61–62.

8. Market implications of shrinking product/service life cycles are explored more extensively in Chapter 7.

9. *Moving Average Commissions and Elimination of Trailing Performers*

Progressive commissions call for the percentage payout to increase with higher sales for the period, without ceilings. A 90-day moving average basis of calculation helps remove distortions and waste that come from meeting artificial end-of-quarter and/or end-of-year target dates. Richard Brown, former CEO of Cable and Wireless and now CEO of EDS, initiates posting of staff ranks by job category at both corporations.

Production: From Parts to Modules

This encompasses (1) parts reduction, (2) vendor reductions, (3) elimination of factory standing inventories, and (4) assembly simplification, all value reduction elements. Additional coverage in Chapter 5, "Value's Engine Room," and "Expense Multipliers/Precedent, Procurement" in Chapter 8.

Replacing Salesforce-Dominated Pricing with Professional Pricing

In response to complaints about bureaucratic delays in responding to pricing requests, management acts to "put pricing closer to the marketplace." But if the goal is to give the salesforce local veto power over pricing, the result can be lower revenues and margins. Swinging the pendulum back toward management by a professional pricing department can mean a two- to three-margin-point improvement, boosting value.

10. *Binary Value*

A third category of value initiatives calls for simultaneous reductions in *both* expenses and revenues at the same time, thus the name "binary."

Several binary value initiatives are described in this book, such as demand-pull/flexible assembly (Chapter 5), in which costs per unit are normally reduced by 30–50 percent. Combined with near-custom ordering (the customers' perception that they can have a custom order as long as commitment is made in advance; Chapter 7), both revenue and expense value factors are affected. Binary opportunities are also explored in the second book in VBM Consulting's series, *Maximum Value Management*.

Ensuring Role of Higher Value, Alternative Providers and Processes to Increase Value (Figure 1-2B and C)

The prospect that *any* service could be assigned to an alternative provider helps ensure the lowest cost/most effective performance on an ongoing basis (see Chapter 8). Understandably, incumbents within the organization seek to own the function, and thus slow or prevent changes regarding *how* that activity is conducted. And by *whom.*

Permitting such an operational straightjacket has the consequence of preventing maximum shareholder value (MSV). Inertia becomes the corporation's principal influence, instead of MSV. Open-ended control of fast-evolving functions is out of step with the gradual movement toward increased project and temporary work assignments, displacing standing salaries.

One thing for sure: As outsourcing grows from exception to viable alternative, the same incumbents who oppose competitive assessment suddenly change their tune. For without pursuit of the service on a maximum shareholder value basis, there's no chance to recapture that function.

11. Intranet-based applications such as this are also addressed in "From Full Service to Self Service: Intranet Revolutionizes G&A Costs, Performance" in Chapter 8; see also Table 8-2.

12. Other examples of changes in staff-to-staff services are described in Chapter 8. An after-effect of internal service approaches to staff functions is that some firms become burdened by a proliferation of marginal internal services, increasing ongoing costs while reducing value.

Major staff-to-staff activities represent a logical starting focal point for process simplification within the firm. Both because of the active value destruction caused when unnecessarily complex processes are allowed to persist, and as holdover "solutions" that are deliberately made overly complex preclude other approaches.

13. "What's the Deal: The ISP Gap," *The Industry Standard,* www.standard.com, September 29, 1999. Simons is managing director of Digital Video Investments, a research firm, and is a regular contributor to www.forbes.com.

14. Reference to Chapter 1 endnote 4.

15. From Chapter 8, Macintosh, James, "Barclays to Set Up E-Market to Cut Supply Costs," *The Financial Times,* October 27, 1999, page 8.

16. From Chapter 8,"Downsizing: One Last Time, from the Top Down": Quote: "Serial downsizing is admission of management failure."

17. *Creating Value as Acquisition Defense*

Closing the corporation's Value Opportunity Gap (the difference between potential value and current value) represents the target management's ultimate acquisition defense. See also "Value Creation as an Acquisition Deterrent," *Beyond the Deal,* pages 93–94.

Standard Synergies Are Already "In the Market"

The efficient market adjusts as soon as a single major intra-industry transaction occurs. As institutional researcher Simons notes, "When AT&T bought TCI and MediaOne, other cable stocks didn't soar past the valuation levels set by the deals. Instead, Wall Street recalibrated its models to reflect them." Op. cit., *Industry Standard*, September 29, 1999.

Standard synergies refer to the market's anticipated efficiencies from a related company acquisition. If and when such synergies are miscounted as available to offset part of the bid premium, this double-counting increases the risk of acquirer overpayment.

Indirect evidence that standard synergies are "in the market" is provided by the actions of analysts and other value influencers. As soon as the major related deal (*Beyond the Deal*, pages 57–60 and 77) occurs in that industry, analysts immediately speculate about the level of synergies. In supportive markets, that source becomes immediately absorbed into current value as reflected by the target company's stock price.

18. A 50 percent improvement in value does not necessarily mean a 50 percent increase in the price-to-cash flow (PCF) multiple. Any value improvement is reflected in the combination of higher multiple *plus* increased cash flow.

19. Regarding adaptation of stock price to an adjusted present value, see Luehrman, Appendix A; also Grant (pages 3 and 4), Copeland/Koller/Murrin (pages 16–25 and 102–106), and *Beyond the Deal*, pages 78–93.

Some issues relating to executive incentive plans that provide maximum payouts for modest value-creation performance are raised in Chapter 4 ("Executive Incentive Packages: Rewards for *Top* Value Creation Performance?").

20. *Beyond the Deal*, pages 16–23, regarding stand alone and comparative TSR measures and their applications.

21. Luehrman, Timothy A. on APV: See Appendix A.

22. *Binary (also noted in Chapter 1 endnote 10)*

The first refers to programs designed from the onset to simultaneously and systematically achieve both revenue increase and expense reduction at the same time, in a systematic manner. Several "binaries" are described in this book, such as the integrated process for combining advance order commitments and demand-pull/flexible assembly.

Acquisition

Claims of "creating value" are standard due diligence for the acquirer in the newly closed deal. But such claims tend to be forgettable sound bites for the financial press. With most deals requiring an acquisition premium of more than 20 percent over full market value, the new acquisition starts in a value hole.

Acquiring management do not know for certain whether the

transaction creates or destroys value until the results of their post-merger value actions can be assessed, three to five years later. The only certainty at the time of the deal signing is that the value result (1) is not yet known and (2) depends on acquiring management's skills at developing new worth.

23. Op. cit., Luehrman (page 150) illustrates that the corporation's future projections are divided into two parts, the primary cash flow analysis period plus terminal value. If analysis terms are assumed to be briefer in anticipation of shrinking product and company lives, terminal value is then moved closer to the present, reducing total company value somewhat.

In Figure 2-3, present value of future growth refers to the period of competitive advantage when the corporation and/or its separate value-driven projects are earning their highest returns. If that "highest return" period is reduced, corporate value also decreases.

Acceleration of decision speed and shrinkage of product life cycles now raise serious questions about discounted cash flow analysis periods beyond three years. It becomes increasingly difficult to defend a discounted cash flow (DCF) projection term of three years or longer in those industries where fundamental changes in that industry's prevailing business models are occurring in half that time. The alternative is a time period for both project and corporate value analysis of 18–30 months, closer to the pace of critical industry change.

24. Reference (see Chapter 1 endnote 3). The fact that value changes in accordance with interpretations of future cash flows rather than reported historical earnings per share (EPS) also arises as the company takes action that reduces reported earnings—but the stock price soars in anticipation of future benefits. One extreme example: Internet companies ("dot-coms") increasing market value as they move into new areas, despite massive spending (burn) rates in 1996–quarter 1 2000.

25. Frequently cited stories of late market entry success by P&G/Pampers and Miller Brewing (Lite Beer) occurred only because the competition was slow moving and underfunded. Chux brand disposable diapers and Gablinger's beer were totally unprepared to deal with major marketing assaults by leading marketers. While throwing money at the problem can occasionally help a late entrant make up for lost time, many have learned the lessons of Chux and Gablinger's and resolve not to let their companies lose their time-to-market advantage so easily.

26. *Demand-Pull/Flexible Assembly (Chapter 5)*
The prospect of two-plus years of shattered formal EPS results

means that many corporations will only consider transition to flow assembly when there is no other choice to prevent: American Standard, Stevenson Furnaces, Clark Shoes, Pratt & Whitney Aircraft Engines.

Corporate Key Contributors (Chapter 3): Take two companies with identical assets and prospects, and the corporation with the rare stellar talent prevails almost every time. Chapter 3 suggests that each industry and each function have a finite number of value star performers who drive the business forward by their personal effort alone. Miss out on acquiring and retaining these Corporate Key Contributors, and the firm languishes in terms of competitiveness and new value development.

Chapter 2

1. Value Opportunity Audit: See Epilogue or VBM Resource Centre (www.vbmresources.com) or VBM Corporate site: www.vbm-consulting.com.

One limitation of some formula-myopic "value" perspectives is their preoccupation with statistical nuances relating to adaptations of Miller & Modigliani's work. Rather than a focus on how best to apply M&M's broad principles to create substantial value, the economist-turned-value-statistician may be intrigued by his own permutations of M&M's Capital Asset Pricing Model, but the measure is at most a scorecard for recording management's value progress—and not a tool for achieving that progress.

Reliance on value models rather than value actions can lead to disappointments. Even one of the better value models (e.g., Adjusted Present Value; see Appendix A) is not designed to originate specific value ideas, a critical difference between the company that achieves MSV and the firm that merely talks about it.

Moreover, two issues threaten the accuracy of some statistical valuation approaches:

1. *Research & Development Add-Backs.* Some statisticians' formulas call for all or a significant part of the company's R&D expenses to be added back to corporate cash flow for purposes of estimating value. But such gross add-backs can easily mislead, as corporations exhibit different patterns when it comes to (1) the split between investment in value-generating new

innovation and either overhead or maintenance R&D and (2) the return and timing from value investment in innovation. One company directs most of its R&D toward maintenance and salaries for administrators, while another firm directs all research and development funding to pursuit of new innovation.

2. *Exaggerated Term Assumptions.* In many technology-based industries, assuming a time (t) period of comparative advantage (see Figure 2-3) of three to four years can be wildly optimistic where revolutionary changes in technology and customer habits occur twice a year. Some DCF valuation models for Internet companies presume terms of ten-plus years. And yet up to 75 percent of business to consumer (B2C) companies in existence as of Qtr. 4 in 1999 are likely to disappear. That's an average life span of two years, three at most.

The necessary conclusion is that canned valuation adjustments may be consistent but are almost always wrong. Companies have unique business models and show different levels of effectiveness in extracting value from those models. No one-size-fits-all adjustment is adequate or accurate. Any adjustments must be adapted to that company's specific circumstances, encompassing both (1) areas of partial value development to date and (2) future value opportunities, by the operations-financial sector (see Chapters 5–8).

Value leadership at the top of the organization can make all the difference between the disappointing initiative that achieves minor improvements only, versus the successful value reform: the program that significantly narrows that firm's Value Opportunity Gap.

Development of a "hit-list" of high probability value candidates as suggested by employees is an important part of the complete value development effort. But if that consultation limits the scope and/or depth of the value development effort as employees defend turf, success of the overall value program may be threatened.

The seminar discussion of value opportunities within the company yields numerous useful development ideas, but almost always within the context of the company's existing cost and organizational structures. Radical changes in both the approaches used (how) and execution (who) are likely to be necessary to maximize value, as contrasted with just increasing value by a small amount. But the internal trickle-up suggestion approach is not designed to extract dramatic value goals.

The answer is to never discourage any valid new-value-creation candidate ideas but to *supplement* those ideas with others unlikely to trickle up from staff.

These additions include intelligence on applicable precedents from other organizations, new processes and technologies, and adapting value strategies for fast-changing market conditions, such as the precedent-shattering market changes described in Chapter 7.

2. Shareholder-owners increasingly treat any reduction from maximum value as money out of their own pockets.

The corporation competes with numerous alternative investments for investors' scarce, sustaining capital. Shareholders are continually comparing their personal/institutional Total Shareholder Returns (TSR) with other, sometimes better alternatives (see Chapter 1, endnote 2). Shareholder insistence on maximum TSR from every investment in their portfolio is no longer limited to a couple of conspicuous activist shareholder groups. Other institutions follow the lead of organizations such as CalPERS and Hermes Lens.

Market's Interpretation of Management's Projected Future Cash Flows

In Chapter 1, "Three Pivotal Value Issues" explains the role performed by influencers in interpreting management's cash flow projections for valuation purposes. Reference: Davis, page 11:

> ... the market doesn't discount management's projections. Instead, the market discounts analysts' and others' collective interpretation of those projections of future cash flows.

3. Cripple the corporation's value development by limiting actions to trickle up value suggestions from self-interested staff within the corporation, and new problems emerge. One department's plan for maximizing value reduces value prospects elsewhere within the organization.

For example, the standing sales organization of the consumer electronics company nominates new cooperative programs with resellers as their key suggestion for enhancing corporate value. Simultaneously, a group within the corporation given the job of finding and applying new high value technologies advocates Internet-only sales of the same goods as its principal value suggestion. Only when the value development candidate programs of separate departments are tied together is this potential threat to value creation lessened.

4. Enduring corporate value is developed one discrete action at a time, so it is that periodic adjustments to Vp, potential value, are

made on a build-up basis, with discrete value programs evaluated separately and then added to the Vp baseline, as appropriate.

The discounted cash flow (DCF) analysis applied to the corporation overall and described in Appendix A (Adjusted Present Value, APV) also applies to discrete value initiatives. An alternative, faster method is to compare the analyzed internal rate of return (IRR) to current cost of capital (WACC) and proceed when IRR is greater. Instead of guessing about how much IRR should exceed WACC to provide a margin for safety, the suggestion here is to use weighted average cost of equity (WACE) as the hurdle instead.

From Chapter 7: In 1991, Encyclopedia Britannica's key value driver is the company's commissioned professional sales staff, agents capable of selling major hard-copy sets at a cost of more than $1,000. Eight years later, the company has changed hands, sells a CD version of the Encyclopedia for less than a quarter of the hardcover price, and gives away other information for free on the company's site on the World Wide Web. Yesteryear's source of value generation becomes 1999's source of rapid value *destruction*.

5. Changes in the external economic conditions have nothing to do with the individual company's performance or the effectiveness of management's value program, but that doesn't prevent the occasional manager from claiming credit anyway. Each of the general economic "tidal effects" described here often also increase market value of specific companies:

- *Reduction in Long-Term Interest Rates*. Reduced cost of capital (WACC) increases corporate value unless there is no debt at all. If the firm is growing at a double-digit pace and applies a value-optimal capital structure, the value increase is probably substantial. Reference: Georgia-Pacific example, Davis, Henry A. and Sihler, William W., *Building Value With Capital Structure Strategies* (N.J. Financial Executives Research Foundation) pages 125–126.
- *Reduction in Risk*. Lower risk (r) generally decreases WACC while increasing corporate value, all other things being equal.
- *Extended Valuation Period*. The longer the term (t) of high cash flow generation, the greater the corporation's value. Figure 2-3, *Beyond the Deal*, pages 81–84; also Copeland, Koller, and Murrin, pages 155–156, Grant, pages 67–68.

6. Circumstances described here apply only under certain situations, such as when: (1) the Board is *not* dominated by insiders; and/

or (2) knowledgeable, activist institutional shareholders are well represented. Crony insider boards are notoriously reluctant to challenge management's value performance regardless of results, sometimes even as competitors' market values soar ahead on a comparative basis.

7. Refer to description of the global Request for Proposal (RFP) preparation at "Grommark-X" in "The Case for Fifty Percent Value Underperformance," Chapter 1.

8. Elements of Miller & Modigliani's analyses are covered extensively in other works and thus are not repeated here. See Copeland, Koller, Murrin, 106; Davis, Henry A., and William W. Sihler, *Building Value with Capital-Structure Strategies* (New York: FERF, 1998), pages 16–21; Grant, pages 66–70; and *Beyond the Deal*, pages 79–80, 90–92.

9. Weighted Average Cost of Capital (WACC) varies over the analysis period with inflows and outflows, even if there is no interim financing involved. Reference: Luehrman, Timothy A., "The Pitfalls of Using WACC," *Harvard Business Review*, May–June 1997, page 153, also included in Appendix B.

Chapter 3

1. *Forbes,* July 7, 1997, page 236.

2. If revenue value opportunities are limited because of a lack of top talent to drive that source of wealth, then attention is directed elsewhere. The outperforming CEO knows that the corporation cannot *shrink* its way to industry dominance and value leadership. The value development program risks becoming dangerously unbalanced if expense reductions and efficiency are emphasized over new internal value development.

Not all Corporate Key Contributors (CKCs) are revenue-side value generators, but many *are.* Such as the top research scientist who can piece together elements of several existing technologies into a high-value combination. Or the marketing ace who discovers, then exploits the high-value target market that others miss. Or the breakthrough salesperson capable of winning whole new relationships, not merely order-taking.

3. The corporation that lives by the Big Bet—the huge innovation breakthrough, the massive account capture—also dies by it. Following years of disappointing internal innovation generation, Digital

Equipment Corporation management emphasized the unfamiliar and ultimately fatal retail personal computer marketplace. Pursuing share just as the segment was deteriorating to a commodity market, Digital's profits plunged. The company was acquired a few years later by Compaq.

4. Quote from Ed Colligan, VP of Marketing and Sales. From Doan, Amy, "Palm Flop," *Forbes Global,* November 29, 1999, page 57.

5. Walker, Sam, "The Price of Victory," *The Wall Street Journal,* June 11, 1999, page B1. Walker cites the following contracts and terms amongst the new players signed by the Major League Baseball team: Randy Johnson, $52.4 mil. (four years); Matt Williams, $45 mil. (five years); Steve Finley, $21.5 mil. (four years); Todd Stottlemyre, $32 million (four years); and Jay Bell at $34 mil. (five years).

6. This refers to focusing CKC additions to those areas of the company/team that are most important to value success. Starting pitchers are arguably a team's most important single player category. Arizona's addition of Stottlemyre and Johnson was instrumental in the team's 100 regular season wins in 1999. By contrast, the Baltimore Orioles also spent heavily for talent prior to the 1999 season, but mostly for position players (non-pitchers) with less impact.

7. Imperato, Gina, "When Is 'Good Enough' Good Enough?," *Fast Company,* (www.fastcompany.com), July–August 1999, page 52.

8. Quote from Imperato, Gina, "How to Hire the Next Jordan," *Fast Company,* December 1998, page 212. Article focuses on Professor John Sullivan at SFSU (johns@sfsu.edu).

9. By definition, the Corporate Key Contributor generates far more value (inflow) than he or she costs in total (outflow). But over the near term, timing differences usually mean negative cash effect for several quarters, at least.

10. "The Art of the Deal," interview by James Daly.

11. Jensen, Michael, "Eclipse of the Public Corporation," *Harvard Business Review,* September–October 1989, pages 61–74. The agent-manager is described by Jensen as an officer with a negligible equity interest in the company he manages. The agent-manager tends to run the company to maximize personal, rather than corporate, goals.

12. Penny-wise and pound-foolish? Directors and managers who undermine offers to CKCs on the basis that the corporation's salary discipline is shattered consider only the cost side. But the corporation languishes when it deprives itself of the critical CKC talent necessary to dominate its sector.

13. Dolan, Kevin A., "GE's Brain Drain," *Forbes Global*, November 1, 1999, page 20. Arguably, any case against special assessment and incentive program payout arrangements is at least partially contradicted at corporations with Executive Incentive Programs for a handful of executives at the top of the hierarchy.

14. "How Microsoft Could Blow It," *Forbes Global*, November 16, 1998, page 47.

15. Ibid. *Business 2.0.*

16. *Maslow on Management* (New York: Wiley, 1998), pages 56–57.

Chapter 4

1. Analysis cited by *Financial Times'* Lucy Kellaway, in "The Short Stay at the Top," June 14, 1999, page 14. Kellaway suggests that "A chief executive taking on a new job can be sure of only one thing: He is unlikely to be able to hold on to it for long."

2. "Thank You and Goodbye," *The Economist*, October 30, 1999, page 91.

3. Being named in a CalPERS (California Public Employee Retirement System) watch list is today's equivalent of being accused of value underperformance. Which helps explain the strident opposition expressed by company officials when they find out that their company is on The List.

Davis (page 11) sees an especially important value development role for such continuing owners in interpreting true value from corporate cash flow future expectations. The FERC official cites comments from administrators of Boeing's SVA plan:

> ". . . value is best understood by institutional investors with a long-term perspective who base their analysis primarily on the estimates of future cash flows discounted at the company's WACC."

Positive (for shareholders' interests) pressure from the "responsible irritant" board member does not necessarily go away with favorable economic times. Markets can and do swing in either direction. The fund or institution relying on the "rising tide effect" of overall indices to bolster TSR results can find itself victimized by the same effects on the way down. The fund has appreciated 30 percent in value, but a key rival's is up 50 percent on a comparable basis. All eyes (including those who award performance bonuses) are on the rankings, not just the absolute returns.

4. The CEO achieving The Value Mandate knows that the company can no longer afford the form-over-function manager, at any cost. One low-risk/high-image tactic of the games player is to generate internal enthusiasm for the new initiative, but then disperse implementation responsibility too widely. If (or rather, when) this poor implementation approach crashes, the nimble coaster remains unblemished.

5. The expected objection from those immersed in nuances of organization charts and reporting relationships is that the CEO cannot, *should not* assign himself as his own implementation manager for the firm's Maximum Value Management initiative. But there is no more important role than maximizing shareholders' wealth. The chief executive is the only plausible project manager, the only one with the power to get the full job done. Moreover, the CEO is the only individual in the corporation whose *entire* performance assessment depends on success or failure in achieving maximum shareholder value.

6. (See Chapter 1 endnote 3.) Copeland, Koller, and Murrin (pages 84–86) examined the relationship between DCF and market value (stock price times shares outstanding) for 35 companies. The McKinsey & Co. consultants' Exhibit 3-7 (page 85 in that book, second edition) indicates a highly significant correlation (R-squared of 0.94).

7. In early 1999, the U.S. Financial Accounting Standards Board (FASB) raised the issue of supplementary cash flow information to supplement historical earnings per share (EPS) information. Some argued against such additional data on the basis that the importance of traditional metrics would be undermined. The opposing position is that when it comes to both managing day-to-day corporate operations and pursuing acquisitions, "cash accounting" is already a reality, as reported data is adjusted to determine value impact. Those raising this argument note that cash flow is not some peripheral value consideration, but rather, the basis upon which market value is determined (see Chapter 1 endnote 3; Chapter 4 endnote 8; and Figure 4-2).

8. The third/third/third split is an approximation based on precedent. Also see Figure P-1. Without attention to all three value development dimensions, only the first third tends to be pursued.

Bernard Merck, Head of HR at France Telecom SA, speaking of his own unit, states that "sixty percent of the personnel work is only (administrative), with no added value." The quote is from Pringle, David, "As Paper-Pushing Tasks Increase, Europe Transfers Them to the Net," *The Wall Street Journal Electronic Edition Europe* (www.wsj.com), October 1999.

9. This describes the hidden value destruction inflicted on the company that misses out on acquiring CKC-caliber talent in a critical area. Both firms described here "have a procurement officer" in the sense that there is a name occupying a box on the organization chart. But the corporation that confuses mere staffing coverage with staffing top value performance is quickly overtaken by rivals in its industry. If not today, soon.

10. "Downsizing: One Last Time, From the Top Down" (Chapter 8) addresses the prospect of uncovering new value by starting any personnel efficiencies with the very top of the organization—the highest paid positions, including deadweight promoted because of past service rather than present and projected value contribution. This top-down approach is the exact opposite of many head-count number-directed approaches.

The deadwood with total compensation around $250K per year costs the corporation a cool million in value terms, minimum. Value-obsessed owners and top management would rather see those funds redirected into high-return internal projects and applications.

11. Actions such as (1) gradual replacement of some salaried positions with project-based assignments and compensation; plus (2) displacing departments' standing budgets with variable expenses incurred only as users require that specific service show great promise in altering the corporation's fixed and variable costs. And by doing so, in lowering the corporation's breakeven level (see Chapter 8).

12. Reference: Figures P-1 (Preface) and Figure 1-7 (Chapter 1). The value program that goes no further than financial value restructuring is positioned to achieve at most a fifth of the corporation's missing value. That percentage estimate is based on the composition of value when both operations and financial value sources are considered.

13. Reference: Figure 1-2. If the (A) "value" actions are already anticipated in the current market value (Vn), then paying incentives for what employees would have done serves to reduce value, rather than increase worth.

The risk management situation described here is not hypothetical. As of 1999, function-specific Web super sites emerge as one of the fastest growing online business-to-business sectors. Standardized functions lend themselves to standard, sometimes online, approaches. A practical consequence is that some corporations logically begin to use intranet technologies for that purpose. See Sherer, Paul M., "Corporate-Finance Executives Trade Financial Products On-line," *The Wall Street Journal Interactive Edition* (www.wsj.com), October 13, 1999.

14. The three examples here plus cash dividend issue relate to "Implementing the Value-Optimal Capital Structure," from part of VBM Consulting's *The Value Challenge* (projected publication date: 2001).

Direct communications with analysts about future cash flow expectations should provide analysts and other value influencers with the data they need, eliminating any need to rely upon dividend levels as an incidental, inexact signal about the future. Note earlier comments about FASB comment drafts on such developments.

But old practices die slowly, and unless the corporation has always had a no-dividend policy, reductions in existing cash dividend levels still tend to be an untouchable subject.

One possible future alternative: issuing interest-bearing debt instead of cash as "dividend." Assuming that the debt has a open market, those who wish to sell immediately can do so, receiving the same impact as outright cash. But by issuing debt, management preserves internal cash for high-yield internal investments, while introducing an additional mechanism for increasing value by decreasing overall WACC.

15. An analyst described the Somerfield/Kwik Save debacle to *Financial Times* reporter Peggy Hollinger: "They replaced Kwik Save (the acquired company) products with Somerfield's, got rid of all the Kwik Save people and completely messed it up." Reference, "Second Warning for Somerfield," *The Financial Times*, September 13, 1999, page 23.

16. The chief executive's enthusiasm for the EIP is partially explained by the fact that he is usually the key beneficiary. The stated rationale is that the EIP is critical to attracting top talent. The CEO's second, unstated message to the Board is more blunt: "Give me a package that I consider to be competitive with my reference group or I may leave."

The EIP takes on additional importance to the extent that corporations adopt Corporate Key Contributor programs. The argument is made in Chapter 3 that CKC incentives must be comparable to the best in the corporation in order to attract top value-creating talent. The value star is notorious for being unimpressed with titles and descriptions of importance that have no basis in fact. When the true

Corporate Key Contributor discovers that some low-value bureaucrat makes a far larger bonus primarily because of his office schmoozing skills, that CKC may go over to the competition.

As an EIP performance measure, Total Shareholder Returns presents some real issues, including:

- *Tidal Effects.* Delete the net cash dividend portion, and what's left in TSR is share price appreciation. A portion of indicated TSR performance has nothing to do with management performance, but rather just reflects overall swings in the market, up or down. Even the most expansive of management teams is usually reluctant to take full credit for appreciation caused by a market boom, fearing that blame will be assigned when share prices go down.

- *Controllability.* No executive or board member would knowingly agree to an award system that a middle manager might manipulate to guarantee his prize. And yet that is what potentially exists when an absolute Total Shareholder Returns level is specified as the threshold. The dividends component of TSR can be changed with the stroke of a pen. Share price level, the major part of TSR, is potentially swung by various management actions, including equity buybacks, changes in capital structure, and premature announcements of future breakthroughs that may never take place. The argument that management will not actually activate such escape hatches to qualify for a higher bonus level is not sufficient protection. The matter is not the integrity of the individuals, but rather the integrity of the value performance system. Unless all potential for manipulation is removed, the value performance measurement system is fatally flawed.

- *Comparability.* Evaluation of company performance to comparable companies on a TSR basis also raises the issue of comparability. Companies' management groups follow different net revenue policies and different actions exerting influence on stock prices over the near term. Unless both factors are normalized to allow comparisons, an apples-and-oranges dilemma arises: "We deserve a bonus because we performed less poorly than the other guys."

Value performance rankings are meaningless if directed at "average" performance. Today, few things ensure special board meetings faster than an allegation that top management is receiving top rewards in return for mediocre performance.

17. Statistics compiled by Towers and Perrin, originally cited in *The New York Times*, January 17, 1999. Also cited in "Which Country Has the Fattest Cats," *The London Observer*, Editor Section, January 23, 1999, page 14.

Quote from Koretz, Gene, "CEO Success Is Its Own Reward," *Business Week*, February 1, 1999, page 13. Article cites *Quarterly Journal of Economics*. Hall's use of the word "value" in the quote is replaced with "market stock price" (in parentheses) in order to be consistent with the context used.

18. *Information Strategy,* April 1998, page 35. Key among Pirelli's value enhancement actions are radical changes to the company's manufacturing operations, designed to significantly reduce ongoing costs and thus improving value.

19. Willman, John, "Diageo Executive Bonus Scheme Attacked," *The Financial Times,* July 16, 1998, page 20.

20. Macintosh, James, "Executive Share Options Reward 'The Average,' " *The Financial Times,* October 18, 1999, page 3.

Chapter 5

1. Some estimates of direct labor costs as a percentage of total product costs are even less. John R. Costanza, president of Denver's Jc-I-T Technology Inc. and developer of that corporation's Demand Flow Technology ™ (DFT™) methodology, estimates labor at 5 percent of total product costs in Figure 11-1, "Product Cost Percentages," 269, *The Quantum Leap in Speed-to-Market* (Colo.: Jc-I-T Inst., 1996).

Emergence of manufacturing and assembly approaches that do not emphasize direct labor costs means a possible opportunity to bring some production and assembly operation back to higher-cost locations in Western nations. In methods such Costanza's DFT, emphasis on labor flexibility is far more important than hourly cost alone.

2. The word "sourcing" reflects the fact that the optimal method for creating product shifts from time to time in accordance with changes in methods and their relative economics. Over time, the optimal sourcing approach may change from manufacturing to assembly to finished goods purchasing. And then back again.

The three primary sourcing methods become more, as hybrids blur distinctions. Major components production integrates procurement and assembly. In two car plants in Brazil, experimentation progresses with component suppliers overseeing part of the production-assembly process.

Limiting corporate sourcing approach to any single solution threatens to reduce value as comparative costs and output patterns change. But in order to take full advantage of such changes, a further progression to primary reliance on contract manufacture is required.

3. There is no full explanation for the historical focus on manufacturing labor costs far in excess of the importance of that component to the corporation's overall costs (see Chapter 5 endnote 1). However, one contributing factor is often the influence of manufacturing managers shifted to supervisory positions as the number of plants decreases. Right or wrong, a perception that high labor costs are a key problem of the company proves to be difficult to overcome.

Management resistance to radical flow approaches is easier to explain. The new approach is such a complete departure from the past that many foremen and manufacturing VPs face the most unwelcome news that their experience is now worthless.

4. Womack, James P., and Jones, Daniel T., *Lean Thinking: Banish Waste and Create Wealth in Your Corporation* (New York: Simon & Schuster, 1996), pages 160–169. Also discussions with Professor Jones, who is the Director of the Lean Enterprise Research Center (LERC) at the Cardiff Business School, University of Cardiff, Wales (lerc@cardiff.ac.uk).

5. Reference Chapter 7's description of tsunami marketing. This refers to deliberately disrupting rivals' market share positions by using model and production flexibility to overwhelm the industry with numerous distinctive models.

6. A problem with such passive investments is that the justification for support may disappear if profitability of the related activity slumps. The product's age advances, and profitability eventually plunges. All of a sudden, there are no funds to support the warehouse operation essential to selling those goods. This dilemma is explored more extensively in Chapter 8, "Unwinding the Crony Bureaucracy."

7. Costanza, page 64: "It becomes marketing's call at that time . . . whether or not the customer commitment will come in for that order . . . if (the order does not materialize) marketing becomes the 'owner' of the inventory until it can be sold."

8. Besides ensuring that the build schedule is stabilized, other preparatory actions include working with key vendors to ensure that

their quality, output, and delivery capabilities fully support the manufacturer's JIT aspirations. In some instances, the manufacturer figures that is in its self-interest to provide extra vehicles for key small suppliers without cost to ensure that just-in-time is true to its name.

Merely dictating delivery terms but doing little more increases the risk of a future supply failure as the suppliers eventually fail, one way or another. LERC's Jones comments that sharing relevant process technology with key suppliers is in that manufacturer's self-interest if it improves the source's delivery performance and reliability.

9. Fearing a revolt from existing dealers comparable to those in some companies in retail stock brokerage and insurance fields, Ford management is careful to describe the traditional dealer network as central to Ford's own advance order online buying service, announced in 1999.

10. It only takes a small number of pure (in this case, non-warehouse) suppliers to effectively force the rest of the industry to unbundle its charges. That is, to limit charges for infrastructure costs such as internal warehousing to only those who specifically request those services. For if the customer has one passion that exceeds avoidance of payment for valueless services, it is subsidizing those services for someone else.

The customer buying computers direct from Dell rather than through a retailer expects to see the lower costs reflected in the price. Lower pricing, in turn, facilitates the firm purchase commitment necessary to schedule on a build-to-order basis.

11. "Perceived custom" is also examined in Chapter 7 in terms of value contribution compared to alternative selling approaches.

12. Statistics from Weber, Joseph, "American Standard Wises Up," *Business Week,* November 18, 1996, page 52. See also Chapter 5 endnote 1.

13. Costanza, page 269.

14. Threaten to write off an old, underperforming plant as an accounting loss and the company's stock price sometimes *increases,* despite the negative impact on reported Generally Accepted Accounting Principles (GAAP) earnings per share. One explanation: Analysts and other value influencers look beyond today's impact in accounting terms to what that action may suggest in terms of management's future performance and orientation. Sometimes the interpretation is that management is now managing for today's and tomorrow's value,

rather than yesterday's reported GAAP earnings, and stock price increases as a surrogate for value.

15. A useful example for companies facing an imperative of implementing an entirely new sourcing structure every few years or be forced from the market has existed since the mid-1980s: the dynamic random access memory (DRAM) chip industry.

New fabrication designs are necessary every three to four years or so for continuing competitors, even with the indicated returns from such new facilities approaching zero. With huge new investments and questionable (or sometimes, negative) returns looming, consolidation accelerates (related article: Hutcheson, G. Dan, and Jerry D. Hutcheson, "Technology and Economics in the Semiconductor Industry," *Scientific American,* January 1966, pages 40–44).

While production replacement challenges in other industries may not be as urgent as in the DRAM industry, comparable forces are at work. In the 1970s, management realized that most plants would have to be replaced before they are written off, as economic lives accelerate faster than accounting lives. At the millennium, even stable industries with growing demand face the prospect that today's business model may be obsolete two years from today. Along with all related investment.

16. Costanza emphasizes the importance of advance inspection of all parts and modules to ensure that there are no interruptions to the production flow that might force profit- and value-diminishing rework.

Womack and Jones urge the importance of sharing company zero-defect approaches with key suppliers as the best way to help prevent problems later. They describe the decision at Toyota to extend JIT to all of Toyota's suppliers in the mid-1960s, explaining that the program initially faltered because of the inability of smaller suppliers to deliver quantities on time and spec to cells on factory floor. The automaker discovered that some of the smaller suppliers were relying on pre-shipment to warehouses near the Toyota plant to meet JIT delivery requirements for delivery several times each day.

17. Modular manufacturing calls on some suppliers to perform a key extra role in the overall production process. As lead supplier at Chrysler's Brazil modular manufacturing plant, Dana Corporation engineers oversee operations on Chrysler's rolling chassis, which represents 78 percent of the car's total parts. Managers from the lead supplier coordinate sub-assemblies and parts from more than 70 suppliers, thus permitting Chrysler to concentrate on what the producer sees as its core role: engines and final assembly. But modular manu-

facturing success is never guaranteed. Limits include (1) the skills of
the master supplier to perform the expanded coordination role (as
Dana did at Chrysler-Brazil) and (2) the completeness of the manufacturer's overall assembly plan.

That's the painful initial lesson learned by Volkswagen at its Re-
sende, Brazil, modular manufacturing facility. Like Chrysler-Brazil,
VW-Resende depends on delivery of major sub-assemblies from a limited range of preferred suppliers. Also like Chrysler, VW in Brazil
relies on suppliers' effectiveness in coordinating preliminary assembly on the continuous flow line.

But unlike Chrysler, VW's early experience at modular manufacturing in Brazil was disappointing. Bloomberg estimates that almost
a third of the vehicles built daily at VW-Resende in early 1998 require
further repairs to pass final inspection. Repairs and stoppages destroy the economies of demand pull/flexible production.

For explanation, some point to the absence of a lead supplier
performing Dana's role. Others believe that the problem is the lack
of a workable design, a deficiency that no master supplier could overcome. Michael Hammons, automotive analyst for Ernst & Young's
Sao Paulo office, is quoted as stating, "VW forfeited too much control
to suppliers . . . nobody was in charge." ("VW's 'Dream Factory'
Wakes Up to Reality," Bloomberg News in *International Herald Tribune*, July 22, 1998, page 13.)

18. Correspondence to Peter Clark, co-author, August 5–6,
1999.

Chapter 6

1. *Smart Organization: Creating Value Through Strategic
R&D* (Cambridge, Mass.: Harvard Business School Press, 1998), page
2. SDG is a research and development management consulting firm
in California and England.

2. Ten percent figure is from von Braun, Christoph-Friedrich,
The Innovation War: Industrial R&D, the Arms Race of the 90's (Englewood Cliffs, N.J.: Prentice-Hall PTR, 1997), page 223. "Even if far
more than 90 percent of these discoveries (referring to new chemical
compound inventions) are of no commercial value. . . ."

On a pure statistical basis, that is, the number of original innovation prospects out of all those created that "succeed," a 10 percent
assumption seems wildly optimistic. That is, if "success" means both

that: (1) the innovation reaches market and (2) the innovation yields a minimum return in line with expectations.

Von Braun's use of "far more than" suggests a sense that the real success percentage may be even lower than 10 percent. A 5–10 percent range is consistent with experience in medical, electronic, and telecommunications new development. A one-in-ten-or-less figure fails to raise eyebrows from many R&D managers, who may be inclined to try to bury the statistic lest it encourages management to cancel all innovation funding: "We have better places to put our money, where it can achieve a higher return."

3. Reference Figure 4-2, Copeland et al., page 85, regarding McKinsey's evidence that changes in company market value (stock prices) correlate far more closely with the discounted value of management's projected cash flows rather than to changes in earnings per share (EPS) performance.

Value is determined by financial marketplace *interpretations* of management's projections of future cash flow (Davis, page 11). The backward-management CEO slashes the R&D budget, hoping that the market will accept his explanation that cutting money will not cut innovation output.

- *Situation 1: Less Money, but No Reduction in Gross Innovation Output.* If *that* explanation is believed, apparent value increases, as the market assumes that R&D's gross yield will be essentially unchanged. But expenses are cut, lending credibility to the claim that management can squeeze more innovation from less funding.
- *Situation 2: Less Money, but Proportional Reductions in Innovation Output.* More likely, the overused "less can be more" proclamation is dismissed as propaganda. If the R&D budget is cut by 25 percent, then that's the anticipated level of decline in innovation output.
- *Situation 3: Less Money, Far Lower Innovation Result.* Gross innovation output declines by an even greater percentage than the budget cut, as anticipation arises that the cuts are symbolic of management's unwillingness to fund organic revenue growth in the future. Or worse, the action is interpreted as management's failure to grow future cash flow from internal sources. Company value plunges, as the market factors in acquisition premiums and other value penalties required to obtain tomorrow's growth from alternative sources.

4. See Chapter 4 endnotes 1 and 2 regarding CEO longevity in office. The shrinking pace of product life cycles (Figure 1-1 and all of Chapter 7) forces a situation in which research departments must radically reduce their internal development cycle time. Either that or face value carnage from trying to generate new innovations at a far slower pace than competitors. Process acceleration tools can help somewhat, but invariably the changes force revisions in the R&D priority list itself.

5. Reier, Sharon, "Trick: Using Discoveries Fast and Well," *International Herald Tribune,* July 4–5, 1998, page 15. Chart, "Innovation Means Success," from a reported Arthur D. Little survey of 669 companies. The survey is described as indicating that managers in ten industries believe that innovation is a "critical success factor," ranging from a low of 75 percent for automotive and metal/resources industries up to a peak percentage of 93 percent for telecommunications.

6. As used here, "partner" does not necessarily mean a joint venture or equity investment in the priority customer, although both relationship-building tactics are expanding in use. The partner may merely be a preferred supplier (Chapter 5). But even that role is of prime importance to the target customer.

7. Data provided to the authors by Company Reporting Ltd. (Edinburgh, Scotland) which monitors R&D spending by companies worldwide. Relating company revenue to company R&D spending is a relatively recent development. The usefulness of same-year comparisons is limited by the lag time factor. The typical R&D investment today requires a minimum of three to five years to manifest itself in the company's cash flow numbers and forward projections.

Effective innovation investment refers to the funds that actually make it through the budget maze, all the way to the corporation's top-value new development targets. A $300 million R&D spend level might look impressive, but if most of that is for department administration plus maintenance of existing innovations with little added profit potential (goldplating), then effective investment is a small fraction of the outlay that appears in the budget figure.

8. *Shooting an Arrow at a Moving Target Three Years in the Future*

Merger analysis provides the closest parallel to the lag time dilemma facing the assessment of discrete R&D projects. While managers seek to control R&D period expenses, the time separating initial investment and expenditure (outflow) and future returns (inflows) points to evaluation on a TSR basis including comparison to other alternative investments (*Beyond the Deal,* pages 3–4 and 21–23). The expenditure made today is *always* justified by a return that exceeds WACC (or WACE, as recommended by VBM Consulting). Otherwise no document is submitted and no funding occurs. Few ask how it is possible that such financial justifications consistently exceed the long-term trend of one-in-ten success (see Chapter 6 endnote 2), maximum.

9. In *The Inmates Are Running the Asylum* (New York: Sams, a division of Macmillan Computer Publishing, 1999), author Alan Cooper describes situations sometimes observed by our project teams. Engineers who assess their *own* performance in terms of the *number* of different solutions keep creating new, unnecessary adaptations, increasing expenses for products in the maintain category. Many times, regardless of whether (1) the added features have any demand and thus any revenue offset and/or (2) other cheaper/better/faster solutions have not already been invented.

Another factor behind goldplating is time budgets. When R&D staff are required to "bill" all of their time to either an active or a development product, a clear bias tends to emerge to bill time to present products, as revenues are available to offset that individual researcher's costs. With the consultants continually prowling, no one wants to be identified as part of a project activity that is a money loser, with the sole exception of an Internet prospect.

10. Any candidate's claims of "creating value" need to be checked against the facts. Just because an impressive innovation emerged while the candidate was head of R&D doesn't necessarily mean that he contributed at all to that value creation. Sometimes it becomes necessary to go to the actual developers (as designated by customers, competitors) if possible to discern whether the candidate increased or decreased innovation-based value at his or her previous company. Lag period between the time of R&D expenditure and generation of revenue means that some well-timed candidates may have benefited from the previous regime's discoveries.

11. The stock price initially rallies, supported by accommodating spin that management is taking control. But if what occurs is that bodies shift and performance doesn't improve, then all the previous positive market sentiments are thrown in reverse, regardless of the spin.

> AT&T—The dominant U.S. long distance carrier responds to the relentless loss of its long distance market share from 1985–1995 with a dizzying parade of different group heads and

different organizational schemes. The first couple of appointments, the first couple of reorganizations, bring excited titters
on the Street in the 1980s that Ma Bell finally has devised a
workable defense strategy. But market share continues to deteriorate anyway.

Sainsburys (UK)—Disappointing results for the U.K.'s chronic
Number Two chain in the 1990s leads to successive management changes, each expertly explained and a golden future
proclaimed. But especially when the appointments are from
within, analysts and others who influence value ask themselves, "Will this make any difference?"

12. Only the major innovation breakthroughs reported in the
trade press make it through to this CEO's consciousness, where they
set the baseline for expectations. A difficult hurdle: If the "successful" innovation is a one-in-ten prospect, the innovation juggernaut
capable of instantly changing market shares and customer habits is
closer to one-in-a-hundred. See Chapter 6 endnote 2.

13. Poor innovation development usually arises for one of two
reasons:

1. *Aiming Low, and Achieving It.* The first reason is that the
   innovation approach is inadequate from the onset. Company
   officials confuse surface awareness of the emerging technology with the far greater level of commitment (and funding)
   necessary to fully exploit the prospect's value potential in the
   marketplace.
2. *Selling the Farm's Seed Corn, Not Planting It.* The second
   reason is that the innovation development budget and approach was once adequate, but over the years, short-sighted
   cost cutting (to make the EPS number) has depleted the corporation's program. Management proclaims that the labs can
   generate just as much with far less funding, and no one can
   fully confront that statement for years to come. Once the
   years have come, the corporation lacks the innovation development base necessary to survive.

Regardless of the reason for the empty innovation pipeline, management at this point exhibits high overpayment increases whenever
the deal is a "strategic imperative." Read: not financially justified
but necessary to prevent going out of business. Reference, *Beyond the*

Deal, page 77, Table 3-1, "Alternative Bid Approaches and Alternative Valuations."

14. Reference Chapter 1, Figures 1-3 and 1-4. Emphasis is on the word "proven." The innovation that has already been demonstrated to be both feasible to develop *and* a commercial success involves very low risk, and thus exhibits a high price to cash flow (PCF) multiple and market valuation. Factor in a required acquisition premium, and the result is a significant front-end offset against future value from the newly acquired unit.

Purchasing unproven technology (either functionality or commercial success, or both) is another matter. Buying the small development lab with some "possibles" represents just another aspect of the corporation's continuing actions to supplement internal innovation developments with other sources.

15. See also Chapter 6 endnote 2. GE's Lexan® was immortalized by GE's commercial featuring a curious cat wandering loose in the lab at night (some sterile lab environment!). Under its first commercial name, Nutrasweet®, the chance discovery emerged as G.D. Searle researchers were examining completely different tastes.

16. "Not Just a Blip on the Screen," *Business Week,* February 19, 1996, page 57.

17. The individual researcher argues that the lingering prospect doesn't cost anything, just some of his own time. But that time has value, so even if the dollars have stopped flowing into the moribund prospect, value is still being destroyed if time is being diverted from areas of promise.

This cost often eludes easy detection: 10 percent of this individual's time here, 20 percent there, and so on. But add up all the slivers of throw-away hours, and the result may be several positions in a large R&D contingent. Time that could be redirected to value creation, rather than value destruction.

Jolly, Vikay J., *Commercializing New Technologies* (Cambridge, Mass.: Harvard Business School Press, 1997) 10. Also "Japan Keeps Its Shirts in Shape," *The Financial Times*, March 5, 1993, page 12.

18. "When Is 'Good Enough' Good Enough?," *Fast Company,* July–August 1999.

19. Buffhiil, Nicholas, "New Breed of Speed Camera Extends Traps," *The London Times,* January 4, 1998, News page 7.

20. Trapp, Roger, "From Masking Tape to Cable," *The Independent*, September 27, 1997, Business page 6; Gibson, Marcus, "Big Results from Thinking Small," *The Financial Times,* November 11,

1997, page 13; Stewart, Thomas A., "3M Fights Back," *Fortune*, February 5, 1996, pages 42–47.

21. "Strider," *ABC World News Tonight*, February 25, 1997; Nuttall, Nick, "Eye in the Sky Helps Blind People to 'See,' " *The London Times*, March 27, 1996, page 21.

22. Transmitters bring the GPS signal into rooms of the hospital, allowing precise positioning inside the building. Mother and baby each wear a sensor. The tracking unit can electronically calculate if parent and child are being separated, and sound an alarm if necessary. *CBS Evening News*, August 19, 1998.

23. Denton, Nicholas, "To Be Taken Internally," *The Financial Times*, March 12, 1997, page 14.

24. Green-Armytage, Jonathan, "Big Blue Adopts Round the Clock Development," *Computer Weekly*, February 25, 1997, page 3. The flow aspect of the global software development effort resembles some of the aspects of continuous flow on the factory floor, where great emphasis is placed on the importance of eliminating start up/shut down waste time.

25. Jackson, Tim, "A Quick Booster for Drug Trials," *The Financial Times*, June 15, 1998, page 17.

Chapter 7

1. Refer to Chapter 1, Figure 1-1, "Shrinking Economic Life Cycles, Some Examples."

Halving product/service life cycles means doubling the number of innovation development cycles over that period. The effect is actually more than a doubling of development investment required on a period basis, as the intensified competition encourages each competitor to exceed the prevailing level of (combination) price, performance, and features by a greater margin.

2. By definition, "in the market" incremental improvements are already incorporated into the company's present value as evidenced by the fact that future projected cash flow increases in subsequent years. As those incremental improvements are already part of value, offering additional incentive payments actually decreases value.

3. When a fundamental new market channel emerges, one of the factors that contributes to the laggard's inability to get on board is sometimes just asking the wrong question. The full-service question

raised here also emerged at the time of the last major channel change before the Internet, outbound telemarketing.

In prior work for the unit of a company, which is referred to elsewhere in this chapter only as Trawlbottom Corp., we encountered the head of that company's communications unit proclaiming defeat before she/hc even commenced, with insistence that "everybody prefers buying from the shops than over the phone."

Inaccuracies of anecdotal research aside, it became quickly apparent that one reason why this individual was failing while others in the same product area were succeeding spectacularly was because the wrong issue was being addressed. Where telemarketing had succeeded, it was where the convenience and speed of the alternative approach advantages had been translated into a new, compelling market offering. Including lower cost, as telemarketing enjoys significant cost advantages over both field- and in-store sales.

A parallel situation emerges within the corporation, where expensive full service support arrangements are replaced with online alternatives (Chapter 8). Again cost/price is a key consideration. If cash can be freed up for more investment in innovation by how the service is provided, why not do so?

4. Kleiner, Kurt, "Making a Killing," *New Scientist*, October 3, 1998, page 6.

While disappearance of browser market profits also reflects Microsoft's strategy with its Explorer browser, the fact is that in many cases, one product once seen as a profit leader gives up that role (along with present profitability) to a successor product and another and another.

5. On a corporate basis, compared to the period of comparative advantage as cited in Chapter 2, Figure 2-3. Knowledge of the product's expected period of advantage is essential for the simple reason that unless the value generation is planned, it doesn't occur. One of the nagging concerns at the millennium regarding some of the less substantial Internet dot-com companies is that management lacks the ability to move the company from high burn rate, money-losing operations to positive cash flow.

On an individual product basis, management must recognize the period of comparative advantage or risk a deteriorating situation in which increasing investment, decreasing life cycles, and limited revenue combine to cause *negative* Internal Rates of Return This was the very real prospect facing the DRAM industry in the mid-1990s. Reference, Hutcheson, G.D. and Hutcheson J.D., "Technology and Economics of the Semiconductor Industry, *Scientific American,* January 1996, pages 40–46, figure showing relationship of profitability to investment, 1971–1994.

6. Blind belief in market share at any cost is often associated with profitless dot-coms in which the CEO has no concrete idea on how soon the corporation will reach profitability, only a hope that investors will not lose patience before the crossover point.

Sustaining the dot-com's pursuit of share is Metcalfe's Law, named for the ex-3Com CEO. *Fortune's* definition for the "law": "a network's value equals the number of its users squared" (Unseem, Jerry, "Hey, Mr. Multibillionaire Hotshot, You Got a Law Named After You?," July 5, 1999, page 25).

Comparable myopic focus on market share alone also haunts some old economy industries and companies. The product manager grabs for share early and often, confident that he can explain away hemorrhaging losses as "investing in growth." By the time that top management discovers that few profits will be achieved, the product manager's early sales momentum has already elevated him elsewhere.

7. A systematic approach to building market momentum and corporate value through planned, systematic product proliferation is described later in this chapter: tsunami marketing.

8. Von Braun offers thoughtful arguments for corporate strategies in pursuit of extended life cycles, citing examples of industries where ever-shorter life cycles destabilized supplier industries and specific companies. At issue is whether extended life cycles are possible to achieve, regardless of desirability. It is all well and good to follow a high-profit, deliberately paced strategy for new product launch, deployment, support, and eventual withdrawal. But if the rest of the industry is running at a full sprint, the jogger cannot be surprised when everyone else passes it.

Over a decade, Honda's timing advantage could mean as much as two whole series of unmatched new introductions to market: market windows that the U.S. manufacturers pass. Stick to longer life cycles? Fine, as long as all major competitors agree to do the same.

U.S. Big Three carmakers attempt to reduce development time to 2.5–3.5 years. Which is impressive progress compared to the six-year cycles of the past. But with Honda aiming at year or more speed to market advantage, the Americans hope that the Japanese manufacturer's advantage cannot be extended to their market.

9. As cited here and in Chapter 8, *value investment* may refer to either investment in innovation, investment in expense reduction/efficiency improvement, or hybrids. The key criterion is projected re-

turn, rather than investment type. Projected returns are not presumed to coincide with past returns, particularly in fast-changing market environments experiencing fundamental changes in IRR-influencing factors.

The argument for diversion of funds from overhead to high-return projects becomes even stronger when it is evident that some zero-return expense outlays compound future negative cash flow. An initial wasted expense, such as for a make-work position, requires additional staff-to-staff support, creating a daisy chain of value reduction (see Chapter 8).

10. Tichy and Sherman describe General Electric CEO Welch's exasperation with those numbers-gatherers who are motivated more by the desire to leave no blank spaces on a form than to ensure that the data are accurate and worthwhile. Historical returns on innovation are especially precarious as fundamental changes in markets shatter the old IRR rules-of-thumb. Fail to reflect *future* conditions and returns in current innovation investments, and management leaves its future to guesswork.

11. Today's high-growth corporate business model is built on a presumption of early, effective, massive investment. More important are investors and others who expect the breakthrough company to generate negative cash flow basis in early years. Some may even argue that the company is not investing enough in its future if early losses are too modest.

- *Multiplier.* The underlying presumption is that the more money spent on investments, the greater future profitability and cash flow. For corporations with an effective value development model and implementation approach, such a presumption *may* be valid. For the corporation that is merely spending lots of money and hoping it all turns out OK, any such multiplier assumption is highly suspect.
- *Static Valuation Models.* Sometimes, the indefensible multiplier assumption is not adequately reviewed because it is hidden with a statistical calculation model. It is a simple matter to insert an equation that automatically converts dollars of investment today into tens of dollars of cash flow and value tomorrow.
- *Advertising.* Investment spending is sometimes expanded to include advertising expenditures, based on the rationale that such outlays help grow and secure market share. Amazon. com's Bezos proclaimed on CNBC in 1998 that "a dollar spent

on advertising today is worth ten tomorrow." But only a miniscule fraction of advertising is effective, and each dollar of
wasted advertising means four dollars of reduced value.

But most companies and many investment projects fail to
achieve the projected returns. The one-in-ten innovation success rate
described in Chapter 6 continues. The end result is that the invest-
to-grow model works, but only for a sliver of companies. Some high-
tech companies go into the red and never reemerge. There is sometimes nothing more than a belief that spending today automatically
translates into positive cash flow tomorrow.

Examining the corporation's specific value business model is essential to help separate the corporation that is investing in the future
from that firm that is merely throwing money away, then mislabeling
it as investment in the future.

12. *Appearance of Instant Whims*

The critical word here is "appearance". Demand-pull/flexible approaches such as described in Chapter 5 depend on a flexible manu-
facturing-assembly process in order to support the largest number
and range of distinct models from the smallest number of components. In the optimal format, the customer *perceives* that he/she has
effectively no limits to what they can order (in advance). Simison,
Robert L., "Toyota Develops a Way to Make a Car Within Five Days
of a Custom Order," *The Wall Street Journal Interactive Edition*,
www.wsj.com, August 6, 1999.

13. Online operations are still the minority in most industry categories as of the millennium. However, the trend lines cause grave
concerns for department heads in traditional business units. Online
brokerage reaches 25 percent of retail trading volume in late 1998.
One year later, the comparable statistic is 37 percent, according to
CNBC.

Only the most secure administrator in the traditional terrestrial
business can resist the temptation to try to command what will un-
doubtedly be the corporation's largest budget category in a decade.
Even if there's good reason to suspect that assigning the online business to the old style/old line terrestrial division will hinder competitiveness against online only, pure-play competitors, that does not
ensure decisions will be based on maximum value considerations
rather than the immediacy of internal politics.

Consequences of placing the fast-growth emerging value business under the control of the slower-moving traditional business are
sometimes severe. The two businesses have entirely different busi-

ness and value models, with the result that what made the emerging business valuable in the first place may be lost.

Absorption of IBM's personal computer group by mainstream IBM deprived the smaller unit of much of its market lead and momentum. In airlines, the problems associated with trying to combine two separate value models within one corporate entity are now recognized as so onerous that few airlines dare setting up a low-cost budget unit except as a separate subsidiary or division.

14. Facing a disappointment with 1992's Alpha product line, Digital Equipment Corp. embarked on an uncharacteristic new big bet by reverting to sales goals in markets slipping toward commodity status. In 1993, Digital set a goal for itself of breaking into the PC world Top Five by 1995. The goal was missed, and Digital disappeared into Compaq in 1997.

15. The automatic assumption that a magic mix of R&D investment, some advertising, promotion, and other market share tactics create value is a key underlying assumption of the limited valuation analysis that never goes beyond the number-crunch model. But building corporate value for real is no MBA simulation play-game.

16. Eight- to twelve-point margin here refers to net income as a percentage of revenues. In very few instances is it possible for the middleman's entire cost to simply be saved by customer and/or seller. There is almost always some substitute service required, in whole or part.

An exception arises when the intermediary service is little more than an excuse for extra charges, with no real service provided. Or when the service is essentially meaningless but is a part of an established check necessary for commercial transaction completion; for example, the fairness opinion for a hugely overpriced acquisition, written in careful language that prevents enforcement.

Eventually, this bureaucratic featherbedding is eliminated, but never fast enough for the principals. New organizations force the pace to quicken. For example, by functioning as mortgage seller, packager, and wholesaler, E-Loan (www.eloan.com) acts to reduce the separate charges claimed by separate groups for each.

17. Use of end-user direct access of services and information on the Internet to bypass alternatives is also addressed in Chapter 8. The perspective here is that of the producer or originating company. But other essential issues of value and even survival face the middlemen organizations themselves. Fail to adapt to the new realities and deny the inevitable, and bypass is accelerated, not delayed. The chal-

lenge for middlemen: to radically change to an alternative industry role before they are forced from the marketplace.

18. Downes, Larry and Chunka Mui, *Unleashing the Killer App* (Cambridge, Mass.: Harvard Business School Press, 1998), page 45; "The Rise of the Infomediary," *The Economist,* June 1999, page 29. Differences between channel costs are not always evident to end-user customers, as pricing doesn't always coincide with costs—especially if the provider company is trying to smooth the path of transition. Eventually, the provider finds it necessary to reflect the full cost differential or risk losing money. Often, the trigger to cost pass-through is surprise market entry of a new, lower-cost competitor.

19. "Reintermediated," *Wired,* September 1997, page 208.

20. Innovation boost: Transformation of existing physical products to new service-product combinations has the advantage of marking the corporation's transition to a new value order with a series of specific new innovation for the marketplace.

21. "Withering Britannica Bets It All on the Web," *Fortune,* November 22, 1999, pages 146–147; "Hi-Tech Slams the Door on Old-Time Salesmen," *The Guardian*, January 13, 1998, page 3.

22. Easton, Thomas, "$800 Billion at Risk," *Forbes Global,* November 29, 1999, page 96.

23. First Boston estimates that an independent agent consumes 30 percent of premium dollars, compared to 20–25 percent for a captive agent or 10–12 percent using the Net or toll free number.

24. *Forbes,* November 4, 1996, page 165. McAfee competitors anguished in 1996 over the problems with different prices to different channels, an invariable challenge that arises with overlapping channel approaches when one of the channels is online. With a clear, consistent, low-cost channel strategy, McAfee quickly dominated the market while rivals dawdled.

25. A dangerous situation arises when the corporation is slow to retreat from an unworkable multiple channel strategy. In personal computer marketing, Dell and Gateway started the movement toward online-only sales of retail machines, with Compaq and IBM gradually withdrawing from resellers but not entirely as of the end of 1999.

26. Dollar value impact based on lower end of sales/revenue range, slightly more than four times the ratio of value-to continuing expense savings.

27. Chapter 5 describes how advance scheduling of the daily build plan on a confirmed order basis is an essential part of demand pull/flexible productivity and value improvements. Fully established,

and with ancillary sub-systems such as JIT and platform assembly and zero error tolerance pre-inspection in place, representative performance improvements include: (1) reductions in total product costs of 30+ percent; (2) time to market halved; and (rather than *or*) (3) significant improvement in product diversity and availability of features.

28. Sometimes the mistake is made that management assumes that funds generated from within the business are without cost, and thus investment in standing finished goods inventories is not a problem, so long as investment remains below internal cash flow levels.

But all funds have cost, and the corporation loses money if those funds yield less than cost, usually set as the company's Weighted Average Cost of Capital (WACC), but sometimes as the Weighted Average Cost of Equity (WACE).

29. Many corporations implement inventory control methods designed to significantly reduce the amount of finished goods stock in the corporation overall. Related car dealers all selling the same brand maintain updated computer lists of all models from all dealers in the area, along with new arrivals from Detroit. Nominally, this serves the purposes of both company and salesman. The former can scale back the funds needed to support company finished goods. The latter are still able to try impulse selling as they can claim that the car of their dreams is available almost immediately.

However, as a corporate direction, this is comparable to trying to sell Edsels by making some cosmetic changes. Starting with a defective approach (stack-and-wait with high inventories) and then seeking to make modifications to correct some of the problems is backwards thinking. Start with a high-value approach (demand pull/ flexible, minimum finished goods inventories) instead.

30. Denton, Nicholas, "Improved Compaq Launches Cut-Price PCs," *The Financial Times,* July 11, 1997, page 23.

31. Any proliferation tactic open to criticism as confusing customers unless the requirement for distinctive, high-demand stand-alone models is enforced. Marketing gurus inclined to attack any multiple model approach as "unfocused" have ammunition to support their claims if products are almost identical in design, features, and performance; for example, the look-alike GM compact models of the 1980s: Cavalier, Sunbird, Cimarron.

32. Honda statistics from: Deschamps, Jean-Philippe, and P. Ranganath Nayak, *Product Juggernauts: How Companies Mobilize to Create a Stream of Market Winners* (Cambridge, Mass.: Harvard Business School Press, 1995), page 34.

Tsunami marketing isn't infallible. *Lean Thinking* co-author and LERC director Professor Daniel T. Jones cautions that model proliferation can deteriorate into customer confusion when one corporation's initiative becomes widely adopted (Correspondence, August 5, 1999):

> Honda's model proliferation . . . is a great way to exploit what is probably the best product development system in the world (which Chrysler copied). And can have a dramatic temporary effect on the competition until they catch up and do the same. Then you have a real problem of confusion in the customers' minds with bewildering choice and a very complex model mix. Striking the right balance between meaningful choice and unnecessary proliferation is tricky!

33. The current estimations of the cost of a single successful field sales call ranges from around $350 to more than $500. Factors influencing each corporation's own cost depend largely on the success rates of individual account managers, compensation amounts, and approach (fixed vs. commission components) and overhead burden.

34. Methods for evaluating the effectiveness of Internet advertising still focus primarily on debate about which metrics to emphasize, and how (Vonder Harr, Steven, "Web Metrics: Go Figure," *Business 2.0,* June 1999, pages 46–47) while the next step of widely accepted methods for converting eyeball "hits" to reliable projections of future sales estimations remain for the future.

No one pretends that sales from Internet ads will be just like other media. And yet, there must be *some* link between hits and later sales for the ultimate Net "business model" to hold up: gain a lot of traffic, support costs plus more with ads.

But the disturbing prospect arises that advertising might be especially hard hit by personal reactions to information overload. Those hockey-stick shaped curves don't just apply to the market caps of the Net Top Five. They also approximate the data overload *caused* by the Net. In seeking to separate forgettable chaff from nuggets of intelligence, new screening devices emerge, both personal and technological, as a matter of necessity. It isn't just that the ads are ignored, but rather, that actions are taken to avoid any contact.

35. Throughout this book, value contribution is assessed on a relative basis, compared to the best/most effective/most efficient alternative. If the optimal sales approach is exceeded by an alternative

by 50 percent, that company's Value Opportunity Gap immediately widens (Chapter 2, Figure 2-1).

Attempts are sometimes made within the sales bureaucracy to justify the caretaker salesperson who merely maintains the existing account relationship (rather than significantly growing that account) based on the logic that customer revenues would otherwise be lost. But the fact that such AM are frequently changed with little effect on ongoing sales undermines this argument.

36. Business specifics are altered to preserve anonymity. One practical question emerging early in the Value Opportunity Gap investigation is that managers wonder why their profits are far less than world competitors'. In the Trawlbottom unit, underperformance had been artificially suppressed for years by internal department insistence that their group was achieving maximum performance, relative to *their* market. But their market was comparable to others in which far greater market success was being achieved, on a consistent basis.

Chapter 8

1. *Deleting the 'S' from SG&A*

The more familiar measure is selling, general, and administrative expenses (SG&A), typically expressed as a percentage of revenues. But revolutionary changes in sales unit costs caused by emerging online sales, industry vertical trade networks, and Net-supported field sales requires that "S" be split out. With a potential 10:1 relative cost difference between the firm that sells online only versus a conventional terrestrial store, cross-comparisons of SG&A/Revenue become unreliable.

G&A/R measures are seen far less frequently than SG&A/R at this writing, but use of the former should increase rapidly as sales and sales costs are split out and addressed separately by management.

One corporation that does evaluate its overhead costs on a G&A/R basis is Xerox Corp., formerly led by Rick Thoman, former CFO at IBM. While at Xerox, Thoman declared a goal of cutting the company's G&A ratio to revenues from 12 percent down to 6 percent by 2001. Based on 1998 annual revenues of $19.4 billion, a six-point decrease would result in $1.16 billion of cash flow available for alternative uses. Assuming that all efficiencies are without offsetting costs or revenue reductions, the result is $3 billion in additional value, based on minimal multiples of value to cash flow.

Thoman says that Xerox requires these funds to help finance new product development, including related acquisitions to generate tomorrow's innovation stream. Network and systems specialist XLConnect was acquired. Product introductions accelerated from 40 in 1996 to 85 in 1998. But Thoman figures that more internal cash is still needed.

The target of cutting G&A from 12 percent to 6 percent is a target goal for 2001 confirmed by Xerox spokesperson Nancy Dempsey, May 7, 1999. Product introduction statistics from Brady, Diane (with Sager, Ira, and Rae-Dupree, Janet), "Xerox," *Business Week,* April 12, 1999, pages 67–68.

2. As applied throughout the book, value destruction here refers to any action that increases the Gap separating potential value (Vp) from current value achieved (Vn). On that basis, both the loss of an existing profitable account *or* failure to implement known cost controls that could reduce HR's budget by 15 percent diminish value.

"Returns" refers to Total Shareholder Returns (TSR), the detached investor-owner's principal basis for assessing performance relative to other available investment opportunities.

3. See Chapter 1, Figure 1-2, Items B and C. The approaches that reach for the *maximum* positive value impact sometimes deliberately depart from prior constraints regarding (1) *how* the function is provided and sometimes also (2) by *whom.*

4. Investment levels envisioned here represent a significant increase from present levels for some companies. Chapter 7 explains that a 50 percent reduction in the economic life cycle of a given product is likely to result in *more* than a doubling of investment, as management seeks to get ahead of the accelerating pace of shrinking life cycles.

The working assumption described here is necessary to prevent the automatic instinct to look to external financing first to finance major investment increases, rather than internal efficiencies. Administrative departments all insist that there are no more savings to be achieved, while resistance to extra borrowing is muted by the fact that weighted average cost of capital goes down.

But unless management adopts a *look inside first* mind-set when it comes to financing increased investment requirements, value-reducing consequences arise, more than canceling any nominal increase in value suggested by reduced WACC:

- *Loss of Administrative Expense Discipline.* Remove a compelling reason for efficiencies, and the savings don't occur. Escaping accountability to generate the funding for new investment, leaders of headquarters departments are inclined to view their units as imperial fiefdoms once again, immune from the expense discipline expected of other parts of the business.
- *Financing: Direct Costs.* All financing has costs as indicated by either the weighted average cost of debt (WACD) or the weighted average cost of equity (WACE). Draw on these reserves, and costs are activated. Increased debt impacts the corporation's servicing ratios, potentially affecting financial risk and rating from outside agencies.
- *Financing: Opportunity Costs.* Forced to accelerate borrowing to meet the corporations' soaring investment requirements with no help from within the company, management loses any timing advantage. Instead of being able to time major debt and equity placements at the best times in terms of long-term overall capital costs, the company must add financing continually, in accordance with the investment schedule.
- *Possible Reduction in Number of Innovation Investments Possible.* Because of the reasons described above, the corporation that does not look first to internal savings finds that it must soon curtail its innovation investment. Artificial limits are imposed because of capital availability constraints, rather than funding all top prospects in the right areas with required returns. If the innovation prospect analysis has been complete, some growth opportunities are missed.

6. Understandably, the increasingly temporary nature of some support roles is disturbing to many. Instead of being able to count on ongoing employment with a stable company in which functions remain consistent or gradually evolve over time, an increasing number of employees face what sometimes may seem to be the worst of all worlds. Manifestations include:

- *Gradual Increase in Alternatives to Full-Time Jobs.* Project and/or temporary work gradually displacing more and more salaried jobs as employers seek to more effectively match work timing with work requirements. Management realizes that they do not require standing staffs for functions ranging from restaurant help to teller services, help desk operators to security personnel. Some other jobs redesigned to change the nature of the job from staff-on-call to staff-as-needed.

* *Changing Functions, Changing Roles.* If the corporation has not changed its basic business model within four years, that corporation is probably in trouble, as it has not adapted fast enough to changing marketplace conditions. Yet each major adjustment changes the key skills valued. In some instances, the changes involve transition from one whole category of expertise to another.

* *Corporate Instability.* CEOs leave office every four years or less, reflecting an increased sense of instability as industries grow in size but shrink in terms of numbers of surviving participants. Employees now know that one way or another, five years from now their paycheck will have a different name at the top.

While most agree on the symptoms, sharp disagreements emerge about actions. One perspective is that intervention at some level is necessary to try to slow the transition to non-guaranteed project work. The opposite contention is that the company that fails to take full advantage of opportunities is quickly eliminated from the global marketplace. The employment problem is resolved, but certainly not in the manner intended.

7. "Yikes! Deadwood is Creeping Back," August 18, 1997, pages 78–79. Author Stewart refers to results developed by Vanderbilt University Professor Germaine Boer, which coincide with data developed for the U.S. Commerce Department.

8. See Chapter 8 endnote 3; also Chapter 1, Figure 1-2.

Radical simplification is an essential prior step to achieving enduring expense reductions. Whether a factory or an office, automating the process with too many steps, staff, and paper (and costs) only makes the expensive, overly elaborate process run faster. Sometimes at an even *greater* total cost than before.

9. If the corporation has changed its assembly process to build to confirmed advance order only (Chapters 5 and 7), stock-out concerns fade, along with many of the costs. The production date and specific materials and supplies are known for several days before the run, permitting JIT purchases of the required amounts only, nothing additional.

10. Quote from Tichy and Sherman, page 8.

11. Then there's the self-promoting senior pure administrator who claims that *he* controls a quarter of his corporation's business as

a make-believe show and an instant profit center. But if this center is nothing more than a bureaucrat's invention, then the claim is a hollow boast. The litmus test question: Is that particular individual seen by key customers and competitors as the key value contributor? If the answer is "no," then the possible situation arises of a senior administrator hiding behind the accomplishments of others.

12. Entrepreneurship, knowledge, risk, future. Part of the internal promoter's tactics to try to elevate visibility of the stylish new topic is the inevitable trade article that calls for creation of the "chief (whatever) officer" position and department.

If the function has real internal demand and use, such extra hype is usually unnecessary. Calls for chief Internet officers were seen in 1996 and 1997, but rarely afterward, as the Internet became part of the corporation's mainstream.

13. Extranets represent extended capabilities and resources for the corporation's intranet accessible by authorized outside groups such as joint venture partners, certain suppliers, and customers previously served by expensive Electronic Data Interface (EDI). And, as applied here, the target external customer accessing a part of the supplier's intranet in order to provide a unique market offering to *its* accounts.

Perceived custom is introduced in Chapter 5 (sourcing) and expanded upon in Chapter 7 (marketing and sales). The demand-pull/flexible producer's capability to offer a wide range of possible products from relatively few components is wasted unless the corporation's marketing tactics are adjusted to reflect the new capability.

Thus, build-your-own PC marketing tactics emerge in 1986 led by Dell, later followed by all of Dell's competitors: Gateway, IBM, even Compaq. Nike now allows customers to make some adaptations on its high-end models sold online.

The demand-pull/perceived custom advantage is extended further when a wholesale customer can use the corporation's added flexibility to help create its different, proprietary offering to *its* customers. The engineering company or advertising firm downloads its best prospects to the target client, inviting modifications within prescribed ranges. The RFP process is circumvented, as the customer becomes part of the *seller's* own pitch.

14. "Sell" is used broadly here. Today, the internal provider is told to assume a customer perspective even when dealing with other groups within the same organization. Sometimes, the point is made even more forcefully with introduction of internal transfer mecha-

nisms that mimic many of the characteristics of the external market-place.

The world-class internal operation that offsets costs by selling its services outside the organization remains more promise than practice. Recognized direct marketing leaders such as L.L. Bean share what they want in response to outside inquiries and "best practices" tours. But these leaders see no benefit to their shareholders in giving away the corporation's precious knowledge capital for nothing.

15. Value contribution occurs on a *relative* basis compared to optimal. Thus management who just get by with whatever internal group has nominal responsibility for that area today actively destroy corporate value *unless* that internal group is the best: within the company, outside the company, anywhere.

And "best" is bestowed only by objective client assessment, never self-proclamation. Internal or external, suspicions arise that any unit that must use world-class three times in every paragraph to describe its services is creating a smokescreen for some purpose.

16. Chairman Dr. Anthony O'Reilley cut back on some continuous advertising on H. J. Heinz brands in the late 1980s, resisting the media buyers' predictable response that such actions only undermine the company's franchises. In the mid-1990s, Heinz acted to reassert its brand presence with special, extra ad spending.

The company's action boosted company cash flow at a time when extra ad spending meant extra wasted images, and not necessarily extra revenues and profits. But after three to four years or so of this policy, the time was ripe to restrengthen the core Heinz line items.

17. The desire to imitate stellar service leaders such as retailer Nordstrom sometimes backfires, as the level of service necessary to act as a marketing magnet costs far more than any incremental cash flow from the upgrade. Corporate value is destroyed, even though management has improved its market offering, to the delight of many end-user customers.

No one advocates inadequate service, ever. But there are different levels of adequate service, at different costs. As life cycles shrink, the corporation finds that an increasing percentage of its products and services portfolio is in the latter half of their economic lives, thus requires flexible support approaches. The support group that only offers one class of service—first—excludes itself from consideration.

Changes in the type of adequate service provided are not without controversy. As toll-free (800) calling becomes a mature market, support in the form of live operators becomes increasingly difficult to afford. A variety of alternatives emerge, including printed directories and online access. But when AT&T announced in November 1999 that it would be phasing out 800 operators in favor of online access, the response from unions representing the call center specialists was vocal and immediate.

18. See also Chapter 8 endnote14. Here we address the illusion of the internal bureaucracy capable of reselling services elsewhere. Such situations are rare, and with reason. The manufacturing corporation's primary purpose is *not* to build specialist functional groups, but to attend to the core business. One result is that the top functional talent goes where specialization and rewards are more focused.

In the short term, the data processing systems manufacturer might try to compensate for its relative lack of Web developers with an advertising blitz, but you can only fool some of the people some of the time.

In terms of *internal* revenue impact, only pricing emerges as a G&A organization that regularly impacts corporate profitability by additions to revenues.

Affectations of other expense units as profit centers or similar embellishments emerge more from the corporate gamesperson's desire to enhance the image of his department than any actual circumstances.

19. Once it was necessary for the internal services provider to merely *match* the best alternative from outside to maintain budget control for that service. As business-to-business becomes a prime post-millennium commercial target, outperforming corporate management insists that the internal group *beats* the best from outside, on a composite performance basis: performance, price, features.

The competitive threshold is continually rising, especially as new entrants to the commercial marketplace enact new approaches to services pricing:

- *30 Percent+ Advantage Entry Hurdle.* Chapter 7 describes how the combination of accelerating change and shrinking life cycles forces new entrants to devise combinations of performance (Po), features (F), and Price (Pr) that exceed the incumbent's best version in the marketplace by more than 30 percent, on a composite basis. Fail to reach and exceed that hurdle, and practical reality for the new entrant is no sales: Most target customers have insufficient incentive to switch.

  Aggressive pricing plays a central role in the overall mix, with the new entrant using unmatchable introductory pricing to increase the composite advantage beyond 50 percent. There exist dual objectives: (a) to accelerate share gain and (b) to set pricing at such a level that others don't even try to compete, and drop out.

- *Pricing According to New Market Share Pricing Theories Enacted.* It would be one thing if concepts such as Metcalfe's Law were just passive theories. But numerous companies are pricing in accordance with concepts that call for pricing far below cost on a sustained basis to gain market share at any cost, especially in Net commerce. Sometimes all charges are eliminated and the service is given away for free or next to nothing based on the curious logic that such actions establish conditions for a future profitable market of other products, sometime in the future.

  As more and more alternative services are provided online, application of such pricing theories becomes an increasing consideration for competitors, including the existing providers of services within the organization.

The self-protective head of the internal services unit argues that such outside substitutes are not legitimate alternatives, as below-cost pricing means that they may not survive for long. But when a continuing series of alternative services emerge at new low prices for years and management decides to retain higher cost in-house alternatives instead, the result is value destruction for the corporation unless management takes advantage.

20. *Continuing Activities*

Changes in the form of staff services and support occur only *after* determination of continuing departments, activities and functions. Attempt to change the form of the service prior to consolidations and elimination of superfluous services, and the intranet becomes clogged with low-value functions.

10-to-1 Transaction Cost Advantages

Chapter 7 endnote 18, Downes and Mui, page 45; *The Economist,* June 26, 1999, page 29.

Commercial Intranet—Refers to the corporate intranet that is developed first and foremost to facilitate support service, logistics, and business development requirements of the corporation. As contrasted with an intranet directed to other purposes.

21. Pringle, David, "As Paper-Pushing Tasks Increase, Europe Transfers Them to the Net," *The Wall Street Journal Interactive Edition* (www.wsj.com).

22. Dodge, John, "Health Care's Soldiers Think The Net Could

Be Their Savior," *The Wall Street Journal Interactive Edition*, November 2, 1999. Analyses—such as those by staunch Republican Farley—are the basis for Bill Bradley's claim that "$45 to $200 billion could be saved if health care administration was moved to the Internet." A hospital's procedures for storage, multiple data entry, and other cost-wasting activities have many parallels to the paper flow–intensive corporate headquarters.

23. The new online entrants price in anticipation of future learning scale efficiencies within their operations, applying the circular argument that unless initial pricing reflects those future expected gains, then there will be no sustaining market share. Realization of such scale efficiencies is accelerated if the online provider uses standardized formats, permitting competitive bids from the widest number of qualifying alternatives.

24. Ibid., Pringle, also Macintosh, James, "Barclays to Set Up E-Market to Cut Supply Costs," *The Financial Times*, October 27, 1999, page 8.

British Telecommunications (BT) estimates that its own intranet resulted in savings of £845 million for its fiscal year ending March 31, 1998 (Upton, Gillian, "Take a Trip to Your Computer," *The Financial Times*, June 28, 1999, page 16). Even presuming that such savings includes some soft dollar costs not directly attributable to the intranet specifically, the true annual and value impact is nonetheless massive.

25. "An intranet should serve all employees—at Ford, 80 percent of those connected log on daily" (Cronin, Mary, "The Corporate Intranet, Ford Motor," *Fortune*, May 24, 1999, page 51). BT's intranet was designed for ultimate use by 130,000 staff worldwide, and management estimates that more than half its employees are frequent users of its intranet (op. cit., Upton).

26. "Mazda Takes the Intranet Road," *Internet Business*, March 1998, page 17.

27. *The Value Challenge* (in development) addresses the cash flow and value contribution of the internal top pricing expert. Changing the number of pricing events from one per month to four to five per month via actively monitored online pricing helps to maximize value from responsive pricing moves.

28. There are always some obvious exceptions to any intracompany travel ban. Two excluded groups: internal audit, inspections. Placing the review point sufficiently high in the organization helps discourage too many exceptions. Setting the requirement of having

to go to the president directly for approval of intra-company travel gets the message across.

29. One answer is to limit comparatively low value, lower priority intranet Web sites to standard, do-it-yourself design and configuration tools. These tools are similar to those available to individuals and small businesses from some of the larger business-to-consumer (B2C) portals.

The self-important executive interested in using the intranet as a stylish display for posturing purposes will not warm to the prospect of being limited to the same design formats as everyone else in the firm. But it is far better for the corporate gamesperson to be limited in terms of his or her ability to waste intranet-related resources than to tolerate such adventures at the steep price of a decrease in the corporation's value. Shareholders aren't interested in paying out of their pockets for spinning logos, anyway.

30. The corporation's intranet emerges as one of the last remaining true captive customer market forums, after airline passengers in flight. And thus, a potentially highly valuable site for online merchants, previously limited to expensive deals with established, "sticky" portals such as Yahoo! to buy traffic.

Any suggestions within the corporation that such arrangements are inappropriate was probably already addressed when the corporation permitted special ads and employee offers in its company newspaper.

With access to the corporation's intranet available to many employees at home (to facilitate telecommuting, remote officing, and other uses), the intranet effectively acts as a front-end gateway for special offers and sponsored services. A barrier to be crossed, even before that employee reaches the general intranet.

Management at the corporation that cannot or will not develop such opportunities diminishes corporate value, as more of the intranet's ongoing running and support funds must come from general corporate funds, instead. Those funds could otherwise be directed toward value investment elsewhere in the corporation.

31. *Head-Count and Dollar-Level Targets*

A combination of both head-count *and* dollar measures is necessary to disarm avoidance tactics of the upper levels of the hierarchy. Impose head-count reduction target only, and the brunt of the reductions are deflected to the lower ranks of the organization, as if the $15,000/year entry-level clerk counts for as much as the six-figure coaster-officer hoping to avoid early detection.

Noninformed supervisor—Such roles still arise in part because of the surprising resilience of some fractured parables from eras long passed, such as a good manager can manage anything. Wrong. The supervisor who lacks a functional understanding of the areas he oversees represents executive featherbedding in its purest form. Reliant on simplistic metrics merely to perform his role, the supervisor is almost always the last to know about the major opportunity or the major problem.

32. Excessive or mismatched staffing levels is an active choice, not a passive consequence. As with other such situations described in this book, passive tolerance of continuing value suppression is presumed to be *the same thing* as overt acts to reduce value.

Both situations lead to the same end result: value destruction. Tolerating five extra EVPs may be a different method of value destruction than the negligent salesperson who loses a key account, but the value consequence is the same.

33. At this writing, revenue/employee (Rev/ E) measures are still used far more frequently than net profit after tax per employee (NPAT/E) or cash flow per employee (CF/ E). As projected cash flow relates directly to the marketplace's valuation for that company, expectations are CF/E usage will increase in the years to come. To ensure accuracy in company-to-company comparisons, "employees" must be adjusted to ensure same treatment of temporaries, project workers, and work performed by third party outsourcing firms.

But CF/E will not necessarily be embraced by all sectors. The dot-com company with no expected earnings or positive cash flow for a few years still has the same resistance to CF/EMPL measures as it does to P/CF, that is, stock price divided by cash flow. Those persistent negative ratios might cause some to think twice about their investments.

34. As corporate value is primarily a function of interpretations of management's future cash flow projections (Davis, page 11; Copeland et al., 1996 and 2000), the corporation that slips into the downward value spiral described here may be unable to pull out. In Telecom Italia's case, years of executive infighting left the base business neglected, with high pre-privatization era costs while high-value market areas were underdeveloped.

Value-underperforming management place their own companies into play. Telecom Italia's huge Value Opportunity Gap caused acquisition bids to emerge from two competing groups, as potential acquirers perceived an opportunity to cover part of their bid cost by the difference between potential value Vp and current value Vn (Figure 1-4). The vicious cycle continues, as the corporation is forced to spend

more money on costs that generate no value, such as acquisition defense fees.

35. The assumption in Chapter 3 and here is that over the near
term at least, Corporate Key Contributors represent a zero sum pool.
Over time, CKC requirements change, and new talent emerges. But
over the 18 to 24–month intermediate term, management assumes
that key talent capable of significantly increasing value is limited.

36. Peter, Laurence J., and Raymond Hull, *The Peter Principle*
(New York: William Morrow, 1969), page 69. Dr. Peter articulated
what everyone already knew: Some managers were being elevated far
beyond their level of competence. Peter's Principle becomes even
more applicable under conditions of accelerating change, as static experience becomes obsolete at a faster and faster pace.

37. The issue of termination costs is highly contentious. One
side argues that such payments are minimal compensation for loss
of employment. The opposite contention is that any payment for an
employee who provides no projected future value to his employer is
too much. Employment laws and informal practices set minimum requirements for departure payouts.

As a practical matter, the well-deserved negative image of downsizing usually assures that departure payments are generous.
AT&T's second and third downsizing announcements in the early
1990s failed to come close to the first announcement in terms of favorable market response. One possible factor: High payouts including
outplacement costs canceled out most or all of the value benefit of
staff reductions.

38. The value contributor continually seeks to adapt and upgrade capabilities to move to other roles of value contribution before
the old one disappears.

39. October 1999: The U.K.'s NatWest Bank takes actions to try
to sidestep takeover bids from two U.K. banks. Rather than discourage acquirer interest, steep reductions in executive ranks made after
an acquisition bid tend to merely whet the raiders' appetites.

40. Hollinger, Peggy, "M&S Axes 34 Top Managers," *The Financial Times*, February 25, 1999, page 29.

41. An *actual* reduction in present staff numbers is necessary
to reemphasize the message to all support staff on salary that their
continuation depends on finding and pursuing high-value activities.
The staff member spending an entire quarter at three symposiums
and exploring two new business areas where others succeed but that
cannot be implemented by his company contends that his time is
being used to great value because he is busy.

But busy doing what? If the activities cannot be easily described in terms of new hard dollar value added, then the suspicion arises that this has instead destroyed value for the quarter: cash flow out (salary, benefits, other costs), no cash flow in or basis for developing new cash flow in the future.

42. The low-value meetings-attendee who makes a career out of doing little more than bouncing from one group discussion to another is among the most difficult of corporate value destroyers to spot. The titles of the meetings are impressive, and the individual always makes sure that his/her comments are preserved. And yet the CEO observing performance and costs in overall terms sees the collective result: *lots* of talk, meetings to set up still more meetings but not necessarily leading to results, as value flows from the corporation: All these players are actually being *paid* for their gab, after all.

Tracking what people do and the resulting benefit is not the only way to try to spot (and then eliminate) the value-destroying meetings attendee before they bring the corporation to its knees. Former CEO of British Airways Robert Ayling acted to eliminate excessive meetings at the source, attempting to change the (poison) meetings culture.

43. Cost includes total costs: salary, benefits, support costs, etc.; 130–140 percent of salary usually works as an approximation of total cost, except here high bonuses are involved that are not truly performance-related.

The five times multiple is suggested here on the basis that it is slightly above the 4x value-to-cash-flow low-estimate multiple referenced throughout this book. There is also the precedent of professional services organizations such as law firms and accounting organizations, where a minimum 5:1 benefit to cost relationship is usually required to ensure continuity at that company.

Index

About the Authors

Peter J. Clark and Stephen Neill are partners of VBM Consulting, an international organization helping corporations worldwide to maximize their shareholder value—on a continuous, priority-set basis, covering all of the principle value source areas.

Stephen Neill (stephen.neill@vbm-consulting.com) is founding partner of VBM Consulting with more than a decade's experience working with management at all levels of client organizations to help those groups achieve their maximum value. Based in London but working on assignments worldwide, Stephen worked with two other shareholder value-oriented consulting groups prior to forming VBM Consulting. Stephen holds a Masters of Philosophy in Economics from Cambridge.

Peter J. Clark (peter.clark@vbm-consuling.com) joined Stephen and VBM Consulting as a partner in the late 1990s, and has nearly two decades' experience with major consulting organizations worldwide. His first book, *Beyond the Deal*, set a new direction for the pursuit of corporate maximum value by emphasizing key actions in the principal parts of the business where value is created. An MBA graduate of Southern Methodist, Peter is based in New York and London.